ISAAC WATTS

His Life and Hymns

by
PAXTON HOOD

AMBASSADOR

Belfast, Northern Ireland
Greenville, South Carolina

Isaac Watts - His Life and Hymns
Paxton Hood

First Ambassador edition 2001

ISBN 1   84030 098 1

Ambassador Publications
a division of
Ambassador Productions Ltd.,
Providence House
Ardenlee Street,
Belfast, BT6 8QJ
Northern Ireland
www.ambassador-productions.com

Emerald House Group Inc.
427 Wade Hampton Boulevard,
Greenville,
South Carolina 29609
United States of America
www.emeraldhouse.com

PREFACE.

MOST men who have left behind them a name so universally honoured and beloved as that of Isaac Watts have shone in many biographies; he reverses the rule, and really has more monuments in stone erected to his memory than there have been readable biographies to record the transactions of his life.

From time to time it seems necessary and natural to attempt some fresh record of the memory of honoured men; even the best biographies wear out, and succeeding ages demand a tribute in harmony with varying impressions or increased information. The life of Watts was one of the most quiet and equable of lives; it flowed on in almost unbroken tranquillity and peace; it was passed in much seclusion, neither his taste nor his health permitting him to come much personally into the presence of the world. The authentic incidents of his career, of which we have any record, are, indeed, very few, yet, such as they are, they should surely be gathered up, and put into some fitting memorial. Besides this, it is a life always good to contemplate. Acquaintance seems to lift the reader almost into that region whose air the good man breathed so freely.

The object of the following pages will be to attempt to do some justice to the various attributes of his mental character. His fame as a writer of hymns has, by its very brightness, obscured departments of work which cost him far more labour. Watts was modest ; in every estimate of himself he disclaimed any title to the rank of a poet ; but in truth his powers, as manifested in his writings, whether we regard him as a preacher, theologian, or metaphysician, are all equally luminous and instructive. Beyond all these, a character exalted by seraphic piety and all-embracing charity makes the narrative of such a life well worthy of the study of all to whom it is pleasant to contemplate human nature in the finer proportions of genius, sanctified and illustrated by Divine grace. It is curious, and almost amusing, to notice that Samuel Johnson quite tamed down his rugged temper and speech when he wrote the life of Watts. He speaks of him as óne who maintained orthodoxy and charity not only in his works but in his innermost nature : not a discourteous or disrespectful word flaws the sketch he has written.

Watts was the Melancthon of his times,—not only in the ranks of Nonconformity, but within the pale of the Establishment there was no other mind so resembling the mild and uniform spirit, and graced by the many-coloured scholarship of the great Reformer. It cannot indeed be expected that those should know or care for Watts, who are not in affinity with his mild and temperate, and yet majestic nature. Equally removed from the servility which would have enslaved, or the fanaticism which would have inflamed, the portrait of Watts is one which will be studied to advantage at all times. When Johnson characterized the philosophical and literary writings of Dr. Watts as " productions which, when a man sits down to read, he suddenly feels himself constrained to pray," he also describes the influence which the reading or the study of his whole life is calculated to have upon the mind. It is not fertile in personal incidents, but it has been well remarked that the Christian biography has other objects—it may be hoped that many other biographies have higher objects—than that of merely exciting the imagination, or agitating the mind by the recital of romantic adventures, brilliant actions, or daring exploits. Watts reminds us of that saying of Richard Sibbes, that "a Christian must be neither a dead sea nor a raging sea." His frequent illnesses, as in the case of Richard Baxter, "set him upon learning to die, and thus he learned how to live." For the greater portion of his life he lived painfully within sight of the world to come ; he hovered on the border-land of life ; he is a fine illustration of power in weakness, and he adds another to the list of those men who surprise us by the results of amazing industry, plied beneath all the interferences of sickness, and a weak and fragile frame.

Thanks are due, and are hereby heartily rendered, to the Rev. Herman Carlyle, LL.B., of Southampton, for permission to engrave the portrait from the vestry of Above Bar Chapel—it has never been engraved before, and is believed to be the portrait presented by his pupil, early in life, to the Rev. John Pinhorne, master of the Southampton Grammar School ; and also to J. Hunter, Esq., of Dr. Williams' Library, for his invariable courtesy, and for permission, obtained through him, to use the portrait formerly the property of Miss Abney, and the bust, of which also. engravings are given in the work.

E. PAXTON HOOD.

CONTENTS.

CHAPTER I.

Birth and Childhood of Isaac Watts.

ISAAC WATTS was born at Southampton, July 17th, 1674, the same year in which John Milton died. He was the eldest of nine children, and was named after his father, Isaac. His father was a truly worthy and respectable man. In the course of the future years of his very long life, he became the master of a school of considerable reputation in the town. Dr. Johnson says it was reported that Watts' father was a shoemaker. In the year 1700 Isaac Watts, of 21, French Street, Southampton, was a clothier or cloth factor; so he is described in legal documents which still exist in that town; so he is described in another deed of 1719; while in 1736 he is described as " Isaac Watts, of the town and county of Southampton, gentleman:"* this was the year in which he died. At the time, however, of Isaac's birth, deep

---

* " Dr. Isaac Watts," a Lecture by Hermann Carlyle, LL.B., seventh minister of the church of which Dr. Watts' father was for forty-eight years a deacon.

grief was round, and heavy distress over the household.
The father was a Nonconformist, and a deacon of that
which is now the Above Bar Congregational Church in
Southampton. It was a cruel time ; the laws were very
bitter against Nonconformists, and the traveller through
Southampton in many months of the year 1674–75 might
have seen a respectable young woman, with a child at her
breast, sitting on the steps of the gaol seeking and waiting for admission to her husband. It was the mother of
Watts, and the daughter of Alderman Taunton. Tradition says, she was French in her lineage, of an exiled
Huguenot family, driven over to England by intolerance
and the massacre of St. Bartholomew, in the reign of
Queen Elizabeth. Thus Watts was the child of persecution, and through all the earliest years of his life his mind
must have been habituated to such impressions and
associations as were well calculated to draw out and give
sharpness and distinctness to his convictions. The old
prison remains very nearly the same as when the young
mother sat with her child looking up to the barred room
in which her husband was confined. It stands upon the
beach of the sweet Southampton waters, which then
rolled much further in, and almost washed the prison
doors. Legend asserts that it was only a few steps from
this spot that Canute fixed his chair when, in order that
he might rebuke the adulation of his courtiers, he commanded the waves to retire. Perhaps the imprisoned man
turned to the incident, and thought of One who is able
to still the noise of the waves and the tumult of the
people, and to say to all billows, "Hitherto shalt
thou come, and no further." If able to climb to the
tower of his prison, a lovely scene opened to his view:
the charming hills of Bittern on the left; the "sweet

fields beyond the swelling floods" opposite, on the right of the Southampton waters; at his foot the old houses of the quaint little town, and his own persecuted abode.

The author of "The Christian Life in Song" has not unnaturally conceived that probably to his mother he was indebted for the lyrical tendencies in which at a very early period his faith sought to express itself. The French Huguenots led the way in the utterance of feeling in sweet sacred hymns; and the grieving young mother might perhaps refresh her faith by some of the strains of her old people, while little knowing that she held in her arms one who was to eclipse the fame of Clement Marot in this particular. As to the imprisonment of the father, a licence had been issued in 1662 by Charles II., under the signature of Arlington, allowing "a room or rooms" in the house of Giles Say to be used for congregational worship, and Mr. Say, himself an exile and refugee from the persecutions of France, to be "the teacher." In a short time this licence of indulgence was withdrawn, and Mr. Say and his chief supporters were thrown into prison; one of the principal of these, as we have seen, was Isaac Watts the elder. It was an unpromising commencement to an illustrious life; and this trouble was no sooner escaped from than it was renewed. Liberated from prison, Isaac was still a very young child when his father was imprisoned again on the same charge for six months. In 1683 he was obliged to flee from home into exile from his family. Where he passed his time we have no exact information, but for two years he was living principally in London; and thus the family continued to pass through a course of domestic suffering until those happier days came which brought the abdication of the Stuart family and in honour of which, on the succession of William, we cannot wonder that Isaac Watts was glad to pour out some of his earliest verses.

Watts sprang from a fairly good family. Alderman Taunton, his grandfather on his mother's side, is still remembered in Southampton by his public benefactions. The grandfather Watts had been engaged in the naval service, and was commander of a man-of-war in the year 1656 under Admiral Blake. He appears to have been a man of great courage and many accomplishments. He had some skill in the lighter recreations of music, painting, and poetry. A story is told how in the East Indies he had a personal conflict with a tiger, which followed him into a river; he grappled with the monster, and got the better in the conflict. In the Dutch war the vessel he commanded exploded, and thus in the prime of life he met his end. It has been tenderly remarked that "the grandmother Lois" is often as influential on the opening mind as "the mother Eunice." The widow of the gallant sailor, and grandmother of the poet, had not only many stories to tell of her husband's adventures, but seems to have been remarkably amiable, if she may be judged by the glowing verses in which her grandson sought to do honour to her memory. She sought to instil into his mind the lessons of early piety, and exercised an influence over his early education during the time when trial and grief were strong in the household of her children. The old people appear to have possessed considerable property, but it was probably much diminished during those persecuting times. Such was the stock whence the poet was descended. We may speak of it as a good strong root, both upon the father's and upon the mother's side. A sap of nobleness and gentleness seems to have given

vitality to both families, and to have left its best influences in their child.

Isaac Watts the elder was a man of great social worth.
In after years his boarding-school became a most flourishing
establishment, and children were sent to it to receive their
training both from America and the West Indies. There
is a document written to his family when he was living
in exile from them, which places his high principles of
character, his prudence and his piety, his strong Protestantism, and his intelligence in a very remarkable light.
He also had a taste for sacred verse, and many of his pieces
have been preserved breathing a saintly meditative spirit.

Mr. Parker, the amanuensis of Dr. Watts, mentions a
singular anecdote to illustrate how his advice was sought
by persons of the town on account of his reputation for
wisdom. A person, a stonemason, in Southampton, had a
dream. He had purchased an old building for its materials ;
previous to his pulling it down he dreamed that a large
stone in the centre of an arch fell upon him and killed
him. Upon asking Mr. Watts his opinion, he said, " I am
not for paying any great regard to dreams, nor yet for
utterly slighting them. If there is such a stone in the
building as you saw in your dream" (which he told him
there really was), " my advice to you is, that you take
great care, in taking down the building, to keep far enough
off from it." The mason resolved to act upon his opinion,
but in an unfortunate moment he forgot his dream, went
under the arch, and the stone fell upon him and crushed
him to death.

This good father lived to the advanced age of eighty-
five ; his son Isaac was then in his sixty-third year, and
only two or three days before his father's death addressed
to him the following tender and satisfying letter :—

" NEWINGTON : *February* 8*th*, 1736-37.

" HONOURED AND DEAR SIR,

"It is now ten days since I heard from you, and learned by my nephew that you had been recovered from a very threatening illness. When you are in danger of life, I believe my sister is afraid to let me know the worst, for fear of affecting me too much. But as I feel old age daily advancing on myself, I am endeavouring to be ready for my removal hence ; and though it gives a shock to nature when what has been long dear to one is taken away, yet reason and religion should teach us to expect it in these scenes of mortality and a dying world. Blessed be God for our immortal hopes, through the blood of Jesus, who has taken away the sting of death! What could such dying creatures do without the comforts of the Gospel ? I hope you feel those satisfactions of soul on the borders of life which nothing can give but this Gospel, which you taught us all in our younger years. May these Divine consolations support your spirits under all your growing infirmities; and may our blessed Saviour form your soul to such a holy heavenly frame, that you may wait with patience amidst the languors of life for a joyful passage into the land of immortality! May no cares nor pains ruffle nor afflict your spirit! May you maintain a constant serenity at heart, and sacred calmness of mind, as one who has long passed midnight, and is in view of the dawning day ! 'The night is far spent, the day is at hand!' Let the garments of light be found upon us, and let us lift up our heads, for our redemption draws nigh. Amen.

" I am, dear Sir,

" Your most affectionate obedient Son,

" ISAAC WATTS."

Troubled as were the early years of his life, the subject of our biography furnishes one of those rare instances in which the precocity of infancy was not purchased at the expense of power in maturity; it is said that before he could speak plainly, when any money was given to him, he would cry, "A book! a book! buy a book!" He began to learn Latin at the age of four years, and in the knowledge of this language and in Greek he made swift progress; it is probable that of Latin, Greek, and Hebrew he had considerable knowledge while yet a child. He is one of those who have been said to "lisp in numbers." His utterances of infant rhyme are not astonishing, but every biography of him has repeated the story how, when he was seven years of age, his mother after school-hours one afternoon offered him a farthing if he would give her some verses, when he presented her with the well-known couplet :

> I write not for a farthing, but to try
> How I your farthing writers can outvie.

It was about the same time that, some verses of his falling into the hands of his mother, she expressed her doubts whether he could have written them, whereupon he immediately wrote the following acrostic; and if some of the lines seem to falter, the last two are certainly remark-able as the expression of a mere child, and have even a kind of prophecy in them of his future years :

> I am a vile polluted lump of earth,
> S o I've continued ever since my birth;
> A lthough Jehovah grace does daily give me,
> A s sure this monster Satan will deceive me,
> C ome, therefore, Lord, from Satan's claws relieve me.
>
> W ash me in Thy blood, O Christ,
> A nd grace Divine impart,
> T hen search and try the corners of my heart,
> T hat I in all things may be fit to do
> S ervice to Thee, and sing Thy praises too.

It was perhaps from the uncertainty of tuition at home, or from the youthful student outstripping the attainments of his father, that he was early sent to the grammar-school at Southampton, of which the Rev. John Pinhorne was the principal. He was a man of good character and attainments, rector of All Saints Church in Southampton, prebendary of Leckford, and vicar of Eling, in the New Forest. The Nonconformist relations of his young pupil appear to have produced no uncharitable effect upon the master's mind. From the first he prophesied the future eminence and celebrity of the young scholar. He died in 1714, when these were in their dawn. Watts held him in most reverent and grateful memory, and illustrated these feelings in a Pindaric Latin ode, which, in its recapitulation of the classical authors, to whose pages the master had guided his knowledge, certainly shows at once the abundant scholarship of the worthy pair.

There, in the grammar-school of the town, in the dark reigns of the Second Charles and James, the little Puritan was the most diligent and advanced scholar, the beloved of his master. He very early exhibited a great proficiency in Latin, Greek, and French. A spare, pale child, there was perhaps nothing peculiarly prepossessing in his features, if we except the bright, intense sparkling eye, and the quivering, nervous expression. There was certainly nothing robust about him, but all the indications of the future scholar. May we not also say the indications of the future saint—a little meditative Samuel—of a time in our history of which we may say " the Word of the Lord was precious in those days, there was no open vision ?"

These first years, when the mind was gathering to itself the many tools of knowledge, were passed in his father's house at Southampton—an utterly different

Southampton from that which we see now—a charming little sequestered town; the gentle river rolled its pleasant and pellucid waves before it, undisturbed by the iron floating bridge, as the nobler Southampton Water rolled along between it and the Isle of Wight. Unsullied by steamboats, it was no depôt for the great navies of the West, but it must have been a charming country town, its streets almost overshadowed by the noble trees of the New Forest. The historian and antiquarian will find no lack of material for observation and suggestion in Southampton; it is rich in old nooks and reminiscences, and as full of material for the artist as for the archæologist. Legend and story of St. Benedict or King Canute, of the knightly Bevis and Ascapart were, we may be sure, not less fragrant then than they are there to-day. Many of the old houses are standing; the old town walls, the monuments of the great Roman road, and the noble bars of the town looked, we may be sure, more perfect then than now; the neighbourhood in which Watts lived still bears traces of being the oldest part of the town; other spots, which bear the marks of nineteenth century improvements in handsome parks and squares and streets, were then only wide, open fields; and many of the objects interesting to those who visit English shrines have altogether passed away. The gaol in which Watts' father was confined, St. Michael's Prison, the old Bull Hall, and the buildings round the old Walnut tree—the town retains the names of these places, and still conveys some impression of what they were. The Blue Anchor Postern still exhibits its massive old masonry, the relics of a building inhabited by King John, and a royal residence of Henry III. Yet more interesting memories gather in another part of the town, round the Widows'

Almshouses,* founded by Mr. Thorner, the friend and
co-religionist of Watts' father. The little town, from
being one of the most inconsiderable, has become one of
the most thriving and famous in the empire.

Still, changed as Southampton is during the last two
hundred years, it is not difficult to realize something of its
ancient character. Its counterpart or resemblance may
still be found in some of those small seaport towns of
France which have been left to their primitive isolation by
the retreating tides of population. Yet a good many
things in the old town of Southampton remain unchanged.
It is full of quaint nooks and corners, gateways and arch-
ways bearing the evident marks of high antiquity. For a
long period Southampton sank into a state of sequestra-
tion and repose ; but her early history was something like
her later, and there was a day when in the most palmy and
splendid time of Venice her connection with that great
commercial republic was as intimate as it is now with the
Eastern and Western Indies. Its glory dates from the
time of the Conquest; and a circumstance ominous to
England in the landing there of Philip II., of Spain, the
husband and ill-adviser of Mary, is the last instance
recorded of its prominence and splendour in the ancient
day. The old parish of All Saints, in which Watts was
born, and the neighbourhood in which his childhood was
passed, remain so little changed as to enable the visitor to
carry in his mind a fair picture of the old lanes and streets,
rambling round the old church, in the middle of the now
rudely paved square.

---

* It is interesting to remember that Isaac Watts the elder was the
first local trustee to Robert Thorner's munificent bequest, which is now
the grandest of all the Southampton charities, and has made the name
of Thorner in that town a household word.

The house in which Watts was born, in French Street, is still standing, and seems to give the assurance of being much the same, although it has so far yielded to the indignities of time that one side of it is a public-house and the other a marine store. It must have been a plain but roomy, substantial building, standing back with its garden behind it, full of lofty rooms and rambling nooks and passages. There he first saw the light, there he passed his play days of childhood; there the dreamy, studious boy accumulated the first spoils of knowledge; returning thither after his academical course was closed, there he wrote his first, and even a considerable number of his hymns; and thither, a celebrated man, he often came to visit his parents, even when he was an old man. A fragrant memory of early piety and matured holiness still lingers over the old place, and consecrates it as one of our English shrines,*

In his childhood circumstances happened likely to produce some effect upon his mind. The memory of the terrible plague of 1665, in which between one and two thousand persons were swept away, was still fresh in Southampton for one hundred and fifty years after. The annalists of the town tell us it did not recover from the state of decay into which it fell from that dreadful visitation. The shops were all closed, all who could fled from the town, and the streets were overgrown with grass. When Watts was six years old the great comet flamed over England, with which were associated in many minds such

---

* The soil of Southampton seems to have been favourable to the production of the lyrical faculty, although it is not probable that many of those whose hearts have been stirred by the holy strains of Watts have been acquainted with the melodies of one of the most national of English song-writers, the laureate of sailors, also a townsman of Southampton, Thomas Dibden.

dreadful portents, and it no doubt lent a colour to many
of his after most imaginative conceptions. It was an object
of singularly marvellous splendour. Several years after he
seems to have put the memory of the impressions it produced
upon him into the couplets in which he alters Young's description, and the words sufficiently show how the surprising
spectacle had excited his youthful fancy :

> Who stretched the comet to prodigious size,
> And poured his flaming train o'er half the skies ?
> Is 't at Thy wrath the heavenly monster glares
> O'er the pale nations, to announce Thy wars ?

The life of Watts had very little in it at any time which
related to the history of the period in which he lived, yet
it is impossible not to notice that these first years of his
life at Southampton were among the most exciting and
memorable of the country's history. What England was
Lord Macaulay has well described in perhaps one of the
most charming chapters of his history—*the State of England
at the death of Charles II.* It was the time of England's
Reign of Terror, and circumstances were happening, the
conversations upon which must have produced a vivid
impression upon the mind of a youth of lively sensibility.
The execution of Algernon Sidney and Lord William
Russell, the trial of Richard Baxter, the rising of Monmouth, the tremendous descent of Jefferies in the Bloody
Assize of the West, the trial of the bishops, the flight of
James, the landing of William at Torbay, and his progress
to London ; these were circumstances such as England had
never seen before, such as England can never see again,
and they all crowded fast upon each other in the years of
Watts' boyhood and early youth.

The period of the youth of Watts calls up to the mind
a singularly contradictory range of associations ; it was a

wild, wicked, and frivolous time, and yet there were men
living then whose names have adorned, and will ever adorn
the literature of our land.   Watts was fourteen years of
age when John Bunyan finished his eventful course.
Samuel Wesley, the father of John and Charles, was just
leaving his academy at Stoke Newington and the Dissenters,
by whom he had been educated ; Henry More, the singular
mystic, preceded Bunyan by one year to the grave ; Ralph
Cudworth was accumulating his immense mass of nebulous
scholarship ; South was preaching his celebrated sermons,
in which coarseness so frequently " kibes the heels " of
wisdom; Robert Boyle was, with intense ardour, prosecuting
his observations and studies in natural history and science,
and blending with equal ardour with them his devotions
to revealed religion and Divine truth ; Barrow was pursuing
his ponderous lucubrations ; Newton was expounding the
system of the universe, and Locke the system of the
the mind ; Howe was indulging in his seraphic ardours ;
Dryden was drawing to the close of an inglorious life, and
writing some of the pieces which have best served his
fame ; John Evelyn, the model of an English gentleman,
was studying his trees at Wootton, or penning his entertaining diary at Sayn Court; Samuel Pepys, garrulous
and silly, was writing a history without knowing it, as
the Boswell or the Paul Pry of the court and the town ;
Lely was flattering a meretricious taste by his paintings,
and Christopher Wren preparing his plans for rebuilding
London.

The persecutions to which the Nonconformists through
this period were exposed of course affected society in
Southampton ; the avenues to prosperity and peace seemed
to lie only in conformity to the Church of England.   It
was then that, in consequence of his great and promising

attainments, his diligence and high character, an offer
was made to Watts by Dr. John Speed, a physician of the
town, on the behalf of several others, to send him to one
of the universities, and very handsomely defray all his
expenses there. He did not hesitate for a second, but
respectfully and firmly replied that he was determined to
take up his lot amongst the Dissenters. Two of his early
friends, in every way incomparably his inferiors, conformed,
and attained to archiepiscopal dignities. Yet, in spite
of all that he afterwards wrote on the relation of the civil
magistrate to religion, there would seem to have been
little in his faith, feeling, or practice which might not
easily have found a home in the Establishment but for the
persecuting spirit of the time. It was the same year that
in his slight, curious autobiographical memoranda,* he
mentions concisely how he " fell under considerable convictions of sin ;" in the year following, his entry runs on,
" and was led to trust in Christ, I hope." In the same
year, 1689, he mentions that he had a great and dangerous
sickness ; and all these events of his life, which look so
brief and cold to us as we put them down on paper, were
great and crucial events to him, settling the foundations
of his character, probably leading him away from the pursuits of scholarship as a mere charm and recreation of
cultivated taste, to regard it as the important means by
which an entrance might be obtained to everlasting truths.
These events would add to those motives which had determined him to renounce the idea of university training,
and to seek an entrance into the ministry through the
humbler portal of a Dissenting academy.

* See Appendix.

CHAPTER II.

In the Academy at Stoke Newington.

THE neighbourhood of London, to which Isaac Watts removed from Southampton for the purpose of completing his studies, and preparing for the work of the ministry, was Stoke Newington, and in that neighbourhood he was destined to pass the greater part of his life. It was probably even then pervaded, as for a long time before and ever since, by an atmosphere of mild but consistent Nonconformity : the academy in which he studied was beneath the superintendence of the Rev. Thomas Rowe, the pastor of the Independent Church assembling in Girdlers' Hall, in the City. It was probably one of the most considerable of the time, and appears to have succeeded to one also well known upon the same spot, of which the principal was the Rev. Charles Morton. Here studied the celebrated Daniel Defoe, also originally intended for the Nonconformist pulpit, as he says in one of his reviews : " It is not often I trouble you with any of my divinity ; the pulpit is none of my office. It was my disaster first to be set apart for, and then to be set apart from, the honour of that sacred employ." The academy had a good reputation, and the effort which old Samuel Wesley had made to sully its fair fame only reflected his own dishonour, and left it untarnished.

Charles Morton was one of those obscure but remarkable men in which our country at that time was so rich. He was descended from a singularly distinguished family —that of Cardinal Morton, Thomas Morton, Bishop of Durham, and many other distinguished men. He took his degree of M.A. at Wadham College, Oxford, and became, and continued until the Act of Uniformity, rector of Blisland, in Cornwall; after preaching for a short time at St. Ives he removed to London, and shortly after opened an academy on Newington Green. Defoe pronounces the highest encomiums upon him and his method as a tutor; and Samuel Wesley, in the midst of his bitterness and ungracious flippancy—for he had been maintained on the foundation under the idea of entering the Nonconformist ministry—ceases from his abuse to honour the memory of his master; he, however, after having trained several men who became eminent in their day, teased by continued persecution, passed over to America; there his fame had preceded him; there he became pastor of a church in Charlestown, and Vice-president of Harvard University.*

Shortly after the departure of Mr. Morton for America, the academy to which Watts was consigned was founded by the eminently learned Theophilus Gale, M.A., the author of that large medley of scholarship "The Court of the Gentiles." He also had been deprived of considerable Church preferments. To his charge the eccentric Philip Lord Wharton committed the tutorship of his sons; with them he travelled on the Continent, adding to the stores of his mental wealth, and contracting a friendship with the learned Bochart. He arrived in the metropolis on his return to see the city in the flames of the terrible conflagration, but to learn that the manuscripts he had left in

* Walter Wilson's " Life of Defoe," vol. i. pp. 26, 27.

the care of a friend were all saved, while the house in
which they had been preserved was destroyed. His mind
was so largely stored with every kind of learning that his
friends entreated him to settle as a professor of theology,
which he did at Stoke Newington, and there he continued
till he died in 1678, at the early age of forty-nine. He
left his personal estate for the education of young men for
the ministry; his library, with the exception of his philosophical books, to Harvard College. Beneath a tutor so
distinguished the interests of the two academies had probably merged into one. The successor of Mr. Gale was
one of his own students, Thomas Rowe, whom we have
already mentioned. He was the son of the Rev. John
Rowe, M.A., ejected from Westminster Abbey, and who was
called to preach the thanksgiving sermon before the Parliament on the occasion of the destruction of the Spanish
fleet, October 8th, 1656. Thomas Rowe very early entered
upon the work of the ministry. At the age of twenty-one
he succeeded his father as pastor of Girdlers' Hall in
Basinghall Street.

Isaac Watts came to the academy of Stoke Newington
in the year 1690; he was then in his sixteenth year.
"Such he was," says Dr. Johnson, "as every Christian
Church would rejoice to have adopted."

There was no doubt a rare congeniality of spirit between
the tutor and his illustrious pupil; the native gentleness of
the latter found nothing perhaps in the former to give to it
either sharpness or force; indeed, the name of Thomas
Rowe would be lost but for the fame of Watts. The pupil
was nearer to manhood than was implied in his years; he
was a well-informed and richly cultivated scholar when he
left his father's house, and his modest bearing was such as
even a tutor might entrust with the responsibilities of

friendship. Friendship soon matured between them; the
tutor testified that he never on any occasion had to give
his pupil a reproof. His academical exercises show with
what diligence he was applying himself to the work of preparation for the work of his future life. A sweet and
cheerful gravity pervaded his manners and his studies, and
it may be boldly said that in the great universities of that
time there were very few who wrought with so much vigour
or to so much purpose. His Latin essays written at this
period " show," says Dr. Johnson, " a degree of knowledge
both philosophical and theological, such as very few attain
by a much longer course of study." This verdict of Johnson is only just. One method adopted by Watts in his
studies he has commended to others in his " Improvement
of the Mind," and it has probably been often successfully
adopted. It was the plan of abridging the works of the
more eminent writers in the various departments of study.
Thus he printed the material more indelibly on his
memory; at the same time, by recasting the thoughts or the
information in his own mind, he was so compelled to analyze
and digest that he made the whole matter more entirely
his own mental property. To this practice he alludes when
he says : " Other things also of the like nature may be use-
fully practised with regard to the authors which you read—
viz., If the method of a book be irregular, reduce it into
form by a little analysis of your own, or by hints in the
margin ; if those things are heaped together which should
be separated, you may wisely distinguish and divide them ;
if several things relating to the same subject are scattered
up and down separately through the treatise, you may
bring them all to one view by references ; or if the matter
of a book be really valuable and deserving, you may throw
it into a better method, reduce it to a more logical scheme,

or abridge it into a lesser form. All these practices will
have a tendency both to advance your skill in logic and
method, to improve your judgment in general, and to give
you a fuller survey of that subject in particular. When
you have finished the treatise with all your observations
upon it, recollect and determine what real improvements
you have made by reading that author."*

There was another plan which reveals the careful
student, and to which Dr. Gibbons refers in his life :
" There was another method also which the doctor adopted,
it may be in the time of his preparatory studies, though of
this we are not able to furnish positive evidence, but of
which there is the fullest proof in his further progress
of life, namely, that of interleaving the works of authors,
and inserting in the blank pages additions from other
writers on the same subject. I have now by me, the gift
of his brother Mr. Enoch Watts, the ' Westminster Greek
Grammar' thus interleaved by the doctor, with all he
thought proper to collect from Dr. Busby's and Mr. Teed's
' Greek Grammars,' engrafted by him into the supple-
mental leaves ; and I have besides in my possession a
present from the doctor himself, a printed discourse by a
considerable writer, on a controverted point in divinity,
interleaved in the same manner, and much enlarged by
insertions in the doctor's own hand." Certainly from
hints such as these no writer could seem by his own
careful diligence to be more admirably prepared to write
to and counsel young men and others concerning the
improvement of the mind.

Most of the biographers of Watts have referred to his
fellow-students. Several of them were interesting men.

---

* " The Improvement of the Mind," chap. iv. of " Books and
Reading."

" The first genius in the academy," to adopt Watts' own descriptive designation, was Mr. Josiah Hart; but very speedily after his removal from Mr. Rowe he conformed, and became chaplain to John Hampden, Esq., the member for Buckinghamshire. Presently after he became chaplain to his grace the Duke of Bolton, Lord Lieutenant of Ireland. Such offices furnished very easy opportunities for advancement in the Church. Before long he became Bishop of Kilmore and Ardagh; and in 1742 he was translated to the archbishopric of Tuam, with which was united the bishopric of Enaghdoen, with liberty to retain his former see of Ardagh; yet he retained friendly relationships with his old fellow-student, and in the "Lyrics" occurs a free translation of an epigram of Martial to Cirinus, which seems to intimate that he was not wanting himself in poetic inspiration :

> So smooth your numbers, friend, your verse so sweet,
> So sharp the jest, and yet the turn so neat,
> That with her Martial, Rome would place Cirine,
> Rome would prefer your sense and thought to mine.
> Yet modest you decline the public stage,
> To fix your friend alone amidst th' applauding age.

Fifty years after the period of their life as fellow-students we find the Archbishop writing to Watts, " God grant we may be useful while we live, and may run clear and with unclouded minds till we come to the very dregs ! I send you my visitation charge to my clergy of Tuam. I submit it to your judgment. Your old friend and affectionate servant, JOSIAH TUAM." If in some part singularly expressed, it gives a not unpleasing idea of the writer's character.

Another fellow-student was Mr. John Hughes; but he also, though dedicated to, and educated for, the Dissenting ministry, upon leaving the academy soon conformed to

the Establishment ; he cultivated the lighter studies
of music, poetry, and painting.   The Lord Chancellor
Cowper, in 1717, appointed him secretary to the com-
missions of the peace ; and after the resignation of the
Chancellor he was still continued in the same office.   He
became a contributor to the "Tatler," "Spectator," and
"Guardian," and he attained to the friendship of some of
the most distinguished men of the age.   Addison admired
him as a poet, Pope held him in veneration for his goodness, and Bishop Hoadley honoured him as a friend.

Others of the fellow-students continued stedfast to the
principles of their Dissenting Alma Mater, and became in
their way also useful and remarkable men ; among these
was Mr. Samuel Say, the fellow-townsman of Watts, and
one year his junior.   After a useful course of ministrations he succeeded Dr. Calamy at Westminster, and continued there until his death.   Through life he was on
intimate friendly terms with his fellow-townsman.   Little
as we know of him, sufficient is known to give to us the
picture of a thoroughly accomplished man, even with
considerable claims to be regarded as a man of genius ;
indeed it strikes us, in reviewing the intercourse of these
young men with each other, and their recommendations
of each other, that there was a thoroughness about
their attainments ; and that while they were faithful to
severer studies they were not indisposed to those graceful
exercises of the mind and fancy which have generally,
but we believe unjustly, been regarded as incompatible
with the severity of the Puritan character.   To this
indulgence, no doubt, the taste of the tutor, Mr. Rowe,
was favourable.   We know that Watts was accomplished
in several departments of taste, although all the exercises
which have come down to us from his college-days are

quite of the severer character—-critical, metaphysical, and theological—but his conscience was probably of that tender order which would esteem it an unfaithfulness to the object for which he was placed in the academy to turn aside to pursuits of a lighter and less sacred description. Another fellow-student of Isaac Watts was Daniel Neal, celebrated as the author of " The History of the Puritans;" he proved ,in an eminent degree his call to the work of the ministry, and after some time spent in travel settled as a pastor in the metropolis.

It is usual in our day, with the Dissenting academies, to receive no one as student for the ministry who has not previously qualified himself by membership with the church which commends him. The practice appears to have been more liberal in Watts' day. He was never a member of the church at Southampton, but in the third year of his residence with Mr. Rowe he united himself with the church of his tutor, as he enters it in his memoranda, " I was admitted to Mr. T. Rowe's church December, 1693." This church also, like so many of the Independent churches in the city, had a very honourable ancestry—as we have previously said, it then held its meetings in Girdlers' Hall, Basinghall Street; after the death of Mr. Rowe it removed to Haberdashers' Hall, but the church itself appears to have originated with the eminent William Strong, M.A., still held in honour by the lovers of old Puritan literature for his folio on the Covenants. He was a fellow of Katherine Hall, Cambridge, and rector of More Crichel, in Dorsetshire. This living during the Civil Wars he was compelled by the Cavaliers to relinquish, and, coming to London, he became minister of the church assembling in Westminster Abbey, and subsequently in the House of Lords. It is singular

that thus both the ministers of the congregation in
Girdlers' Hall were originally pastors of the church in
Westminster Abbey. Mr. Strong died in 1654, and was
buried in the Abbey church, but upon the restoration his
remains had, with those of Cromwell, Blake, and Pym,
the honour of exhumation. Still, in the church when
Watts became a member of it, lingered some of the old
elements which first composed it; perhaps the most conspicuous of these was Major-General Goffe, the well-known
name of one of the judges of Charles I.

Such was the church with which Watts held his first
communion, and from which he was only transferred to
become the pastor of that over which he presided for the
remainder of his life. It need hardly be said that whatever interest attached to its memory in connection with
the circumstances which we have recited, his name confers
upon it the most permanent human interest. The union
must have strengthened that intimacy we have already
pointed out between himself and his tutor, pastor, and
friend. It is not probable that even at this period Mr.
Rowe had the large scholarship and keen insight into the
beauties of the most famous classics possessed by his
pupil, if we may form a judgment from the Pindaric ode
to Mr. Pinhorne, but a quiet mind will often marshal ideas
into order, and give a military usefulness in commanding
materials it could not recruit. Watts was probably never,
at any period of his life, wanting in the accoutrements of
discipline; but this was the service chiefly rendered at.
the academy, this and the more earnest entrance upon
philosophical and theological studies. We are sure also
that he and his tutor well harmonized in their sense of
the duty and the dignity of moral independence; Watts
had already shown himself to be possessed of this by his

entrance into the academy. In his lines "To the much honoured Mr. Thomas Rowe, the director of my youthful studies," he says :

> I hate these shackles of the mind
>   Forged by the haughty wise ;
> Souls were not born to be confined,
> And led, like Samson, blind and bound ;—
> But when his native strength he found
>   He well avenged his eyes.
> I love thy gentle influence, Rowe,
> Thy gentle influence like the sun,
> Only dissolves the frozen snow,
> Then bids our thoughts like rivers flow,
> And choose the channels where they run.

And here we may say farewell to the tutor ; he lived just long enough to see his scholar settled in the ministry ; but for his companion pupils he occupied a solitary home ; he was never married, and in 1705, riding through the city on horseback, he was seized with a fit, fell from his horse, and instantly died. He was one of those men of whom the world makes little mention, and finds little recorded ; he was a comparatively young man. We have dwelt upon the furniture of his mind, the attractiveness of his manners, the docility and beauty of his disposition ; to these it may be added that he was also probably possessed of an engaging manner in the pulpit, as he retained what was then considered a large congregation to the time of his death.

While referring to the Dissenting academies of those days, it may be interesting to notice that from one of them in Gloucester, beneath the tutorship of the Rev. Samuel Jones, two eminent men received their first training for the ministry of the Church of England, although intended for the Nonconformist communion—Samuel Butler, the distinguished author of the " Analogy," and

Bishop of Durham; and Thomas Secker, Bishop of Oxford, and afterwards Archbishop of Canterbury. The Archbishop probably found one of his earliest patrons in Dr. Watts, by whom, as the following letter testifies, he was introduced to the academy. The biographers of the Archbishop, Dr. Porteus and Dr. Stinton, pass over the Archbishop's first studies, as conducted by "one Mr. Jones, who kept an academy at Gloucester;" but the following letter from Secker, written when about the age of eighteen to Dr. Watts, gives a very admirable idea of the manner in which he directed the work of study in the academy:

"GLOUCESTER: *Nov.* 18*th*, 1711.
" REV. SÍR,

" Before I give you an account of the state of our academy, and those other things you desired me, please to accept of my hearty thanks for that service you have done me, both in advising me to prosecute my studies in such an extraordinary place of education, and in procuring me admittance into it. I wish my improvements may be answerable to the advantages I enjoy; but, however that may happen, your kindness has fixed me in a place where I may be very happy, and spend my time to good purpose, and where, if I do not, the fault will be all my own. I am sensible how difficult it is to give a character of any person or thing, because the most probable guesses we make very often prove false ones. But, since you are pleased to desire it, I think myself obliged to give you the best and most impartial account of matters I can.

" Mr. Jones, then, I take to be a man of real piety, great learning, and an agreeable temper; one who is very diligent in instructing all under his care, very well qualified to give instructions, and whose well-managed familiarity will always make him respected.   He is very strict in keeping good order, and will effectually preserve his pupils from negligence and immorality.   And accordingly, I believe, there are not many academies freer in general from those vices than we are.   In particular my bedfellow, Mr. Scott,* is one of unfeigned religion, and a diligent searcher after truth.   His genteel carriage and agreeable disposition gain him the esteem of every one. Mr. Griffith is more than ordinary serious and grave, and improves more in everything than one could expect from a man who seems to be not much under forty; particularly in Greek and Hebrew he has made a great progress.   Mr. Francis and Mr. Watkins are diligent in study and truly religious.   The elder Mr. Jones, having had a better education than they, will in all probability make a greater scholar; and his brother is one of quick parts.   Our logic, which we had read once over, is so contrived as to comprehend all Hereboord, and far the greater part of Mr. Locke's Essay, and the Art of Thinking.   What Mr. Jones dictated to us was but short, containing a clear and brief account of the matter, references to the places where it was more fully treated of, and remarks on, or explications of the authors cited, when need required.   At our next lecture we gave an account both of what the author quoted and our tutor said, who commonly then gave us a larger explication of it, and so proceeded to the next

---

* Afterwards, says Dr. Gibbons, Dr. Daniel Scott. He was a very learned and amiable man. After he had studied under Mr. Jones he removed to Utrecht for further education; there he took the degree of doctor of laws. In the year 1741 he published a new version of St. Matthew's Gospel, with critical notes, and an examination of Dr. Mills' various readings. He published, also, in the year 1745, an " Appendix to H. Stephens' Greek Lexicon," in two volumes.

thing in order. He took care, as far as possible, that we
understood the sense as well as remembered the words
of what we had read, and that we should not suffer ourselves to be cheated with obscure terms which had no
meaning. Though he be no great admirer of the old logic,
yet he has taken a great deal of pains both in explaining
and correcting Hereboord, and has for the most part made
him intelligible, or shown that he is not so. The two
Mr. Joneses, Mr. Francis, Mr. Watkins, Mr. Sheldon, and
two more gentlemen, are to begin Jewish Antiquities in
a short time. I was designed for one of their number, but
rather chose to read logic once more; both because I was
utterly unacquainted with it when I came to this place,
and because the others having all, except Mr. Francis,
been at other academies, will be obliged to make more
haste than those in a lower class, and consequently cannot
have so good or large accounts of anything, nor so much
time to study every head. We shall have gone through
our course in about four years' time, which I believe
that nobody that once knows Mr. Jones will think too
long.

" I began to learn Hebrew as soon as I came hither, and
find myself able now to construe and give some grammati-
cal account of about twenty verses in the easier parts of
the Bible, after less than an hour's preparation. We read
every day two verses apiece in the Hebrew Bible, which
we turn into Greek (no one knowing which his verses
shall be, though at first it was otherwise). And this, with
logic, is our morning's work. Mr. Jones also began about
three months ago some critical lectures, in order to the
exposition you advised him to. The principal things contained in them are about the antiquity of the Hebrew language, letters, vowels, the incorruption of the Scriptures,

ancient divisions of the Bible, an account of the Talmud, Masora, and Cabala. We are at present upon the Septuagint, and shall proceed after that to the Targumim, and other versions, etc. Every part is managed with abundance of perspicuity, and seldom any material thing is omitted that other authors have said upon the point, though very frequently we have useful additions of things which are not to be found in them. We have scarce been upon anything yet but Mr. Jones has had those writers which are most valued on that head, to which he always refers us. This is what we first set about in the afternoon, which being finished we read a chapter in the Greek Testament, and after that mathematics. We have gone through all that is commonly taught of algebra and proportion, with the first six books of Euclid, which is all Mr. Jones designs for the gentlemen I mentioned above, but he intends to read something more to the class that comes after them.

" This is our daily employment, which in the morning takes up about two hours, and something more in the afternoon. Only on Wednesdays, in the morning, we read Dionysius's Periegesis, on which we have notes, mostly geographical, but with some criticisms intermixed; and in the afternoon we have no lecture at all. So on Saturday, in the afternoon, we have only a Thesis, which none but they who have done with logic have any concern in. We are also just beginning to read Isocrates and Terence, each twice a week. On the latter our tutor will give us some notes which he received in a college from Perizonius.

" We are obliged to rise at five of the clock every morning, and to speak Latin always, except when below stairs amongst the family. The people where we live are very civil, and the greatest inconvenience we suffer is, that we fill the house rather too much, being sixteen in number, besides Mr. Jones. But I suppose the increase of his academy will oblige him to move next spring. We pass our time very agreeably betwixt study and conversation with our tutor, who is always ready to discourse freely of anything that is useful, and allows us either then or at lecture all imaginable liberty of making objections against his opinion, and prosecuting them as far as we can. In this and everything else he shows himself so much a gentleman, and manifests so great an affection and tenderness for his pupils as cannot but command respect and love. I almost forgot to mention our tutor's library, which is composed for the most part of foreign books, which seem to be very well chosen, and are every day of great advantage to us.

"Thus I have endeavoured, sir, to give you an account of all that I thought material or observable amongst us. As for my own part, I apply myself with what diligence I can to everything which is the subject of our lectures, without preferring one subject before another; because I see nothing we are engaged in but what is either necessary or extremely useful for one who would thoroughly understand those things which most concern him, or be able to explain them well to others. I hope I have not spent my time, since I came to this place, without some small improvement, both in human knowledge and that which is far better, and I earnestly desire the benefit of your prayers that God would be pleased to fit me better for His service, both in this world and the next. This, if you 'please to afford me, and your advice with relation to study, or whatever else you think convenient, must needs be extremely useful, as well as agreeable, and shall be thankfully received by your most obliged humble servant,

"THOMAS SECKER."

Secker's first communion was with a Dissenting church —the Rev. Timothy Jollie's—and he preached his first sermon in a Dissenting meeting-house at Bolsover, in Derbyshire.   He retained his feelings of affectionate indebtedness to his early friend to the close of Watts' life.

His term of study closed at Stoke Newington, Watts, still little more than a youth, returned for some time to his father's house at Southampton.   Worshipping with the congregation there, under the ministry of the Rev. Nathaniel Robinson, he felt that the psalmody was far beneath the beauty and dignity of a Christian service.   He was requested to produce something better, and the following Sabbath the service was concluded with what is now the first hymn of the first book ; and a stirring hymn it is— as an ascription of praise or worship, and as a confession of faith it is remarkably comprehensive and complete.

> Behold the glories of the Lamb
>   Amidst His Father's throne;
> Prepare new honours for His name,
>   And songs before unknown.
>
> Let elders worship at His feet,
>   The church adore around,
> With vials full of odours sweet,
>   And, harps of sweeter sound.
>
> Those are the prayers of the saints,
>   And these the hymns they raise;
> Jesus is kind to our complaints,
>   He loves to hear our praise.
>
> Eternal Father, who shall look
>   Into Thy secret will?
> Who but the Son shall take the book,
>   And open every seal?
>
> He shall fulfil Thy great decrees,
>   The Son deserves it well;
> Lo! in His hand the sovereign keys
>   Of heaven, and death, and hell.

Now to the Lamb that once was slain,
  Be endless blessings paid;
Salvation, glory, joy, remain
  For ever on Thy head.

Thou hast redeemed our souls with blood,
  Hast set the prisoners free;
Hast made us kings and priests to God,
  And we shall reign with Thee.

The worlds of nature and of grace
  Are put beneath Thy power;
Then shorten these delaying days,
  And bring the promised hour.

This is the tradition of the origin of the first hymn. It was received with great alacrity and joy. It was indeed "a new song." The young poet was entreated to produce another, and another. The series extended from Sabbath to Sabbath, until almost a volume was formed, although their publication was long delayed. This was the interesting result of his return to Southampton.

CHAPTER III.

In the Hartopp Family.

RETURNING from Southampton, Isaac Watts entered the family of Sir John Hartopp, the first of those two influential friends whose names will always be associated with his own; it was October 15th, 1696, he being then twenty-two years of age, when he went to reside with him. Within the memory of some of the old inhatants of Stoke Newington there stood on the north side of Church Street the remains of a red brick house, with large casement windows; once they were all handsomely painted, and bore the arms of Fleetwood, Hartopp, and Cook. But no one of these later generations saw that old mansion in all its original greatness. In later years it came to be divided into houses, and parts of it drifted down from the abode of statesmen to the boarding-school for young ladies. Still it retained even to its close, traditionary relics and reminiscences of the old days of its pride and importance. On the ceilings of its principal rooms were the remains of the arms of the Lord General Fleetwood; and in the upper part there was a little door concealed by hangings, through which the persecuted Nonconformist passed into a place of safety and concealment, in the days of Charles II. The old house

was built towards the close of the reign of Elizabeth, so
that even at the period when it comes before our readers
it was ancient. It was purchased by Charles Fleetwood,
Lord General of the army of the Commonwealth, and under
Cromwell one of the Council of State. It is quite unnecessary here to dwell upon his transient importance and
power; he was one of the last of those remarkable men in
that singular interregnum of our history, and the very last
after the resignation of Richard Cromwell who held some
of the shadows of the departed substance of greatness.
He spent the remainder of his days in the mansion of
Stoke Newington before his final departure for Bunhill
Fields. To this place, in time succeeded Sir John Hartopp,
by his wife Elizabeth Fleetwood, a grand-daughter of the
General; and to this old red brick building, with its secret
chambers and armorial casements and ceilings, Isaac Watts
came as a tutor in the family.

Sir John Hartopp was not a mere city knight, and indeed city knighthoods meant much more in those days
than now. He was of an old Leicestershire family of
Dalby Parva, in the register books of which place the name
is written Hartrupte. The family was able to trace a very
interesting history back to the time of Richard II.; the
baronetcy dated from the time of James I., and the family
received considerable honours from Charles I., and, what
is more to the purpose of the present memoir, it was in his
house that Richard Baxter planned, if he did not partly
write, "The Saint's Everlasting Rest." Sir John Hartopp,
the friend of Watts, was born at the commencement of the
Civil Wars. In his early youth the whole of his neighbourhood was alive with marchings and counter-marchings.
Buckminster was the place of the family residence, and the
steeple of the parish church was used as a watch-tower for

reconnoitring. The house was alive and perpetually on the guard against the incursions of the Cavaliers. Sir Edward Hartopp, the first baronet, died at the commencement of the Protectorate of Cromwell, and was buried at Buckminster; his son, the father of Sir John, died a short time previous to the Restoration, and about this time we find the family removed to London and settled at Stoke Newington. Sir John became an eminent Nonconformist; as he cast in his lot among the Independents, he was a member of the Church of Dr. Owen, with whom he maintained a very close and intimate friendship; and there is in the library of the New College, in St. John's Wood, a volume of the sermons of Owen, very carefully written down after hearing them, copied, probably for use in the family, in Sir John's handwriting. Many of Dr. Owen's manuscripts came into his possession upon his decease, and were contributed by him to the complete collection of the Doctor's sermons.

Sir John Hartopp was an ardent and active patriot. He was three times chosen representative for his native county of Leicestershire. In 1671 he was high sheriff, and he afterwards distinguished himself by his earnest advocacy of the Bill of Exclusion to bar the Duke of York's succession to the throne. He became the subject of much persecution, and paid in fines apparently the larger portion of £7,000. He died in 1722, when the affairs of the nation had long, through the active exertions of such men as he was, settled themselves into comparative tranquillity and prosperity. Watts preached in his memory his sermon " On the Happiness of Separate Spirits made Perfect," and he dwells at some length upon certain personal characteristics, from which we gather that Sir John was an accomplished man, with a taste for universal learning, and the pursuit of knowledge in various forms—mathematics in his younger days, and astronomy in his old age ; keeping alive his early knowledge of Greek for an intelligent acquaintance with the New Testament, and so late in life as at the age of fifty entering upon the study of Hebrew. His house became the refuge of the oppressed, while by some happy disposition of Providence he himself was saved from those more severe and painful persecutions to which so many were not only exposed but subjected. His ardent attachment to Dr. Owen assures us of the temper and character of his religious convictions, and altogether he shines out before us as one of those beautiful and luminous examples and illustrations of the men to whom our country owes so much. So far as we can gather from what is left on record of him, he appears to have been a true Christian gentleman, a fine harmonious combination of characteristics blending in him the severity of high principle with a gentle and tenderly affectionate nature.

Sir John Hartopp, as we have seen, became by marriage connected with the family of Cromwell ; he married Elizabeth, one of the daughters of the Lord General Fleetwood, and his sister married a son of the old general—thus there was a double connection. When Fleetwood's house was first built in the village of Stoke Newington it must have been a stately mansion. In his day it was probably divided, and had all the characteristics of the old mansions of the earlier part of the seventeenth century. Hither the General retired after the Restoration, and here, singularly enough, he was permitted to pass his days in tranquil obscurity. He died while Watts was studying at the adjoining academy. Watts no doubt knew the old Ironside, for he was on terms of close intimacy with his son, Smith Fleetwood. Such were some of the collateral connections of the Hartopp family. And there was another, Sir Nathaniel Gould, to whom Watts inscribes a poem, who married Frances, the daughter of Sir John and Lady Hartopp. Such was the circle in which it appears he moved to and fro with a pleasant and indulged affability. All of these people were members of the church over which Dr. Owen had presided, and of which Watts was hereafter, and shortly, to be minister. It was no doubt owing to the intimacy he sustained with all these eminent persons, that he by-and-bye received the invitation to become their pastor, in which relation he preached a funeral sermon, as we have seen, for Sir John, so also for Lady Hartopp, and Lady Gould, of whom he remarks, " I would copy a line from that most beautiful elegy of David, and apply it here with more justice than the Psalmist could to Saul and Jonathan, ' Lovely and pleasant were they in their lives, and in their death they were not divided,' silent were they and retired from the world, and un- known except to their intimate friends ; humble they were and averse to public show and noise, nor will I disturb their graves by making them the subject of public praise."

It was a house full of daughters and two sons. Two had already gone to the family vault, and one—born the year of Watts' entrance into the family—was soon to follow. But there were nine daughters in the household ; of these two had died before the days of Watts' residence, seven survived ; these were Helen, and Mary, and Martha, and Elizabeth, and a second Anne, and Bridget, and Dorothy, and Frances. Was Watts their tutor ? It was a dangerous neighbourhood for a young man, amidst all those bright glances and radiant young faces in the Puritan house- hold; perhaps the danger had been greater had there been fewer of them. Fancy indulges herself in picturing the life of the young student there. As we have seen, Frances married Sir Nathaniel Gould, and died in 1711, six days after her mother, Lady Hartopp. The other six daughters all lived and died unmarried in the family home. How solitary, one thinks, the last of that bright circle must have felt, dying there in 1764, sixty-two years after Watts first took up his abode among them.

Isaac Watts entered the family as the tutor of the future baronet, and many of those pieces which he afterwards gave to the world were the productions of this time, many of his " Miscellaneous Thoughts," the chief portions of his " Logic," and probably much of his " Improvement of the Mind." We have said already he furnishes, like John Calvin and some others, an instance of a singular prematurity of intelligence, not however interfering, as is so frequently the case, with future eminence, usefulness, and advance= ment.

Here, then, was for some time Watts' home. He studied hard and diligently, drawing forth and putting into shape the results of previous years of scholarship. Behind the house there were extensive gardens and remarkably fine trees, and especially a noble cedar, said to have been planted by General Fleetwood, concerning which Robinson tells a singular story : That long years ago a scythe had been hung up in the fork of the tree, and was left there unnoticed and untouched until years after it was discovered, the body of the tree having completely overgrown it and enclosed the blade so fast that it could not be removed. " And," says Robinson, " it is at this day to be seen, the point of the blade on the one side, and the end on the other." *

* " History and Antiquities of Stoke Newington." By William Robinson, LL.D., F.S.A.

The young man to whom Watts was tutor died at the age of thirty-five. He had succeeded his father in the baronetcy. Watts had given to him a noble training. Upon the publication of his "Logic" it was dedicated to him, and the writer reminds him that it had been prepared for him to assist his early studies. Some of the most animating verses in the "Lyrics" are addressed to him, and many other scholastic pieces also were prepared for his pupil while residing at Stoke Newington. Amidst the shades of its trees were written many of those essays so pleasing to read now, his "Miscellaneous Thoughts" and "Juvenile Relics." Here the young man was indeed training himself as well as teaching his pupil, when we remember that many, if not most, of his hymns had already been written at Southampton, and that his "Institutes of Logic" and his whole method of thought were matured and written here ; truly he appears to have been an industrious athlete. Neither egotism nor egoism seems to shadow his studies by any morbid self-consciousness, or any wondering dreams as to what his future destiny might be. He appears to have been one to whom faith and duty were sufficient. He had found his Saviour, and he believed ; he had his work to do, and he wrought at it like a living conscience. By-and-by he left the old house which had yet a singular history. His pupil was very wealthy, and he appears to have given during his life, and to have left upon his death a maintenance, with the family mansion, to his six maiden sisters. There they lived, and there they died ; and it is remarkable, as has been already said, that one of them died in 1764, aged eighty-one, ninety years, as the church register shows, after the death of a young sister in 1674, the year in which Watts was born ; this, we may be sure, was throughout his life one of the houses he would frequently revisit, and renew his impressions of youthful days amidst its elm and cedar shades. Gradually all the members of the family dropped away, each in turn gathered one by one, till one and all were re-united in the vaults of Stoke Newington Church. But we are stepping on too fast for our life of Watts, whose more obvious and active career was all before him yet.

CHAPTER IV.

Pastor of a London Church.

WATTS preached his first sermon on his birthday, July 17th, 1698 ; he was then twenty-four years of age. He probably mingled with his duties as tutor those of chaplain to the excellent family in which he resided. The ice once broken, he began to preach constantly. Sir John Hartopp and his family were members of the church of Dr. Chauncy, in Mark Lane ; and it was, no doubt, greatly in consequence of this friendship that Watts was invited to become the assistant of the doctor.

It is curious to compare the dearth of chapels and preachers in the City in the present day with the many remarkable for their importance at the time when Watts became a pastor. Still a few places stand out, dating from that time ; but, for the most part, all have gone, leaving only the memories of certain men of remarkable attainments, wit, and eloquence behind them. To the distinguished circle of ministers, and to the church which had known, before him, men so eminent, Watts, all but unknown, brought a name which was to give to them a crowning reputation. His qualities as a preacher all accounts represent as rather solid than shining. His sermons were beautiful in their clear harmonious symmetry of powers, rather than startling. Surely never a man who poured into his verse so much rich brilliancy of expression —sometimes, it must be admitted, with questionable rhetorical afflatus and pomp of utterance—preserved through all that we know of his public teaching so quiet and equable a flow of language and ideas, so instructive, while so entirely removed from all that can unduly agitate the spirit. In Jeremy Taylor we wonder that the poet seems to abandon every ambitious attempt when he writes verse, while his sermons possess a gorgeous and overwhelming splendour of diction and imagery. In Watts, on the other hand, it is equally surprising that so sprightly and splendid a fancy, so rich a command over sacred verses and images, should express itself with such calmness and modesty in words intended for the pulpit; but this was probably of a piece with his whole character. His hymns are often raptures and ecstasies, but he reserved these for his most private life, for his own heart, for his closet and study. There was nothing in his character bustling, prominent, or obtrusive. In an evening conversation he would shrink as far as possible from taking any prominent part, and would never in ordinary company lead it. In the home circle, among close and well-known friends, he shed around himself a genial atmosphere; but he was too essentially a student and a book-man to be in any high sense a popular preacher. Eminent and eminently honoured, his greatness was not of that order which easily finds itself at home in multitudes. His person was not striking, although we can conceive it to have been very impressive; and his mode of setting forth all things upon which he wrote or spoke was so purely thoughtful, demanded so intimate a sympathy with pensive and meditative moods, and required so close an acquaintance with high and abstract thoughts, that it is not to be wondered at that his fame as a preacher and scholar was rather reserved for the intimate circle than for more extended, not to say vulgar, spheres.

The City of London at present conveys no idea of what it was then; and what it was very materially affects our estimate of the position of Watts as one of its Nonconformist ministers. The City of London was the chief bulwark of English freedom. Happily all the needs and occasions for what it was in those days have long since passed, and England itself has greatly become what London was then. The City of that date calls up the idea of some such spots as the great mediæval cities, the burgher strongholds of the middle ages. Not many years before it had been the refuge of the five members whom Charles I. sought to attach for high treason. It had been committed to the cause of Puritanism, Protestantism, and William; some of its chief men had become martyrs to the cause of civil and religious liberty. The governments of Charles II. and James II. scarcely permitted to active minds and public men a middle way. Nonconformity was imposed by the exactions of tyranny upon spiritually minded men. Hence, leaving the fanes and structures then very pleasantly standing in many a retired close, surrounded by pleasant trees, sequestered places in the midst of the graves of many generations, such persons were compelled to assemble for worship where they best could, in some old guild hall or place of trade, some loft over offices and warehouses.* Most of the congregations we now should consider small. No company composed of faithful souls meeting for Divine service

---

* The interested reader consulting that singular monument of patient and painstaking industry, "The History and Antiquities of Dissenting Churches and Meeting-Houses in London, Westminster, and Southwark," by Walter Wilson, will probably feel astonishment, not less at their number than at the singular places in which they assembled.

beneath the blessing of Him who said, "Where two or three are gathered together in My name, there am I in the midst of them," * can be held contemptible; but their congregations were largely composed of persons who had figured prominently in the great actions of the immediately preceding years, officers and soldiers of that great army which had overawed the world by their fame, persons to whom Nonconformity was no mere negation, but the profession of all that was dearest to human freedom or to human hopes, men of substance and position, the most eminent merchants, to whose sense religious and civil liberty were so closely related that it was impossible to do injustice to the one without aiming at the heart of the other, and who knew that to injure either was to hurt the lesser, but still eminent interests of trade and commerce, and industry, and national prosperity. Nonconformity in the City of London has grown in representative wealth and importance; but it may be safely affirmed that it could not show such congregations of noble men as those which thronged its contemptible meeting-houses in Watts' day.

Referring back to those times, entering one of the chapels during the time of service, we should, perhaps, be astonished and chilled by the want of animation and ardour, if these are to be tested by the apparent excitement. Indeed, to our taste, the service must have appeared very formal and frigid; not merely in the fact that no instrumental music of any kind would have been tolerated, no response or chant, but, in many congregations, there was no singing at all. To the stricter Puritan sensibility this would have been merely intolerable. We have instances of ministers who were made uncomfortable in their churches, and compelled to relinquish them, because they desired to

* Matt. xviii. 20.

introduce some religious melody; in other instances it was the minister who disapproved such extravagant piety in his people.   The Society of Friends was not alone in its renunciation of all the adornments and flights of religious song.   Even where singing was indulged, it was Patrick's or the Scotch version, or some such literal translation of the words of Scripture.   Paraphrases and more expanded religious sentiments had never been heard of, and were regarded, when first introduced, as seditious and dangerous innovations, disturbing the purity of so reasonable a service, which derived all its life and interest from its most perfect conformity to a spiritual order; the simple voice of the minister in prayer, and in preaching, meandering in many instances through roads of uncommon length.   We have instances on record of a prayer itself taking the entire length of that time we now ordinarily allot to a public service.   This state of things in the congregation must have greatly influenced the religious life of the times where it existed at all.   It became cold, remote, and abstract; not that there were wanting instances, both of ministers and congregations, who maintained, in the midst of so much lifelessness, a high spiritual state and intercourse.

The Nonconformists throughout the country were, in the latter part of the seventeenth century, for the most part men disposed to social quiet.   They had now recovered in some measure a state of religious tranquillity, and they were rather interested quietly to preserve what they possessed, than to attempt any occupation of new ground, either in principle or in practice.   They made few efforts to correct the vices of men, or to convert them from their life of sin. The round of Nonconformist duty and piety was a quiet, staid, and respectable service; nothing, we suppose, could be more unlike the satires so often pronounced upon it.

Most of its ministers were men of considerable scholarly attainments, their minds fed by the rich and strengthening food to be found in some of the oldest fathers and the earliest reformers ; at the same time they were accustomed to abstractions and questions, which at once enlarged and strengthened the understanding. They had no acquaintance with our large varieties of nature and language ; but they were keen observers of *human* nature, and they submitted their knowledge to the test and use of daily life. As to their people, in many instances, no doubt, they were humble, perhaps even of obscure rank, but this was not always the case. Nonconformity in those times included others than those we should even call the respectable middle classes ; it represented an order of political opinion quite as much as religious doctrine and practice, not only as we have seen in London, but in many districts of the country. Some of the highest and oldest families formed the staff and stay of congregations. It was a respectable but cold piety, in many instances with assured tendencies towards Socinianism and Unitarianism. The Nonconformity into which Watts came, and with which during the whole of his life he mingled, is quite removed from that Nonconformity of Methodism and Revivalism which became the great religious movement of the last century. It was a Nonconformity educated, solid, rooted in certain principles and assurances, inclining too exclusively to a life of thought ; the religion of intelligent multitudes who could not conform, especially to what the Church of England was, in that coarse and intolerant time, when her nets gathered fish of every sort, among them some chiefly remarkable for their rapacity and impurity.

It was over one of these old City churches, probably the most famous of them, that the youthful Isaac Watts was called to preside as the pastor. The congregation or church contained a number of eminent persons ; its pastors had been eminent men ; here a few years before ministered Joseph Caryl. From the pulpit of this place probably were poured forth those prelections on the Book of Job, assuredly in more than one sense a monument to the memory of Patience ! Vast and mammoth-like, a megatherium of books, the most huge commentary ever written, but a structure of learning, with eloquence and evangelical truth, if large in bulk almost equal in worth. Over this church, more recently, had presided a greater man in the person of the mighty John Owen, the friend of Cromwell, and, during the Protectorate, Vice-Chancellor of Oxford. The place of meeting was in Mark Lane, and in the congregation there were present some whose character and lives might a little daunt any preacher, much more a very youthful one. There were many in that congregation able to carry the memory back through the days of England's fiery trials, through the years of war and of persecution, and the times when the City was alive in its own defence. They had heard the cry, " To your tents, O Israel !" when, in an ill-omened hour, Charles I. came to the City ; they had seen the Thames alive with barge and boat as the members were escorted back to Westminster ; some had served in the camp with the Ironsides, and some had seen Sir Harry Vane hailed to the scaffold ; there were officers of the old Commonwealth army, members of the old Long Parliament, strong merchants and magistrates who had stood up for the liberties of the City and of England ; there, in that congregation, scattered over the place were clustering remnants of the immediate members and descendants of Cromwell's family, none more remarkable than that most singular woman, Mrs. Bendish,.

Bridget Ireton, the grand-daughter of Cromwell, of whom all contemporaries spoke as bearing just the same relation to her grandfather in character that Elizabeth bore to Henry VIII.—a woman with a most remarkable life ; there was Charles Fleetwood, her mother's second husband ; there was Charles Desborough, the brother-in-law to Oliver Cromwell ; there was that fine old English gentleman Sir John Hartopp, and Lady Hartopp, who was a daughter of Charles Fleetwood, and thus allied to Mrs. Bendish ; there was Lady Vere Wilkinson, and Lady Haversham, a daughter of the Earl of Anglesey, and the wife of John Thompson Earl of Haversham ; and there, last as we mention them, but far from least in importance in the life of Watts, Sir Thomas and Lady Abney.

As we have said already, the Independent churches of the City were in that day greatly composed of such characters as these. Look into any one, and you will see such persons of rank and influence, although probably a kind of Cromwell clannishness gave distinctness and importance to the little church in Mark Lane ; there was a respectability and dignity about those churches in general which we should in these days but little appreciate. They were snug little spiritual corporations, held together by several bonds which have ceased to be distinctive now ; a strong faith in certain great first principles in religion ; a strong faith also in certain political principles, quite essential to the freedom of their faith and their religious life and its usages. Nor can we conceal from ourselves that there was also a conservative spirit of an aristocratic flavour ; there was nothing in the communion which savoured of our modern more heterogeneous assemblies : the members were usually persons of strong character, considerable culture, and thought. Their idea of liberty

was no more cut out after the modern type than was
their theology; indeed both were ideal. If the Harringtons
and Sidneys dreamed their republics, not upon the wild
democratic inclusiveness of complete suffrage, the pro-
clamation of the sanctity of ignorance, and the wisdom of
vice, but upon the models of classical times,—these for
the most part idealized the republic of the saints, and
formed their conceptions of church life and political freedom upon the unattainable standard of the college of the
apostles, and the traditions of the community of the
saints. Yet it is very easy to perceive how, ensconcing
themselves in religious life as in a comfortable arm-chair,
while perfectly faithful themselves, they became the
parents of that large declension of such churches to
Arianism and the cognate Socinian ideas which in the
later periods of his life vexed the spirit of Watts, and
led his thoughtful philosophic nature into an arena of
mild, but not the less earnest conflict.

Watts, accepting the charge of the church, was ordained
over it March 8th, 1702, the day on which King William
died. The young minister's immediate predecessor was
Dr. Isaac Chauncy, who, like most of his coadjutors in the
ministry of that period, was a gentleman of good and
ancient family; originally coming over with the Conqueror, settled at Yardley, Berkshire, in the time of
Elizabeth, and by the drift of circumstances conducted to
considerable eminence among the Puritans and Nonconformists. The father of Isaac Chauncy had been professor
of Greek in the University of Cambridge, and vicar of
Ware, in Hertfordshire. He took up his testimony for
Nonconformity when the "Book of Sports" was published,
commanding him to desist from preaching on the Sabbath
afternoon, that the people of his parish might indulge

themselves in profane amusements; he fell beneath the
vengeance of Archbishop Laud, and was twice cited before
the Court of High Commission; he made a recantation,
which he afterwards so regretted and bewailed that he
threw up everything and withdrew to New England. His
son Isaac held the living of Woodborough, in Wiltshire,
from whence he was ejected, and after ministering a short
time in Andover came to London, intending to practise as
a physician, when the church in Mark Lane called him to
become its minister; but he was not popular as a preacher,
however eminent in other qualifications.

The congregation had exhibited signs of decline when
Watts was called in, probably as one on whom the eyes
of leading Nonconformists were fixed, especially as the
friend of Sir John Hartopp. Although so young, his
knowledge of mathematics, of the classics, of Church history, of theological science, especially his piety, must have.
made him already well known in Nonconformist circles.
This knowledge extended back to the early part of 1698,
so that for nearly two years he must have been the
preacher, and it may be presumed very considerably the
pastor of the church before, upon the resignation of Dr.
Chauncy, he succeeded him in his office : the members of
this distinguished church must have invited him with
their eyes completely open to all that he was as a preacher
and as a man. But he gave no indications of ability to
enforce by his bodily powers the manifestations of his
genius—his health appeared to be constantly failing. For
some months before his ordination he had been laid aside
from preaching, and in search of health had, by the advice
of physicians, visited Bath. And then again we find
him for some time resting at home at his father's house,
now, no doubt, a comfortable residence, a flourishing

school, and released from all the terrors which had
shadowed it in his infancy.   And from thence again by
physicians we find him sent to Tunbridge Wells, so that
he says, "I was detained from study and preaching five
months by my weakness, except one very short discourse
at Southampton in extreme necessity."   He was of a
slight and most fragile frame throughout his life.   His
works constitute an amazing monument of industry.   But
during the years he had been tutor in Sir John Hartopp's family he must have performed these duties in a
spirit of remarkable conscientiousness, for he prepared
some of the works which afterwards delighted and in-
structed the world, as the necessary means of the course
he was pursuing in the education of the young man, his
pupil.   Very remarkably this is the case with his " System
of Logic," which when it was published many years after
was adopted and continued to be until recently the text-book
for the Universities of Oxford and Cambridge ; this appears
also to have been the case with his "Scheme of Ontology."
He refers to many of his writings published at a much
later period of his life, as for the most part the productions
of these his earlier years.   We shall have occasion to speak
of these again ; at present it is sufficient to refer to this
persistency of mental labour and assiduous industry as not
only the sufficient cause for the illness which suspended
him from labour, but the foundation of future years of
painful infirmity which accompanied him through life.

There must have been much about him not only to
command respect but to enchain affection.   Long hesitating
as to whether he should accept the proffered pastorate, he
had not long entered upon the real responsibilities of his
office before he was again seized with a painful and
alarming illness ; almost immediately he was compelled

again, in July, 1702, to renew his rest in Southampton, and then returning to London he mentions, in the memoranda we have already quoted, that he was "seized with violent gaundise and colic three weeks after my return to London, and had a very slow recovery, eight or nine weeks' illness. From September 8th, or thereabouts, to November 27th or 28th. This year, viz., 1702, by slow degrees removed from Newington to Thomas Hollis's, in the Minories."

During a period of about six years Watts appears to have resided in the family of Sir John Hartopp; in the paragraph above quoted he refers to his removal to the house of Mr. Hollis, in the Minories. The names of the places associated with the ministrations or the residence of Watts and his fellow ministers in the City, sound to our ears now strange and singularly unromantic and uninteresting; but what they are now we must not for a moment suppose they resembled then. Even the Minories —now the last place in which one could wish to reside— lay, at that time, open and fresh towards the pleasant fields of the east end of London, a rather distinguished neighbourhood beneath the shadows of the Tower, and pleasantly refreshed by the breath from the waters of the then really silvery Thames, whose banks were alive with the songs of watermen. The Minories or Minoresses—so called from the nuns of the Order of St. Clair—had once been the region of noble residences; here had been the residence of Sir Philip Sidney, here his body lay in state. The spot was, and is, full of interesting memories. The family of the Hollis's was from Sheffield, in Yorkshire, and having founded churches in Doncaster and Rotherham, removing to London, the father of Watts' friend became one of the most helpful representatives of Nonconformity

in the City, immediately connected with the church
assembling in Pinners' Hall, beneath the pastorate of Dr.
Jeremiah Hunt.   To this place, in consequence of the
narrow and dilapidated state of the building in Mark Lane,
Watts and his people were compelled to remove in the
year 1704.   Pinners' Hall had for years been used by
Nonconformists, and in their turns Baxter, Owen, Bates,
Manton, and Howe had all preached in it to crowded
congregations, hence the reason, most likely, of the friendship of the minister and Mr. Hollis.

We have few particulars of Watts in his pastoral work.
From the first days of his pastorate his health was a
frequent source of interruption to his activity.   The hymns
and poems frequently expressing the experience of pain,
weakness, and weariness are no fancies ; they express a
very devout spirit of resignation, with regret, as he expresses it, that "many other souls are favoured with a more
easy habitation, and he hoped with a better partner, accom-
modated with engines which have more health and vigour;"
but he instantly recovers his spirits to exclaim, " Shall I
repine then, while I survey whole nations and millions and
millions of mankind that have not a thousand's part of
my blessings ? "   He was laid aside by sickness for five
months soon after he became assistant to Dr. Chauncy,
1698 ; he was the subject of another illness soon after
his settlement in the pastoral charge in 1701 ; a violent
fever seized him in 1712, his constitution was shattered by
it, his nerves weakened and unstrung, and he prevented
from returning to his public work until October, 1716 ; we
find from his own record that he was confined by illness in
1729 ; and many other occasions might be discovered of
these sharp bodily afflictions.   Life around him was usually
beautiful and serene ; he seems to have possessed a very

large revenue of love, but he unquestionably possessed this "thorn in the flesh," nor can we doubt that such experiences to such a faith as his, gave personal meaning to his hymns. He sung very often as one stretched on a rack, and not the least of his pains must have been that his incessantly active nature, his constant design and desire to carry out some purpose or to pursue some task found itself checked and arrested. Dr. Gibbons quotes a paragraph from a very beautiful letter to a friend, a minister, in affliction, through which there runs a vein of true spiritual friendship, and a pathos which his own experience of trials would very naturally inspire : " It is my hearty desire for you that your faith may ride out the storms of temptation, and the anchor of your hope may hold, being fixed within the veil. There sits Jesus our Forerunner, who sailed over this rough sea before us, and has given us a chart, even His Word, where the shelves and rocks, the fierce currents and dangers are well described, and He is our Pilot, and will conduct us to the shores of happiness. I am persuaded that in the future state we shall take a sweet review of those scenes of Providence which have been involved in the thickest darkness, and trace those footsteps of God when He walked with us through the deepest waters. This will be a surprising delight, to survey the manifold harmony of clashing dispensations, and to have those perplexing riddles laid open to the eyes of our souls, and read the full meaning of them in set characters of wisdom and grace."

It is not extraordinary, therefore, that even so early as 1703 the church relieved Watts by choosing a co-pastor, Mr. Samuel Price, a native of Wales, but a student from Attercliff, in Yorkshire. As it was necessary to have a co-pastor, he was chosen upon the express desire and earnest recommendation of Watts ; but many years appear to have passed between the choice of the church and his ordination as joint pastor, for Watts' autobiographic memoranda says : " June, 1703, Mr. Samuel Price was chosen by the church to assist me ; " but he was not ordained to the office of co-pastor until 1713. This relationship continued until it was dissolved by death. They were colleagues considerably upwards of forty years, and Price succeeded his beloved and amiable friend, whom he survived about seven years ; he died in 1756, having been connected with the church fifty-three years. Watts mentions him in his will as his faithful friend and companion in the ministry, and leaves some little legacy, " as only a small testimony of his great affection for him, on account of his services of love during the many harmonious years of their fellowship in the work of the Gospel." Watts several times, in the course of the prefaces and dedications to his published works, refers affectionately to his colleague ; and his colleague when he died expressed a wish that he might be buried as near as possible to his honoured friend. It may be incidentally mentioned that he was uncle to the celebrated Dr. Richard Price.

Although his companion in the ministry neither as a preacher nor man of letters approached the eminence of Watts, it would seem that he was in every way acceptable as a preacher and a pastor, " judicious, and useful, and eminent in his gift of prayer," says Gibbons. Certainly, the old place in Mark Lane became too small, for, after a temporary sojourn in Pinner's Hall, in 1708 the congregation removed from Mark Lane* to Duke Street, St. Mary Axe.

It had been the site of one of the most celebrated metro-

* Originally Mart Lane.

politan ecclesiastical establishments previous to the Reformation, the Priory of the Holy Trinity, the founder of
which was Matilda, Queen of Henry I. ; it became a huge
establishment and enormously wealthy, the richest convent
in England, some have said ; rich in lands and ornaments,
and incomparably surpassing all the other priories in the
same county. The prior was always an alderman of
London, although, if he happened to be exceedingly pious,
he appointed a substitute to enact temporal matters ; and
on solemn days this clerical alderman rode through the
city with the other aldermen, but arrayed in his monastic
habit. On the dissolution of the monasteries this became
one of the earliest spoils, and it was given by Henry VIII.
to Sir Thomas Audley, the Speaker of the House of Commons, and afterwards Lord Chancellor. On the site of the
old priory he erected a splendid mansion, in which he resided
until his death in 1544. His daughter and sole heiress,
Margaret, married Thomas, Duke of Norfolk, so the estate
descended to the Howard family, and became the Duke's
place ; he lost his head ; passing to his eldest son, he sold
it in 1592 to the mayor, corporation, and citizens of London.
This is a singular piece of history, which Wilson, in his
" History of Dissenting Churches," has gathered from
Strype, Maitland, and Pennant.

In the time of Watts the neighbourhood had scarcely
fallen from its high estate. Time had been since the period
of the Reformation when Sir Francis Walsingham, Sir
Thomas Wyatt, and the Earl of Northumberland had their
houses here ; and Bury Street derived its name from the
abbots of Bury, who also had a residence on this spot.
Since the time of Cromwell, however, the region had
become a kind of *Juden Strasse.* The Jews, who now form
its principal inhabitants, then first settled there. The spot

on which the chapel was built was part of a garden, although removed from public observation, a necessity laid upon the Nonconformists of that time, who were compelled to retreat into obscure recesses to escape the vigilance of prowling informers.   The building has now entirely passed away, but we very well remember it, one of the old square substantial buildings with its galleries, exactly an ideal conventicle of those times, one of those in which the Nonconformists seemed to teach that there was no beauty in architecture which they particularly desired.   The rich furniture and attainments of the ministers' minds contrasting singularly with the plain and altogether unornamented and even barn-like simplicity of the scene of their ministrations : almost the only buildings which now retain the entirely unornamented architecture of the Puritan times are those of the members of the Society of Friends.   Such was the building opened in Bury Street, October 3rd, 1708 ; it is also interesting to notice that it was erected at the costly sum of £650 !   In the present year of the publication of this volume a building has been erected in the City of London for the same order of communicants as those in Bury Street, at a cost of £55,000.   The two sums are very suggestive of a comparison and contrast between the Nonconformists of the time of Watts and of to-day.

CHAPTER V.

First Publication as a Sacred Poet.

THE fact that the first work published by Watts was the "Sacred Lyrics" may justify this early estimate of his character as a sacred poet. It is probable, nay it is certain, that the time bestowed by Watts upon poetry was very slight and insignificant compared with that which he devoted to the graver pursuits of life, and the various studies connected with philosophy, theology, preaching, and education. He first, however, appeared in print as the author of the "Horæ Lyricæ," the Lyrical Poems : and Dr. Johnson judges that they entitled him to an honourable place amongst our English poets. Watts himself thought very modestly of his claims in this way, and speaks concerning his own compositions in the humblest language. "I make no pretences," he says, "to the name of a poet, or a polite writer in an age wherein so many superior souls shine in their works through the nation." In many of his hymns he unquestionably deserves the highest honour : but for the most part it is not in the lyrics we are to seek, as we certainly shall not find, the noblest illustrations of his poetical genius; nor, perhaps, is it probable that we should turn to them with much interest or expectation but that they are the production of Dr. Watts, and that he was the author of those hymns so dear to the Church of Christ, and the "Divine and Moral Songs for Children." In all our judgments and criticisms upon Watts as a poet, two things must be borne in mind : first, as we have seen above, that he not only disclaimed the character himself, but proved his sincerity by regarding it only as the recreation of grave and serious studies, and the very natural occupation of a man of fine taste and largely cultivated sensibility ; and next, we must remember that the poetry of the age in which he lived was artificial, formed for the most part upon classical models, whose rules were very greatly inapplicable to English verse. The sweetest and most perfect poet in any near approach to those times was Oliver Goldsmith, and he was the writer least imbued with classical lore, and the one who left all classical rules and allusions furthest behind him, content to express himself in simple and pleasing English. Johnson was a poet, and Joseph Addison, but although so much more ambitious and devoted to the pursuit, they neither of them have produced sentiments or expressions which charm us more than those we find in the productions of Watts. Thomas Gray was a poet, but only in two or three instances did the simplicity and purity of the English language, and the simple metre, succeed in winning him from the trammels of classical formularies. Indeed there was something ludicrous in the poetry of the time ; and the great genius of Pope, which really was equal to anything in verse, seemed almost to struggle in vain against the pedantic rules he imposed upon himself. It was the age of fantastic ornament and of formal symmetry, of artificial gardening, of trimmed yews, when even Nature herself in her trees, hedgerows, and flower-beds was made to look ridiculous. A sort of tulip-mania, a false admiration in colour and in form, took possession not merely of the speculators in the market, but of the devotees of the fine arts. Years passed on before English poetry liberated itself from these false trammels, and the first great English writer who subsequently gave freedom and freshness, a combination of sublimity and simplicity to English verse, was William Cowper.

We must separate and distinguish between Watts as a poet, the author of the "Lyrics," and Watts as a hymnologist, and the author of those pieces which, as they have been, so we trust they will continue to be, a precious legacy of the Church, and the expression of its deepest, highest, and tenderest emotions. In a letter to the "Gentleman's Magazine," when his judgment was appealed to for a poetical decision, he said, "Though I have sported with rhyme as an amusement in younger life, and published some religious composures to assist the worship of God, yet I never set myself up among the numerous competitors for a poet of the age, much less have I presumed to become their judge." There is a writer of one or two immortal hymns in our language who sometimes suggests a comparison with Dr. Watts. Watts was capable of poetry. He was not only a poet in his hymns, but a poetic nature often broke through the turgid pindarics he adopted as the vehicle of his expressions. But Ken was no poet at all, and yet, unlike Watts, who disclaimed the character, this was Ken's one vanity. A writer in the "Quarterly Review," which may be accepted here as an unexceptionable umpire, says, "If there was any vanity in the good man's heart, it would seem to have been on the subject of his poetical skill. He expresses, indeed, a belief that his verses are open to the assaults of criticism, but he must have thought something of them, for he left them for publication, and they fill four thick volumes.

The contrast is strange between the clear, free, harmonious flow of his prose, and the barbarous, cramped, pedantic language, the harsh dissonance, the extravagant conceits, which disfigure the great mass of his verses. Mr. Anderson has tried the ingenious experiment of reducing some passages from metre to prose, and no doubt they gain considerably! But there is no getting over the fact that these four volumes are altogether a mistake."* Such a criticism as this can never be pronounced on Watts, but it is yet true that some of the vices of Ken disfigure the pages of the "Horæ Lyricæ," and they are traceable to the same cause — the forsaking simplicity and nature, and following artificial models and straining after affected diction.

He was essentially a hymn writer, and among the lyrics the most beautiful and effective pieces are those which either are hymns or approach nearest to that order of composition. The modern reader will be impatient of the frequent apostrophe, and, although "personification, that is, the transformation of the qualities of the mind, and abstract ideas, and general notions into living embodiments," has ever been regarded as one of the noblest exercises and proofs of the poetic faculty, we suppose few will be disposed to regard Watts' excursions in this way with favour. He possessed this power in an eminent degree: instantaneously, apparently, a sentiment became an image, and the image pointed to a tender and pathetic treatment. His elegy on the death of William III. has often been cited as a fine piece of elegiac personification; should it seem extravagant to the reader, it would scarcely seem so to Lord Macaulay; and it must be remembered that Dr. Watts was one who regarded himself and the

* " Quarterly Review," vol. lxxxix. pp. 303, 304.

nation as profoundly indebted, surely not unnaturally,
for freedom and prosperity to the arms and government
of the deceased king. He was young when he wrote
these verses. William, as we have said, died the day on
which Watts was ordained to the work of the ministry,
1702. The verses present a picture of the illustrious
hero lying in state, surrounded by the weeping arts and
graces of society. Dr. Gibbons, not inappropriately, speaks
of the piece as "the largest constellation of personifica-
tions occurring amongst the Doctor's Odes:"

> Preserve, O venerable pile,
> Inviolate thy sacred trust;
> To thy cold arms the British isle,
> Weeping, commits her richest dust.
>
> Rest his dear sword beneath his head;
> Round him his faithful arms shall stand:
> Fix his bright ensigns on his bed,
> The guards and honours of our land.
>
> High o'er the grave *Religion* set
> In solemn guise; pronounce the ground
> Sacred, to bar unhallowed feet,
> And plant her guardian virtues round.
>
> Fair *Liberty*, in sables drest,
> Write his loved name upon his urn;
> William, the scourge of tyrants past,
> And awe of princes yet unborn.
>
> Sweet *Peace*, his sacred relics keep,
> With olives blooming round her head,
> And stretch her wings across the deep
> To bless the nations with the shade.
>
> Stand on the pile, immortal *Fame*,
> Broad stars adorn thy brightest robe;
> Thy thousand voices sound his name
> In silver accents round the globe.

> *Flattery* shall faint beneath the sound,
> While hoary *Truth* inspires the song;
> *Envy* grow pale, and bite the ground,
> And *Slander* gnaw her forky tongue.
>
> Night and the grave, remove your gloom;
> Darkness becomes the vulgar dead;
> But glory bids the royal tomb
> Disdain the horrors of a shade.
>
> *Glory* with all her lamps shall burn,
> And watch the warrior's sleeping clay,
> Till the last trumpet rouse his urn,
> To aid the triumphs of the day.

But he had a simpler manner, and even in his stronger expressions rose to the majesty of simple strength, as in the following:

LAUNCHING INTO ETERNITY.

> It was a brave attempt! advent'rous he,
> Who in the first ship broke the unknown sea:
> And leaving his dear native shores behind,
> Trusted his life to the licentious wind.
> I see the surging brine: the tempest raves:
> He on the pine-plank rides across the waves,
> Exulting on the edge of thousand gaping graves:
> He steers the winged boat, and shifts the sails,
> Conquers the flood, and manages the gales.
> Such is the soul that leaves this mortal land,
> Fearless when the great Master gives command.
> Death is the storm: she smiles to hear it roar,
> And bids the tempest waft her from the shore:
> Then with a skilful helm she sweeps the seas,
> And manages the raging storm with ease:
> (Her faith can govern death) she spreads her wings
> Wide to the wind, and as she sails she sings,
> And loses by degrees the sight of mortal things.
> As the shores lessen, so her joys arise,
> The waves roll gentler, and the tempest dies,
> Now vast eternity fills all her sight,
> She floats on the broad deep with infinite delight,
> The seas for ever calm, the skies for ever bright.

The weight and grandeur of his thoughts, the radiance
of his perception, the far-reaching, remote grandeur of the
objects of his verse, must always be taken into account,
pondered, and allowed an adequate influence over the
reader's mind, whenever attempts are made to estimate
what he was as a sacred poet. Not the less was his mind
in ready accord with objects of Nature. He had seen,
probably, little of Nature in her more grand and exciting
moods. Men like him, born to London life, and only
occasionally escaping thence to some near and quiet
watering-place, saw little of those ample pages which,
in our own or other lands, are now unrolled to almost
every designing eye. But his verses abundantly show
with what perfect sympathy every object touched him,
how all the smaller or greater things of Nature impressed
the subtle sense within him, and awoke the mystery and
the awe. The following lines, not composed as a hymn,
but included in his " Miscellaneous Thoughts," have always
seemed to us very cogently to illustrate this :

> My God, I love, and I adore;
> But souls that love would know Thee more.
> Wilt Thou for ever hide, and stand
> Behind the labours of Thy hand?
> Thy hand unseen sustains the poles
> On which this huge creation rolls:
> The starry arch proclaims Thy power,
> Thy pencil glows in every flower;
> In thousand shapes and colours rise
> Thy painted wonders to our eyes;
> While beasts and birds, with labouring throats,
> Teach us a God in thousand notes,
> The meanest pin in Nature's frame
> Marks out some letter of Thy name.
> Where sense can reach, or fancy rove,
> From hill to hill, from field to grove,

> Across the waves, around the sky,
>   There's not a spot, or deep or high,
> Where the Creator has not trod,
>   And left the footstep of a God.

And in the same strain, with what strength and majesty he sweeps every chord of Nature in his sublime version of the 148th Psalm :

> Loud hallelujahs to the Lord.

The strong nervousness of his expression, the passionate personification (always the mark of a great poet) with which his verses abound, sometimes, but more especially in his lyrics, give the appearance of inflation to his expressions. But when attempting to describe adequate themes, they only fitly represent the subject, as in the following fine description of the glory of God in the clouds :

> Thy hand, how wide it spreads the sky !
>   How glorious to behold !
> Tinged with a blue of heavenly dye,
>   And starred with sparkling gold.
>
> There Thou canst bid the globes of light
>   Their endless circles run ;
> Where the pale planet rules the night,
>   And day obeys the sun.
>
> The noisy winds stand ready there
>   Thy orders to obey ;
> With sounding wings they sweep the air,
>   To make Thy chariot way.
>
> There like a trumpet loud and strong,
>   Thy thunder shakes our coast ;
> While the red lightnings wave along,
>   The banners of Thy host.
>
> On the thin air, without a prop,
>   Hang fruitful showers around ;
> At Thy command they sink, and drop
>   Their fatness to the ground.

Strong exception has been taken to Watts' verse, on the score of its frequent, almost passionate, expression of Divine love; in this he frequently writes like Madame Guyon, or like some of those old monastic spirits who passed their days in cloisters; and Watts' life was almost as cloisteral as that of a monk. Unlike his amiable friend, Philip Doddridge, he was never diverted from any of the solemn pursuits of his life by the claims of human passion or affection, although there are not wanting verses which, perhaps, show that he had not been altogether insensible to female charms:

> Virgins, who roll your artful eyes,
> And shoot delicious danger thence;
> Swiftly the lovely lightning flies,
> And melts our reason down to sense.

But perhaps his poem " Few Happy Matches," reveals some reason why his timid spirit refused to seek its happiness in matrimonial chains, and so he turned to the higher affections, singing—

> Life is a pain without Thy love;
> Who can ever bear to be
> Cursed with immortality,
> Among the stars, but far from Thee?

But the author of many of these hymns must often have been wafted away with a true mystic ecstasy. The warmth of this rapture has been objected to; the objection lies, also, against the works of most of the great mystics.

> My God, the spring of all my joys,

is one of countless illustrations—

> My God, my life, my love,
> To Thee, to Thee, I call.

or—

> Dearest of all the names above.

In such as these, if the reader feels unable to rise to them amidst the delights of family joys—wife, and children, and society—let him remember how Watts lived, his solitary nights, in a family where, no doubt, his presence was a charm and blessing, but in which he must have been to himself, comparatively, lonely as a monk, feeding his mind with thoughts until they became passions and ecstasies to him, and even found their vent in such words as the following:

> His charm shall make my numbers flow,
>   And hold the falling floods;
> While silence sits on every bough,
>   And bends the listening woods.
>
> I'll carve our passion on the bark;
>   And every wounded tree
> Shall drop and bear some mystic mark
>   That Jesus died for me.
>
> The swains shall wonder when they read,
>   Inscribed on all the grove,
> That Heaven itself came down and bled
>   To win a mortal's love.

To this same order of sacred personification also belong those verses, which are certainly remarkable, and when properly apprehended among the most tenderly antithetical in our language, on the Death of Moses:

> Sweet was the journey to the sky
>   The wondrous prophet tried;
> "Climb up the mount," said God, " and die;"
>   The prophet climbed and died.
>
> Softly his fainting head he lay
>   Upon his Maker's breast;
> His Maker kissed his soul away,
>   And laid his flesh to rest.

In God's own arms he left the breath
That God's own Spirit gave;
His was the noblest road to death,
And his the sweetest grave.

And while remarking upon the poet, we may notice that many of his pieces reflect that quiet scholarly spirit of the age, in which not only Watts, but so many other writers delighted to indulge; that Seneca-like musing and moralizing, that contented dreaming beneath umbrageous woods and by the side of purling streams. It has been said that Samuel Rogers, in his "Human Life," portrays the Twickenham side of existence. The Stoke Newington side was very much like it, certainly wholly unlike the stir and heat of the vivid passions, the painful introspections, and diseased musings, which have forced their way into modern poetry. If Watts described or dealt with these it was not in his verse, although many of his prose writings seem to reveal that he was not ignorant of them; such is his often quoted piece:

TRUE RICHES.

I am not concerned to know
What, to-morrow, fate will do:
'Tis enough that I can say,
I've possessed myself to-day:
Then, if haply midnight death
Seize my flesh, and stop my breath,
Yet to-morrow I shall be
Heir to the best part of me.

Glittering stones, and golden things,
Wealth and honours that have wings,
Ever fluttering to be gone,
I could never call my own:
Riches that the world bestows,
She can take, and I can lose;

But the treasures that are mine
Lie afar beyond her line.
When I view my spacious soul,
And survey myself a whole,
And enjoy myself alone,
I'm a kingdom of my own.

I've a mighty part within
That the world hath never seen,
Rich as Eden's happy ground,
And with choicer plenty crowned.
Here on all the shining boughs
Knowledge fair and useful grows;
On the same young flow'ry tree
All the seasons you may see;
Notions in the bloom of light,
Just disclosing to the sight;
Here are thoughts of larger growth,
Rip'ning into solid truth;
Fruits refined, of noble taste;
Seraphs feed on such repast.
Here, in a green and shady grove,
Streams of pleasure mix with love:
There, beneath the smiling skies,
Hills of contemplation rise;
Now, upon some shining top,
Angels light, and call me up;
I rejoice to raise my feet,
Both rejoice when there we meet.

There are endless beauties more
Earth hath no resemblance for;
Nothing like them round the pole,
Nothing can describe the soul.
'Tis a region half unknown,
That has treasures of its own,
More remote from public view
Than the bowels of Peru;
Broader 'tis, and brighter far,
Than the golden Indies are;
Ships that trace the watery stage
Cannot coast it in an age;
Harts, or horses, strong and fleet,
Had they wings to help their feet,

Could not run it half-way o'er
In ten thousand days or more.

Yet the silly wand'ring mind,
Loath to be too much confined,
Roves and takes her daily tours,
Coasting round the narrow shores—
Narrow shores of flesh and sense,
Picking shells and pebbles thence:
Or she sits at Fancy's door,
Calling shapes and shadows to her;
Foreign visits still receiving,
And to herself a stranger living.
Never, never would she buy
Indian dust, or Tyrian dye;
Never trade abroad for more,
If she saw her native store:
If her inward worth were known,
She might ever live alone.

Nor, much in the same vein, was he indisposed occasionally for a gentle kind of satire, as in the following vigorous paraphrase, which some readers may perhaps be surprised to find falling from the pen of Watts. "When I meet with persons," he says, "of a worldly character, they bring to my mind some scraps of Horace :"

"Nos numerus sumus, et fruges consumere nati,
Alcinoique juventus
Cui pulchrum fuit in medios dormire dies," etc.

PARAPHRASE.

There are a number of us creep
Into this world, to eat and sleep;
And know no reason why they're born,
But merely to consume the corn,
Devour the cattle, fowl, and fish,
And leave behind an empty dish.
The crows and ravens do the same,
Unlucky birds of hateful name;
Ravens or crows might fill their places,
And swallow corn and carcases.

Then if their tombstone, when they die,
Ben't taught to flatter and to lie,
There's nothing better will be said,
Than that " They've eat up all their bread,
Drank up their drink, and gone to bed."

And the following verses are surely very pleasing to the
discontented and unquiet :

'Tis a dull circle that we tread,
Just from the window to the bed,
To rise to see, and to be seen,
Gaze on the world awhile, and then
We yawn, and stretch to sleep again.
But Fancy, that uneasy guest,
Still holds a longing in our breast :
She finds or frames vexations still,
Herself the greatest plague we feel.
We take great pleasure in our pain,
And make a mountain of a grain,
Assume the load, and pant and sweat
Beneath th' imaginary weight.
With our dear selves we live at strife,
While the most constant scenes of life
From peevish humours are not free ;
Still we affect variety :
Rather than pass an easy day,
We fret and chide the hours away,
Grow weary of this circling sun,
And vex that he should ever run
The same old track ; and still, and still
Rise red behind yon eastern hill,
And chide the moon that darts her light
Through the same casement every night.

We shift our chambers and our homes,
To dwell where trouble never comes :
Sylvia has left the city crowd,
Against the court exclaims aloud,
Flies to the woods ; a hermit saint !
She loathes her patches, pins and paint,
Dear diamonds from her neck are torn ;
But humour, that eternal thorn,

Sticks in her heart: she's hurried still,
'Twixt her wild passions and her will:
Haunted and hagged where'er she roves,
By purling streams, and silent groves,
Or with her furies, or her loves.

Then our native land we hate,
Too cold, too windy, or too wet;
Change the thick climate, and repair
To France or Italy for air.

Happy the soul that virtue shows
To fix the place of her repose,
Needless to move; for she can dwell
In her old grandsire's hall as well.
Virtue that never loves to roam,
But sweetly hides herself at home.
And easy on a native throne
Of humble turf sits gently down.

Without claiming then for Watts a pre-eminent place among those who are called poets, these citations will be sufficient to show that however he might disclaim the dignity, he deserved the designation. And there are poets whose eminence is in general more unquestioned, who deserve it less. He was unjust to himself in this particular; verse and rhyme fell from him easily, happily, naturally. Perhaps he succeeded least when he most ambitiously attempted; but he had a remarkable and pleasant power of instantly translating some sentiment which crossed his mind from the classics into English verse, as in those well-known lines,—

Seize upon truth where'er 'tis found,
On Christian, or on heathen ground.
Amongst your friends, amongst your foes,
The flower's divine where'er it grows,
Neglect the prickle and assume the rose.

In which he elevates the sentiment of Virgil,—

"Fas est ab hoste doceri."

Referring to his translations, it has been very justly said
that he seldom translates or imitates a heathen poet but
he either makes him a Christian in the end, or shows his
deficiency in not being one.   He consistently maintained
throughout his writings, as a poet, the determination
expressed in the lines—

> Thy name, Almighty Sire, and Thine,
> Jesus, where His full glories shine,
>   Shall consecrate my lays.*

His familiar method of remembering the signs of the
Zodiac is an illustration of the rapid and neat way in
which he could bind up knowledge in a verse:

> The ram, the bull, the heavenly twins,
> And next the crab the lion shines,
>   The virgin and the scales;
> The archer, scorpion, and the goat,
> The man that holds the water-pot,
>   The fish with glittering tails.

And his receipt for the orderly conduct of Divine worship,
for sustaining a mental effort in prayer, is useful, beautiful,
and perfect:

> Call upon God, adore, confess,
>   Petition, plead, and then declare
> You are the Lord's, give thanks and bless,
>   And let Amen confirm the prayer.

The devout purpose which ruled and governed the whole
life of Watts is of course manifest in his poems.   Such as
he is, he is always a sacred poet; he never forgets that his
life has been consecrated and set apart to religious teaching and to the promulgation of useful knowledge; his
moralities are recreation, never mere dreams; and if he
never attempts the great flights of poetry in epic or
dramatic writing, we may remember that in this, as in his

* " Ode to Mr. Pinhorne."   Translated by Dr. Gibbons.

yet more sacred pieces, he was a lyrist, and reserved all
his greater efforts for his work in the ministry, seeking
thus to make more sweet and serviceable the whole service
of the House of God.

Throughout these remarks we have left it to be inferred
that the verse-making, great as was the fame it procured
the author, was regarded by him merely as the *accident* of
his work ; at the same time his nature seems to have been
truly in sympathy with all those impulses derived from
external scenery, calculated to stir a poetic sensibility.
We fancy his modest nature would almost have assented,
without a rejoinder, even to some of the very severe
criticisms which modern fastidiousness has pronounced
upon him ; but Dr. Gibbons assures us how swiftly and
instantly his spirit caught every impression of natural
scenery and life ; how he delighted in the rural verdure,
or the waving harvest-field, or the resounding grove ; how
his nature was awed almost equally by the wonderful and
subtle labours of the industrious bee, or the sun walking
through the heavens in the greatness of his strength. In
his lyrics, classical forms, perhaps, rather hampered than
aided him ; he was fascinated by the majestic roll of the
Pindaric Greek ; but from this fault the best of his hymns
are entirely free.

We have dwelt thus at length upon some of the
characteristics of Watts' verse, feeling that criticism upon
it is far from exhausted; and that, amidst its various
representatives in our language, in spite of that modern
contempt which is creeping even into the circles of those
who profess to hold his faith and follow in his footsteps,
he still deserves to retain a place in the history of English
poetry. We have referred rather to those more striking
and obvious marks of his genius ; but we must still

prefer him in his more quiet and subdued strains of devotion, those peaceful, pensive lines with which his works abound. It is equally certain that he wrote a number of verses and lines perfectly indefensible on the score of good taste : this is the more remarkable, because his taste does seem to have been cultivated to the highest pitch of excellence ; and his mind was remarkable, not merely for the plenitude of its ideas, but for the easy elegance with which he ordinarily gave expression to them. However this may be, their bad taste and strange conceits have not greatly repressed the reverence with which we regard the works of George Herbert or of Henry Vaughan ; nor does the frequent turgidity of Milton much interfere with the admiration and awe with which we read most of his poems.

CHAPTER VI.

Residence in the Abney Family.

IT was at that period of Watts' life, when he felt in a very especial manner his loneliness, and fever and infirmity were reducing him to a painful sense of abiding weakness, that Sir Thomas and Lady Abney invited him to spend a week with them at their magnificent house of Theobalds, in Hertfordshire. He accepted the invitation, and the hosts and their guest seemed to have been so mutually pleased with each other that Watts continued in the family until his death, a period of thirty-six years. Watts must have then been about thirty-eight years of age. Johnson remarks upon this friendship that " it was a state in which the notions of patronage and dependence were overpowered by the perception of reciprocal benefits ; it deserves a particular memorial ;" and he refers to Dr. Gibbons' interesting account, which is, indeed, one of the most pleasant pieces of his biography, and compels the wish that he had more frequently broken the monotony of the book by pages so pleasing. The event was one of those kind providences which those who watch the lives of eminent men, who have served their generation and the cause of God, will not fail to perceive. Think of the solitary student, the shrinking, sensitive man, the modest and fearful spirit who could not

command service, and recoiled from giving trouble, how
fearfully life might have dragged along through a few years
of languor and pain, unequal to much service, unable to
gather round him any, or but few, of the comforts of life,
suddenly transferred to all the affluent comforts of this
magnificent abode, to its rooms, capacious and luxurious,
the abode of order, and harmony, and holiness, not only a
pious household, but entirely after the type favoured by
the thoughtful guest.   There were the rich rural scenes,
the delightful garden, the spreading lawn, and the fragrant
and embowered recess, all wooing the body back to health
and the heart to peace ; and although a few years after his
entrance into the household Sir Thomas Abney dies, yet
the guest cannot be permitted to depart.   The same affection and respect are continued by Lady Abney and her
daughter.   Lady Abney was the sister of the chief friend
of Watts' younger days, Thomas Gunston ; her wealth was
very great, and, says Gibbons, " her generosity and munifi-
cence in full proportion."   There must have been a
pleasant fellowship and community of tastes, certainly a
fitting harmony of character, reminding us of Robert Boyle
with his sister Lady Ranelagh, or William Cowper with
Mary Unwin ; such relationships are very beautiful in
their serene, unselfish character.   Beneath the roof of Lady
Abney Watts died.   Within two months of his departure
to Bunhill Fields, she was taken to her resting-place in
the vaults of Stoke Newington Church.   But the family
in which Dr. Watts was for more than half his life an
honoured guest merits some more particular mention.

Sir Thomas Abney was descended from an ancient and
respectable family in Derbyshire.   His father was James
Abney, Esq., of Wilsley, whose ancestors had enjoyed that
estate upwards of five hundred years.   The son came to

the City of London, and appears to have passed through
the honours of Alderman, Sheriff, and Lord Mayor.   For
the services he rendered to King William he received the
honour of knighthood, and was chosen chief magistrate
some years before his turn.   He appears to have had in
those troublesome times great influence in the City, though
holding at that time a strong opinion adverse to the Stuarts.
He was chosen in 1701 to represent it in Parliament;
he was a director of the Bank, and president of St. Thomas'
Hospital; and when, upon the death of the exiled James,
the King of France, Louis XIV., caused the Pretender to
be proclaimed at St. Germains King of Great Britain, and
by the recall of the Earl of Macclesfield war seemed to
be unavoidable, Sir Thomas Abney, in the Court of Common Council, proposed, in opposition to the majority of his
brethren on the bench, an address to William III., declar-
ing that they would support him against France and the
Pretender: it was carried and transmitted to the King,
who was then on the Continent.   It is impossible now to
estimate the vigour this imparted to the King's affairs—it
was the note which roused the nation.   It was said that
this act of Sir Thomas Abney served the cause of the King
more than if he had raised for him a million of money.

It is a singular circumstance that although Watts received such marks of favour from the Abney family, Sir
Thomas and Lady Abney do not appear to have, in the first
days of their acquaintance, belonged to the church of which
Watts was pastor.   Sir Thomas was a member of that
church during the pastorate of Mr. Caryl, whose daughter
was his first wife.   After Mr. Caryl's death he united
himself with the church of which John Howe was the
minister.   Nonconformists were at that time, as they
have been frequently since, Lord Mayors of the City,

usually complying by occasional conformity so far as
to attend one part of the Sunday at church, the other
at their own place of worship.　When Sir Humphrey
Edwin, who was a member of Pinners' Hall congregation,
was Mayor, he very unwisely caused the regalia of the City
to be carried to his meeting-house, and it created a vehement storm.

But it is remarkable that Mr. Milner, usually very
accurate, in his life of Dr. Watts quotes a paragraph
from "The Shortest Way with the Dissenters," speaking
of it as a piece of High Church vituperation, apparently
unaware that this was the very production of Defoe, the
satire for which he was put in the pillory; Mr. Milner,
misled by the heartiness of the composition, like many of
Defoe's day, came to the conclusion that it was the work
of an enemy to those whose interests the pamphlet was
intended to serve.　The paragraph points immediately to
Sir Thomas and his friend Watts, as the reader will
perceive by the designations italicized : "But a lady,
Queen Anne, now sits on the throne, who though sprung
from that blood which ye and your forefathers spilt before
the palace-gates, puts on a temper of forgiveness, and, in
compassion to your consciences, is not willing that you
should lose the hopes of heaven by purchasing here on
earth.　She would have no more Sir Humphreys tempt
the justice of God, by falling from his true worship and
giving ear to the cat-calls and back-pipes at St. Paul's;
would have your *Sir Thomas's* keep to their primitive
text, and not venture damnation to play at long spoon and
custard for a transitory twelvemonth; and would have
your *Sir Tom* sing psalms at Highgate Hill, and split
texts of Scripture *with his diminutive figure of a chaplain,*
without running the hazard of qualifying himself to be

called a handsome man for riding on horseback before the City trainbands."

It may be noticed now how much the interest of King William and the Hanover succession to the throne of England were served by the Protestant dissenters of the City of London, and by no one more than by Sir Thomas Abney. He lived to a good old age, dying at his house at Theobalds in the year 1722. Nor can we wonder that his friend should pay a high tribute to his memory in a funeral sermon, and seek to give it a more durable place in a sketch in his " Miscellaneous Thoughts."

Theobalds was a fine old palace, and has been celebrated in the verses of poets and the pages of novelists, and the memoirs of historians ; but no biography of Watts gives any specific account of the magnificent old building in which he spent the greater number of the years of his life. It was as much Watts' home as if it had been his own property ; and he was in the habit of saying his poetical contributions would have been much more numerous had he, in his early life, been privileged with the means of retirement among such shades and gardens, and ample grounds. Theobalds was, and had been, everything that could excite the memory, or stir or soothe and lull the imagination. Situated a little more than a mile from Cheshunt, in Hertfordshire, and within an easy ride from the metropolis, on the borders of Enfield Chase, it possessed a very remarkable history ; it had been the favourite residence of the mighty Cecil, Lord Burleigh ; to this place he fled with eagerness to enjoy his short intervals of leisure ; amidst its shades he planned and plotted schemes in which the whole future of England's history was interested ; he laid out immense sums of money upon the grand pile, and kept up great state with extraordinary magnificence, while he might be seen ambling along upon a mule through the groves of his magnificent domains, overlooking his workmen or the parties of pleasure he had gathered around him. Here, at this old house, Queen Elizabeth had repeatedly rested in the course of her great progresses. Here, when Burleigh and his mistress had both passed away, came James I., and held his masques, written by Ben Jonson, and enjoyed his pleasures. It was in his reign that it was given up by the Earl of Salisbury to Queen Anne of Denmark, amidst such strange pageantries of most intemperate folly that Sir John Harington writes, contrasting the days of James I. with what he remembered of the same place in the days of Queen Elizabeth, " I never did see such lack of good order, discretion, and sobriety, as I have now done."

In Watts' day there was living in the neighbouring village of Cheshunt that remarkable man, also a member of Watts' church, Richard Cromwell, although, somewhat to shroud himself in obscurity, he usually went by the name of Mr. Clarke. An eminent novelist * has woven into his fiction very naturally one of the most striking incidents of his story from the casual meeting of his hero and the son of the Protector on this very spot, when Cromwell became his host and entertainer. Richard Cromwell died probably before Watts became a constant resident at Theobalds ; and indeed Cromwell removed from Cheshunt some time before his death.

Cheshunt churchyard once contained a number of inscriptions upon the tombs from the pen of the poet; most of them have probably long been obliterated, but two or three have been snatched from oblivion ; an inscription for the tomb of Thomas Pickard, Esq., citizen of London, who died suddenly, probably a member of Watts' church :

* Lord Lytton, in " Devereux."

> A soul prepared needs no delays,
> The summons comes, the saint obeys;
> Swift was his flight and short the road,
> He closed his eyes and saw his God.
> His flesh rests here till Jesus come
> And claims the treasure from the tomb.

Another epitaph :

> Beneath this stone Death's prisoner lies.
> That stone shall move, the prisoner rise
> When Jesus with Almighty word
> Calls His dead saints to meet their Lord.

The following lines were not long since in existence, written upon a ceiling dial at a western window of Theobalds :

> Little sun upon the ceiling
> Ever moving, ever stealing
> Moments, minutes, hours away;
> May no shade forbid thy shining
> While the heavenly sun declining
> Calls us to improve the day.

There was another, indeed there appear to have been several ; it was the taste of the times to line the avenues with these moralities in verse :

> Thus steal the silent hours away,
> The sun thus hastes to reach the sea,
> And men to mingle with their clay.
> Thus light and shade divide the year,
> Thus till the last great day appear
> And shut the starry theatre.

If we are able to discriminate Watts in his various abodes here and at Stoke Newington, certainly it is not his biographers we have to thank for it. They have jumbled up his residences in a very heterogeneous fashion, and leave us very much in doubt whether their descriptions of his rooms apply to his earlier or later abode.

Assuredly he lived in a mansion large enough for him. One of the smallest of mortals, he had one of the largest homes. We can readily believe that good Sir Thomas was very well pleased from such a pile to deliver up a suite of apartments to such a guest. His own rooms were a kind of true literary hermitage, adorned with paintings from his own pencil, and his collection of portraits of eminent persons he had known, or great contemporaries he admired ; at the entrance of his study on the outside were the fine lines from the first book of Horace's satires, in which he denounces the faithless friend : " He who reviles his absent friend, who does not defend him while another defames him, who aims at the groundless jeers of people, and the reputation of a wit, who can feign things not seen, who cannot keep secrets, he is the rancorous man." The spaces within, where there were no shelves, were filled up with prints of distinguished friends, or eminent persons. Of course, there was a spacious old Elizabethan fireplace, panelled on either side, and in each panel an inscription from the beloved Horace. On the one side :

Locus est pluribus umbris.

And on the other :

Quis me dolorum propria dignabitor umbra.

There we are permitted to fancy him. Such were his haunts among those pleasant and sequestered shades, and such was his home. His rooms well arranged and tasteful, as one biographer has depicted them. The lute and the telescope on the same table with the Bible, a treatise on logic in one hand, and hymns and spiritual songs in the other. Few writers in our language seem to suggest a finer illustration of the mingled powers of faith and reason.

With so small a family what a silent household it must have seemed, sustained in its grand and memorable stateliness. There passed what we may believe to have been the happiest years of Watts' life, amidst scenes inviting to rest, and with little to disturb the equanimity of his quiet spirit, receiving and reflecting its own peace, peace not to be disturbed even by much bodily restlessness and pain. Those numerous allusions in his hymns to the wakeful hours of night were not mere poetic fancies, "the comforts of my nights" were not unneeded; for many years he knew little of sleep, except such as could be obtained by medicine; intense mental application, working upon a weak and nervous constitution, brought about the consequences of insomnia, or sleeplessness; yet his mind seems to have been too calm, too equally balanced, and too completely under the control of highest principles, ever to know such agitations as shake to their centre some poetic natures. Even public agitations did not disturb him much. Almost the severest trial he knew was the vehement and intolerant persecution he sustained from the tongue and pen of Thomas Bradbury; but to him we may refer in subsequent pages.

CHAPTER VII.

Hymns.

SO early as the year 1700 Watts' brother, Mr. Enoch Watts, wrote a letter to him from Southampton, urging upon him the publication of his hymns. It sets not only the mind of the writer as a member of the Doctor's family in a favourable light, as well as it expresses the probable general feeling of desire for some hymns suitable for Divine service. We quote it here :

" SOUTHAMPTON : *March*, 1700.

" DEAR BROTHER,—

" In your last you discovered an inclination to oblige the world by showing it your hymns in print, and I heartily wish, as well for the satisfaction of the public as myself, that you were something more than inclinable thereunto. I have frequently importuned you to it before now, and your invention has often furnished you with some modest reply to the contrary, as if what I urge was only the effect of a rash and inconsiderate fondness to a brother ; but you will have other thoughts of the matter when I first assure you that that affection, which is inseparable from our near relationship, would have had in me a very different operation, for instead of pressing you to

publish, I should with my last efforts have endeavoured
the concealment of them, if my best judgment did not
direct me to believe it highly conducing to a general
benefit, without the least particular disadvantage to yourself. This latter I need not have mentioned, for I am
very confident whoever has the happiness of reading your
hymns (unless he be either sot or atheist) will have a very
favourable opinion of their author ; so that, at the same
time you contribute to the universal advantage, you will
procure the esteem of men the most judicious and sensible.
In the second place, you may please to consider how very
mean the performers in this kind of poetry appear in the
pieces already extant. Some ancient ones I have seen
in my time, who flourished in Hopkins and Sternhold's
reign ; but Mason now reduces this kind of writing to a
sort of yawning indifferency, and honest Barton chimes us
asleep. There is, therefore, a great need of a pen, vigorous
and lively as yours, to quicken and revive the dying
devotion of the age, to which nothing can afford such
assistance as poetry, contrived on purpose to elevate us
even above ourselves. To what may we impute the prevalency of the songs, filled with the fabulous divinity of
the ancient fathers, on our passions ? Is it, think you,
only owing to a natural propensity in us to be in love
with fable, and averse to truth in her native plainness ? I
presume it may partly be ascribed to this, that as romance
has more need of artifice than truth to set it off, so it
generally has such an abundance more, that it seldom fails
of affecting us by making new and agreeable impressions.
Yours now is the old truth, stripped of its ragged ornaments, and appears, if we may say so, younger by ages,
in a new and fashionable dress, which is commonly
tempting.

"And as for those modern gentlemen who have lately exhibited their version of the Psalms, all of them I have not seen I confess, and, perhaps, it would not be worth while to do it unless I had a mind to play the critic, which you know is not my talent, but those I have read confess to me a vast difference to yours, though they are done by persons of no mean credit. Dr. Patrick most certainly has the report of a very learned man, and, they say, understands the Hebrew extremely well, which, indeed, capacitates him for a translator, but he is thereby never the more enabled to versify. Tate and Brady still keep near the same pace. I know not what sober beast they ride (one that will be content to carry double), but I am sure it is no Pegasus: there is in them a mighty deficiency of that life and soul which is necessary to raise our fancies and kindle and fire our passions, and something or other they have to allege against the rest of adventurers; but I have been persuaded a great while since, that were David to speak English, he would choose to make use of your style. If what I have said seems to have no weight with you, yet you cannot be ignorant what a load of scandal lies on the Dissenters, only for their imagined aversion to poetry. You remember what Dr. Speed says:

> So far hath schism prevailed they hate to see
> Our lines and words in couplings to agree,
> It looks too like abhorred conformity:
> A hymn so soft, so smooth, so neatly drest,
> Savours of human learning and the beast.

And, perhaps, it has been thought there were some grounds for his aspersion from the admired poems of Ben. Keach, John Bunyan, etc., all flat and dull as they are; nay, I am much out if the latter has not formerly made much more ravishing music with his hammer and brass kettle.

"Now when you are exposed to the public view these calumnies will immediately vanish, which, methinks, should be a motive not the least considerable. And now we are talking of music, I have a crotchet in my brain, which makes me imagine, that as chords and discords equally please heavy-eared people, so the best divine poems will no more inspire the rude and illiterate than the meanest rhymes, which may in some measure give you satisfaction, in that fear you discover, *ne in rude vulgus cadant,* and you must allow them to be tasteless to many people, tolerable to some, but to those few who know their beauties, to be very pleasant and desirable; and, lastly, if I do not speak reason, I will at present take my leave of you, and only desire you to hear what your ingenious acquaintance in London say to the point, for I doubt not you have many solicitors there, whose judgments are much more solid than mine. I pray God Almighty have you in His good keeping, and desire you to believe me, my dear brother,

"Your most affectionate kinsman and friend,

"ENOCH WATTS."

But notwithstanding this and other solicitations, the first edition was not published until 1707. The copyright of the hymns was sold to Mr. Lawrence, the publisher, for £10 ; about half a century before the same sum was given to Milton for his "Paradise Lost;" the volume instantly obtained a very large acceptance, and he then directed his attention to his version of the Psalms; this was only completed by him during the painful and distressing illness from which he suffered about 1712 and the following years, but the Psalms were not published until the year 1719.

" Dr. Watts," says James Montgomery, in his introduction to the " Christian Psalmist," " may almost be called the inventor of hymns in our language, for he so far departed from all precedent that few of his compositions resemble those of his forerunners, while he so far established a precedent to all his successors that none have departed from it otherwise than according to the peculiar turn of mind in the writer, and the style of expressing Christian truths employed by the denomination to which he belonged." And, again, he says, " We come to the greatest name among hymn-writers, for we hesitate not to give that praise to Dr. Isaac Watts, since it has pleased God to confer upon him, though one of the least of the poets of this country, more glory than upon the greatest either of that or of any other, by making his ' Divine Songs ' a more abundant and universal blessing than the verses of any uninspired penman that ever lived. In his ' Psalms and Hymns ' (for they must be classed together) he has embraced a compass and variety of subjects which include and illustrate every truth of revelation, throw light upon every secret movement of the human heart, whether of sin, nature, or grace, and describe every kind of trial, temptation, conflict, doubt, fear, and grief, as well as the faith, hope, charity, the love, joy, peace, labour, and patience of the Christian in all stages of his course on earth, together with the terrors of the Lord, the glories of the Redeemer, and the comforts of the Holy Spirit, to urge, allure, and strengthen him by the way. There is in the pages of this evangelist a word in season for every one who needs it, in whatever circumstances he may require counsel, consolation, reproof, or instruction. We say this without reserve of the materials of his hymns ; had their execution only been correspondent with the preciousness

of these, we should have had a Christian Psalmist in
England next (and that only in date, not in dignity) to
the 'Sweet Singer of Israel.' Nor is this so bold a word
as it may seem. Dr. Watts' hymns are full of 'the
glorious Gospel of the blessed God;' his themes, therefore, are much more illustrious than those of the son of
Jesse, who only knew 'the power and glory' of Jehovah
as he had 'seen them in the sanctuary,' which was but the
shadow of the New Testament Church, as the face of
Moses holding communion with God was brighter than
the veil he cast over it when conversing with his
countrymen."

His attention was very early awakened to the importance and necessity for some improvement in this department of Divine service. Our readers will remember that
after he had closed his academical studies at Stoke
Newington, before he entered on the ministry, he returned
home and lived during the years 1695 and 1696 in the
old house with his father; he devoted those years, the
twenty-first and twenty-second of his life, to systematic
reading, meditation, and prayer; and during those years he
appears to have composed the greater number of his hymns.
Thus, if they are among the first effusions of his poet's
pen, they are among the best; and in this circumstance
they resemble the first and chief volume of one of his
successors in the art of sacred poetry in our own day,
John Keble, whose "Christian Year" was the production of his earliest manhood, and all whose subsequent
efforts in verse seem to be a vain striving to overtake the
beauty and harmony of his first performances. Many of
Watts' later hymns are very noble and beautiful, but the
greater number appear to have been composed in those
early Southampton days. Dr. Gibbons says, " Mr. John

Morgan, a minister of very respectable character now
living at Romsey, Hants, has sent me the following information : ' The occasion of the Doctor's hymns was
this, as I had the account from his worthy fellow-labourer
and colleague, the Rev. Mr. Price, in whose family I
dwelt above fifty years ago. The hymns which were sung
at the Dissenting meeting at Southampton were so little
to the gust of Mr. Watts, that he could not forbear com-
plaining of them to his father. The father bid him try
what he could do to mend the matter. He did, and had
such success in his first essay that a second hymn was
earnestly desired of him, and then a third, and fourth, etc.,
till in process of time there was such a number of them as
to make up a volume.' "

It is remarkable that in England the power of the
popular hymn was so late in discovering itself. It does
not appear to have been known here in the old Roman
Catholic days as assuredly it was in other countries,
while in Germany the Reformation was born and brought
forth amidst the chanting of noble and triumphant hymns.
It appears to be impossible to realise the services of the
Church without the hymn. Canon Liddon, curiously ana-
lyzing the texts of several of the Pauline Epistles, seems to
demonstrate that those "faithful sayings" quoted by the
apostle as the embodiment of the belief of the Church,
were apostolic hymns sung in the Redeemer's honour.
And certainly the early Church expressed its faith and
its best aspirations in hymns. Of this we have many and
very beautiful illustrations ; as we descend from that time
along the line of the ages, the great Divine truths united
themselves to experiences and hopes in the hearts of
many, and as we read the great hymns of the Church we
behold her travelling along as beneath a series of triumphal

arches reared out of the service of sacred song, expressing
the emotion of multitudes of spirits. For the history of
holy hymns is really the history of the Church. Our
sacred books carry us back, indeed, to the airs of Pales-
tine; the voices of the soul strong, intuitional, and clear,
rising from the sands of Arabia; from the tabernacle in
Shiloh, from the forests of Lebanon, from Moses and David,
from Asaph to the sons of Korah, from the majestic
antiphones of the temple; the murmur of captives by
Babylonish streams; and then rich and strong the raptures
of the apostles, touched from the altar flame of heaven,
they were not less than sacred hymns; and from their
times what gushes and wails of sacred song come sounding
to us, clear and shrill, over the roar of persecuting multitudes, or from desert caves or the lonely Churches of the
catacombs! The rich hymns of the early Fathers are still
amongst the most treasured legacies of the Church. Christian hymnology is the treasure-house into which all the
best devotions of the men " of whom the world was not
worthy," exiled kings, bishops, confessors, and seers, and
souls of lowlier state, have been poured, giving to us in
some instances the doxology of a life-time, and associat-
ing through all ages the martyr's or the musician's name
with that one particular chord. We have no collection
yet, at all such as we desire to see, in which the varied
tones of human hearts through all times are collected; the
surges of old cathedral aisles; low, thrilling tones of old
monks; thunder-peals of the wild, old, rugged people;
chants of the ancient martyrs at the stake; the glorious
and wonderful hymns of the Greek Church; the treasuries
of Latin hymns, and even many of the more popular of the
great vernacular German chants. For the hymns of the
Church are the lamps of the Church; they are the myriad

lights which stream through the darkness of the dark centuries, and they furnish the fresher beam of the new illumination, lighting the shrines and altars and chapels of modern times. What is a hymn? St. Augustine has, in a well-known passage, defined a hymn to have necessarily a threefold function. It must be praise; it must be praise to God; it must be praise in the form of song. These limitations, essential as they seem, would perhaps curtail many of our selections. We should then have to exclude much of that meditative devotion with which our best books abound; much also of that too painful and curious self-anatomy which many of our best hymnwriters permit their strains to exhibit. Yet we are very far from thinking that to be the test of sacred song which Augustine has supplied, and with which a very able writer in the "Quarterly Review," in an article on hymnology, has quoted with approbation.* This test, applied to the great hymnals and hymnologists of the Church of the middle ages, would, we apprehend, be quite a failure. It is true that praise, and praise to God, and praise to God through Christ, in the form of song, should be the grand criterion for the structure of sacred verses for the use of congregations; but to what extent should these be mixed with the strains of simple devotion, the dwelling of the spirit upon the perfections of the Almighty; and with confession, the laying bare of the heart—its wants and its woes—in no morbid tone or strain, before the Divine and searching eye? Our impression surely is that hymns should represent all that the spirit desires to express in its moods of praise and prayer. By a more earnest appeal to the senses, the soul is opened; and it has been well said that so closely and mystically knit together are

* " Quarterly Review," No. 222, April, 1862. Art. Hymnology.

our higher and lower natures, that to neglect the one is
to neglect the other. In prayer—the long, earnest, ex-
temporaneous prayer—the spirit becomes abstracted, and,
perhaps, even in the highest states, in the most subduing
states of ecstacy, there are few of the congregation who
rise as the preacher rises, or rest as he rests. The hymn,
in its throbbings and tremulous and pendulous vibrations,
breaks through the monotony and *ennui* the body imposes
on the soul, and, therefore, we are quite away from that
increasing number in our more immediate midst who are
indisposed to avail themselves of the bursts of sensuous
song. We remember that it is not long since grave
exception was taken by some among us to the singing—

There is a land of pure delight,

on the ground that it contains no recognition of, or praise
to, the Redeemer. But, surely, as long as beautiful sights
and beautiful sounds, the solemn gloom and glory of the
everlasting hills, and the endlessness of the pure sky are
to be apprehended by men, so long it must be not only a
desirable, but an imperative thing, that they should all be
transferred to the keys of the Christian organ and of
Christian speech. We are not unaware of the danger
of the defence of æsthetic beauty, to spiritual Christianity, but a wise and balanced nature will know how
far to advance and when to stop, and we quite believe
that our doxologies, and thanksgivings, and moments
of Christian fervour should lay under contribution
every faculty of the soul, and that each faculty may
be moved by a Divine affection, speak to the heart's
inner chambers, and relate them to the most consecrated
heights.

For song being a natural expression of inflamed emotion,

man must become an unnatural creature if he disdain to
sing, and those who cannot themselves sing do not therefore always the less delight in the happy jubilant expressions attained by others ; for man, happily, can enjoy that
to which he cannot attain, and in this consists one of the
great moving powers of his soul.   Unconverted people
sing.   They have airs and melodies wafted from the ground
of the nature in which they live and have their being ;
and when they learn and feel their heritage of salvation
and immortality, the joy in God through Jesus Christ
demands its appropriate expression in suitable elevated
strains and tones.   And Christians feel their unity, not so
much in reading or in preaching as in those great expressions which rise above the colder forms of the understanding, and touch each other at the centre of some great
affection of faith or hope.   It is, we must think, to
Protestantism that the Church is indebted for the ample
and sweeping robes of spiritual melody.   Papists indig-
nantly deny this.   Cardinal Wiseman has told us in a
well-known article, that Protestantism is essentially
undevotional.   Our devotional practices and services
might be improved and increased ; but for the multitudes
of its hymnologists, and the multitude of their songs,
and for the fulness and the fervour of those same songs
Protestantism seems to leave Western and Eastern
Churches far behind.   Although some of our spiritual airs
and aspirations need the hallowing touch of time before
they can receive the consecration of affection which crowns
the words of Basil, and the hymns of Ambrose, and the
chants of Gregory.

Thus, the history of the hymn, and of hymns from the
earliest ages, their originals, their writers, their associations, would form one of the most charming chapters of

Church history. To read how the great hymns grew, what study of Church history can be more delightfully entertaining? Down the long line of the ages the hymns pass on, and they, more than the creeds of councils and the clangour of warriors, seem to shape the spandrels from whence leap up the great arches of the Church. The great Church hymns, by these greatly its unity of faith is proclaimed. In what simple incidents many of the chords arose. That is a very sweet, solemn, pathetic line in our wonderful Burial Service, "In the midst of life we are in death"—in fact, it seems to be the adaptation of the first line of the rare old Latin hymn, the "Media Vita," composed by Notker Balbulus, born of a noble family of Zurich. He attained to great eminence at St. Gall by his learning and skill in music and poetry, and his knowledge of the Holy Scriptures. No one ever saw him, say the old stories of him, but he was reading, writing, or praying. The faint sound of a mill-wheel near his abbey, moved him to compose a beautiful air to some pious verses, and looking down into a deep gulf, and the danger incurred by some labourer in building a bridge over the abyss, suggested the celebrated hymn, the "Media Vita." What a singular and interesting history there is in the hymn, "Jerusalem, my happy home." Through what generations of variations it has passed!

The history of hymns, from the earliest to the latest times, furnishes one of the most interesting chapters in the history of the Church. In the hymn the spirit seems to bound into a higher life, and expressions which are scarcely admitted in cold conversation, which almost seem like exaggerations in an essay, or inflated even in a sermon, are felt to be a sweet, fitting, and natural utterance; in some happy moment a nature gifted by genius, subdued by sorrow, but lifted up to a region of serene vision and glowing consolation, found itself caught and compelled to utter an experience which to itself was not always abiding, but which often became afterwards an exceeding joy to it to remember, and which the Church at large retained as the expression of what it believed, and desired yet more fervently to believe through all subsequent ages. Thus the great hymns grew, and the Church has never been without them. Thus many of the portions of the Common Prayer Book of the Church of England and many of its collects are "the golden fruit in a network of silver;" and we in the present day are singing hymns of the holy men of old, who were moved by the Divine Spirit to utter forth the words of prayer and praise. In his Life of Dr. Watts, Dr. Johnson has many remarks which have been the subjects of criticism and exception, but in none are his remarks more open to exception than when he says that "his religious poetry is unsatisfactory." "The paucity of its topics," he continues, "forces perpetual repetition, and the sanctity of the matter rejects the ornaments of figurative diction; it is sufficient for Watts to have done better than others what no man has done well." If this is kindly said, still it is not true ; perhaps Johnson was confining his observation, which he ought not to have done, to sacred poetry as belonging to that order represented by Milton or Phineas Fletcher; and yet this could scarcely be the case; and if he referred to his productions as a hymn-writer, then, through the long ages past, men innumerable had done well, as many a noble Latin and German hymn abundantly shows. In the first ages of the Church, the whole city of Milan was alive with hymns, and Augustine tells us how his soul was moved by the power of sacred psalms ; the passage is well worth remembering. "The hymns and songs of the Church," he says, "move my soul intensely; by the truth distilled by them into my heart the flame of piety was kindled, and my tears flowed for joy. The practice of singing had been of no long standing in Milan, it began about the year when Justinian persecuted Ambrose; the pious people, watched in the church, prepared to die with their pastor; there my mother sustained an eminent part in watching and praying; then hymns and psalms, after the manner of the East, were sung, with a view of preserving the people from weariness; and thence the custom has spread through Christian Churches." Johnson was a pious man, the truth as it is in Jesus was held by him very heartily, but we are compelled to believe that, with all his amazing knowledge, he had not seen the innumerable hymns which through the successive ages had rained down their beautiful influences on the Church.

Luther, as is well known, ushered in his great Reformation with a voice of joy and singing. There is a pretty little anecdote telling how one day he stood at his window and heard a blind beggar sing. It was something about the grace of God, and it brought tears into his eyes, and then the good thought rushed into his soul, and it wrought its results there. "If *I* could only make gospel songs which would spread of themselves among the people." And he did so. The songs were fashioned, and flew abroad like singing birds—"like a lark singing towards heaven's gate," says one writer; "the song shot upward, and poured far and wide over the fields and villages; and though the snare of the fowler sometimes captured the preacher, and military mobs dispersed the congregation—like the little minstrel among the clouds, too happy to be silenced, too airy to be caught, and too high to dread man's artillery—the little song filled all the air with New Testament music, with words such as 'Jesus,' 'Believe and be saved,' 'Gospel,' 'Grace,' 'Come unto Me,' 'Worthy is the Lamb that was slain,' and thus they became the passwords and watchwords of the Church." *

Watts has been styled the Marot of England; he must receive far higher praise than could be implied by this designation; but there are resemblances between the two. Clement Marot was the favourite poet of Francis I. of France; Bayle ascribes to him the invention of modern metrical psalmody. He was a free and even profane writer, but Vatable, the Hebrew professor, suggested to him the translation of the Psalms into French verse. He did so, or rather he translated fifty-two Psalms " from the Hebrew into French rhyme." They quite took the taste of Paris; they found universal reception, and became favourites with Francis I., who sent a copy to Charles V. Most of the pieces were set and sung to the tunes of the gay ballads of that day. They were quite the favourites of the court of Henry II. and Catherine de Medicis, especially they became the favourites of the Huguenot party; Marot, it is said, had himself belonged to the party of the Reformation. Ere long, however, the dangerous tendency of the pieces was perceived by the Sorbonne, the book was denounced; Marot fled to Turin, where he closed in poverty a life which had passed in singular vicissitudes, but which only just before had been sunned in the rays of the courtly magnificence of Paris in that splendid time. Marot's small collection was completed by Theodore Beza, and the pieces continued long in use among the Reformed Churches; some, we believe, are, with many additions, still sung.

* " British and Foreign Evangelical Review," 1865.

Our chief concern at present is with our own country, but the other reforming peoples of Europe appear to have preceded us in this holy art, although some indications are given of the existence of a very hearty and earnest religious song; in the Zurich Letters, published by the Parker Society, we find, even so early as 1560, the following letter from Bishop Jewel to Peter Martyr; he says: " Religion is now somewhat more established than it was; the people are everywhere exceedingly inclined to the better part; the practice of joining in church music has very much conduced to this; for as soon as they had commenced singing in public in one little church in London, immediately, not only the churches in the neighbourhood, but even the towns far distant, began to vie with each other in practice. You may sometimes see at St. Paul's Cross, after the service, 6,000 persons, old and young, of both sexes, all singing together and praising God. This sadly annoys the mass priests and the devil, for they perceive that by this means the sacred discourses sink more deeply into the minds of men, and that their kingdom is weakened and shaken at almost every note."

As time went along in our country, there appeared a race of poets of the highest order; we need scarcely mention such names as Quarles, Vaughan, Herbert, Jeremy Taylor, Richard Baxter, John Norris, Thomas Ken, and with these names we certainly ought to include John Milton, who attempted a version of several of the Psalms, one of which is a great favourite with us to this day. Poets not remarkable for sanctity, like John Dryden, were compelled to the service of sacred song, as in the instance of his fine hymn,

Creator, Spirit, by whose aid.

Richard Baxter leaves a beautiful testimony as to the power of sacred hymns over himself; he says, "For myself I confess that harmony and melody are the pleasure and elevation of my soul; I have made psalms of praise in the holy assembly the chief delightful exercise of my religion and my life, and have helped to bear down all the objections which I have heard against church music and against the 149th and 150th Psalms. It was not the least comfort I had in the converse with my late dear wife, that our first in the morning and last at night was a psalm of praise, till the hearing of others interrupted it. Let those that savour not melody leave others to their different appetites, and be content to be so far strangers to their delights."

With all this it is singular that an amazing prejudice existed until the time of Watts against the indulgence of congregational psalmody. Josiah Conder simply expressed the fact, when he says, "Watts was the first who succeeded in overcoming the prejudice which opposed the introduction of hymns into our public worship." It is quite remarkable that the prejudice against congregational singing was quite as great with many of our English Churches as amongst the Papists themselves; among the Presbyterians especially, this prejudice obtained a considerable hold and lingered long. "No English Luther," says Conder, "had risen to breathe the living spirit of evangelical devotion into heart-stirring verse adapted to the minds and feelings of the people. Are we to suppose the want was not felt, or was there anything in the aristocratic genius of the Presbyterian polity that forbade or repressed the free expression of devotion in the songs of the sanctuary ?" *

It was about the time that Isaac Watts came to London that some of the assemblies of the saints were shaken

* "The Poet of the Sanctuary," etc. By Josiah Conder. 1857.

by the innovation of singing. The Baptists appear to have been most indisposed to the doubtful practice; and in the church of the well-known Benjamin Keach, of Southwark, the pastoral ancestor of Charles Spurgeon, when the pastor, after long argument and effort, established singing, a minority withdrew and " took refuge in a song-less sanctuary," in which the melody within the heart might be in no danger of disturbance from the pertur-bations of song. * The Society of Friends was not alone in regarding with distaste all the exercises of song in the house of the Lord. Those who are interested in the curious literature of that time may easily discover pamphlets and lectures which show " great searchings of heart" upon the question "whether Christ, as Mediator of the New Covenant, hath commanded His churches under the Gospel in all their assemblies to sing the Psalms of David, as translated into metre and musical rhyme, with tunable and conjoined voices of all the people together, as a Church ordinance, or any other song or hymn that are so composed to be sung in rhyme by a prelimited and set form of words ? " The dispute was mainly confined to the Baptist churches. But in 1708 one of the Eastcheap lec-tures, in a discourse by Thomas Reynolds, replied to the "objections of singing." A few years before the contro-versy had run strong and high. Isaac Marlow very angrily maintained the ordinary songless usage, in the year 1696, in his "Truth Soberly Defined" and in the "Con-troversies of Singing Brought to an End." Benjamin Keach seems to have been the first to lead on in this sus-picious diversion by the publication of his " Breach Re-paired in God's Worship ; or, Singing of Psalms, Hymns,

* "The Psalter and the Hymn Book.'' Three Lectures by James Hamilton.

and Spiritual Songs, proved to be an Holy Ordinance of Jesus Christ." This appeared in 1691.* The controversy is forgotten now, except by those who explore the more curious nooks and corners of Church history. Among the followers of Christ the Quakers are the only people who have consistently maintained their first profession, a profession, however, in which they do not imitate their founder, George Fox, of whom we especially read that he sometimes led his services with singing.

It was into this state of things that Isaac Watts was introduced. "I almost think," says Alexander Knox, "that he was providentially appointed to furnish the revived movement of associated piety, which Divine Wisdom foresaw would take place in England in the 18th century, with an unexampled stock of materials for that department, which alone needed to be provided for, of their joint worship. Examine his poetry, and you will find that, though ability to converse with God in solitude is not absolutely overlooked, the sheet-anchor is what he calls the sanctuary. In particular in the Psalms you will find him generally applying to Christian assemblies what David said of the Temple services, as if public ordinances occupied the same supreme place in the inward and spiritual as in the outward and carnal dispensation." This judgment of Knox is curiously involved, and its latter portion seems to contradict its former. Acquaintance with Watts' hymns will show that Knox was quite wrong, that Watts by no means overlooked the inward and the spiritual; but his object seems to have been to provide a congregational, joint, and united service. And for this it does seem as if he in an especial manner was raised up by the providence of God; and this becomes more evident as we notice how

* See Crosbie's " History of the English Baptists " (1740), vol. iii.

it is from his day, and apparently very greatly from the
method he created that the popular hymnology of our
country, which is now surely—may we not dare to say ?—
the noblest, of any church or of any nation in the world,
dates its true original.

We have claimed for Watts already a far higher rank
than is implied by the Marot of England, but it is certain
that exception will be taken to our judgment when we
say that no other writer of this order approaches near to
him in the elevation, not merely of expression, but of sentiment ; the very grandeur, the majesty of his epithets, the
inflamed utterances may be to some more quiet natures a
ground of exception.   To them they seem sometimes to be
open to the charge of inflation.   Yet every order and
variety of expression, from the loud swelling jubilant
rapture to the softest and sweetest strains of tenderness,
find fitting utterance in them.

The efforts he made to create a sacred congregational
psalmody exposed him, as we know, in his own times to
obloquy, singular as it seems, even to contempt, and this
contempt has been renewed in our own day.   In a paper,
understood to be from the pen of John Keble, in the
" Quarterly Review," it is said, " Watts was an excellent man, a strong reasoner, of undoubted piety, and
perhaps—a rarer virtue—of true Christian charity ; but in
our opinion he laboured under irreparable deficiency for
the task he undertook—*he was not a poet !*   He had a great
command of Scriptural language, and an extraordinary
facility of versification ; but his piety may induce us to
make excuses for his poetry—*his poetry will do little to
excite dormant piety.*"   The writer then goes on to remark
upon the rude, homely, and unequal strains of Watts, there
follows something like a history of psalmody in England,

but not another word about our author.*   George Macdonald, the novelist, has condescended to sneer at Watts
and to travesty his verses, while another writer in a fierce
attack upon evangelicalism—the predominance of which
in Watts' verses we presume to be the spring of the hatred
they often inspire—informs us that " most of Dr. Watts'
hymns are doggerel ; " and after quoting some passages he
considers to deserve this appellation—and which some of
them do—he closes by saying, " These may possibly be
poetry, but if they are, it is extremely plain that ' Paradise
Lost ' and ' In Memoriam ' are not poetry." Thus by
many it has come to be settled that Watts must take a
very low place in English literature, if, indeed, he can be
considered in any sense worthy of a place at all.   Let us
see how the case stands.   The man who has no sympathy
with Nature is not to be expected to find beauty or melody
in the poetry of Burns or Wordsworth.   Men who have no
sympathy with evangelical truth can scarcely be expected
to have much admiration for Watts; yet the gifted
nobleman, who was the Mecænas of the past age, was
not an indifferent critic, and when called on to cite
the most perfect verse in the language he immediately
instanced

> There shall I bathe my weary soul
>   In seas of heavenly rest,
> And not a wave of trouble roll
>   Across my peaceful breast.

A friend who, to his other attainments adds those of
scholar and a critic, suggests how interesting it would be
to analyze the verses of Watts, for the purpose of noting
how often he evidently thought in foreign languages, and
especially the Latin, with which he was so familiar ; and

* " Quarterly Review," vol. xxxviii.   Art. Psalmody.

hence we have lines which, while to some readers they appear to be doggerel, are indeed illustrations that he was using words in their real etymological sense, and thus imparting to his verse a singular beauty; thus:

> How *decent* and how wise,
> How glorious to behold,
> Beyond the pomp that charms the eyes
> And rites adorned with gold.

Thus, again, of God:

> He sits on no *precarious* throne,
> Nor borrows leave to be.

And thus again:

> Let every creature rise and bring
> *Peculiar* honours to our King.

Every poet is to be judged by what he is on the average. Homer has been said to nod; Milton is frequently very turgid, and innumerable passages sink quite below the usual sustained magnificence of the poem; in Shakespeare there are lines, conceits, and redundances which all good taste would wish away. The reader who judged of Keble's capacity for poetry by his version of the Psalms, or many of his later pieces, would not form a very lofty estimate of his powers. And there are many more expressions and passages than we shall care to count among the psalms and hymns of Watts which are wholly indefensible by any standard of good taste, good sense, or good theology. Upon these, critics, like those to whom we have referred, have pounced, these they have quoted, and to the crowds of passages sublime or pathetic, strong or tender, they have most adroitly closed their eyes or their ears.

Watts has suffered in many ways. Accused by one

class of critics of bad taste, and sneered at for the absence of poetic gifts by another class, his theology has been called in question as leaning towards heresy. How this charge could ever have been made by any man who had read for himself Watts' hymns passes all our conception. But the Unitarians, with a mendacity singularly their own, have in many instances taken his hymns and garbled them to suit their own theology. The Unitarians are clever at taking possession of other people's property, their churches, their endowments, their books, their great names, and, in Watts' instance, their hymns. We have even seen the *Te Deum* adapted to a Unitarian service. The Unitarians are regarded as an exceedingly moral people, and it has often been supposed that what they lack in doctrine they make up in duty, but it is quite true that they are singularly dishonest; and the most eminent Unitarian minister in England in our day, the Rev. James Martineau, does not hesitate to charge such dishonesty upon his community; he shows how the term Unitarian has to be kept out of sight in order that certain property may be obtained. He says, " How could an organization with a doctrinal name upon its face, the Unitarian Association, go into court and plead our right to our chapels, on the ground of their doctrinal neutrality? Accordingly, another association had to be got up specially for the purpose, the Presbyterian Association, in order to evade the inconsistency; and I know it to have been the opinion of the two founders of the Unitarian Association that they committed a disastrous mistake in giving a doctrinal name to the society." And he says to Mr. Macdonald, to whom he is writing, " Upon what ground can you claim a rightful succession, as you have so nobly done, to Matthew Henry and the founders of Crook Street, if you place the essence

of your Church in doctrines which he did not hold!" *
And thus Unitarians have constructed a science of equi-
vocations, and tread a plank of double meanings; it
expunges the term Unitarian as designative of their creed,
and it takes the words representative of the creed of the
great Church through all ages, and, reversing the miracle
of our Lord, they use them as vessels in which the wine is
turned into water.   This is the principle which has
governed in Unitarian hymn-books.   The selection of
many of the hymns from Watts, even his sacramental
hymns, have in several instances not been permitted to
pass unmutilated; and then, putting the top stone upon
the column of injustice, the further indignity, amounting
to insolence, of claiming him as a Unitarian.

It is a curious thing to find a writer in the "Wesleyan
Magazine" for 1831 boasting that none of the Wesleyan
hymns have ever been used for the purpose of Unitarian
or Socinian worship, while Watts' have been thus frequently employed.   The writer admits that in such
instances they have been altered, but says that "Charles
Wesley's hymns are made of too unbending materials ever
to be adapted to Socinian worship."   He was quite mistaken in the fact, they have often been "bent" for this purpose; but it is the very peculiarity of Watts that he rises to
the pre-existent and uncreated realms of majesty, of which
our Lord speaks as "the glory I had with Thee before the
world was."   It would be interesting to know how any
Socinian or Unitarian could "bend" that magnificent hymn,

> Ere the blue heavens were stretched abroad,
> From everlasting was the Word:
> With God He was; the Word was God,
> And must divinely be adored.

* "Letter to Rev. S. F. Macdonald," by James Martineau, 1859.

> By His own power were all things made;
> By Him supported all things stand;
> He is the whole creation's Head,
> And angels fly at His command.
>
> Ere sin was born or Satan fell,
> He led the host of morning stars:
> Thy generations who can tell,
> Or count the number of Thy years?
>
> But lo! He leaves those heav'nly forms,
> The Word descends and dwells in clay,
> That He may hold converse with worms,
> Dressed in such feeble flesh as they.
>
> Mortals with joy beheld His face,
> The Eternal Father's only Son;
> How full of truth! how full of grace!
> When through His eyes the Godhead shone.
>
> Archangels leave their high abode
> To learn new myst'ries here, and tell
> The loves of our descending God,
> The glories of Immanuel.

But, indeed, the sum of the matter is that the theology —the evangelical theology of Watts' hymns—is the chief reason of the exception taken to the poetry. He is in a very eminent sense the poet of the Atonement; he saw the infinite meanings in that great expression " the blood of Jesus Christ His Son cleanseth us from all sin." We have heard some quote and speak of what they have called that dreadful verse!—

> Blood hath a voice to pierce the skies,
> Revenge the blood of Abel cries;
> But the dear stream, when Christ was slain,
> Speaks peace as loud from every vein!

He saw infinite attributes in the Incarnation of Jesus Christ, God manifested in the flesh, and he saw infinite consequences involved in the sacrifice of Christ. It was all to him "the wisdom of God in a mystery," it was all the great power of God. Thus we have called him the evangelical poet, the poet of the Atonement. Hence those who have a distaste for his doctrine will dislike his verse.

It was the nature of Watts' theology that it entered more into the heavenly places, the timeless, and the unconditioned purposes of the Infinite and Eternal Mind. He was a student, a real and a hard student, and the speculations of his intellect whenever he betook himself to verse, presented themselves to his mind suffused in the glowing but ineffable lights of eternity ; he seemed to be fond of revolving eternal truths. We hope not to be misunderstood if we speak of him as a mystic. Although in his prose writings so little of the mystic appears, in his hymns he is perpetually moving amidst the adumbrations of uncreated mind. What an illustration of this is in that extraordinary hymn,

> Lord we are blind, we mortals blind.

Much of the mystic spirit which pervades his verse is perceptible in the fine paradox in the following expressions of the last verse :

> The Lord of Glory builds His seat
> Of gems unsufferably bright ;
> And lays beneath His sacred feet
> Substantial beams of gloomy night !

It is quite vain work to argue with those who take exception to these expressions. If they are not felt they will not be seen. If we say Watts was a mystic, the expression will astonish some of our readers. The hard abstract lines of cold creeds, and bodies of theology, suddenly in his verse flashed out radiant and visible as planets in southern heavens ; and his words expressing truths which seem cold in the creed of Calvin or the rigid framework of the confessions and catechisms of Puritanism, became like wings of ardent fire, tipped with seraphic light. There was even an oriental splendour about his expressions. He was mighty in the Scriptures, and we believe it will not be possible to find a verse or phrase which is not justified by Scriptural expression. His verse—the verse of the man who has been claimed as a Unitarian—was incessantly struggling up to express in glowing metre those sublime flights of thought which have always been at once the prevailing glory and gloom of what is called the Calvinistic theology. We note this in such pieces as

> What equal honours shall we bring
> To Thee, O Lord, our God, the Lamb ?
> Since all the notes that angels sing
> Are far inferior to Thy name.

Or,

> When I survey the wondrous cross
> On which the Prince of Glory died,
> My richest gain I count but loss,
> And pour contempt on all my pride.

Or,

> Up to the fields where angels lie,
> And living waters gently roll,
> Fain would my thoughts leap out and fly,
> But sin hangs heavy on my soul.
>
> Thy wondrous blood, dear dying Christ,
> Can make this load of guilt remove,
> And Thou canst bear me where Thou flyest,
> On Thy kind wings, celestial Dove !

Or,

> Descend from heaven, immortal Dove,
> Stoop down and take us on Thy wings,
> And mount and bear us far above
> The reach of these inferior things.

Or the hymn commencing

> Oh the delights! the heavenly joys!

Or that,

> Now to the Lord a noble song!

Watts, we have said, has suffered in many ways. No hymns, we will be bound to say, in our language have suffered so much from garbling and mangling; many of them have passed through a perfect martyrdom of maltreatment. Dr. Kennedy, of Shrewsbury, in his "Hymnologia Christiana," will not admit "When I can read my title clear" to be a hymn, because it is gravely wrong in doctrine; and "There is a land of pure delight" is not admitted, because it is seriously faulty in style. But if an impartial reader should desire to sum up the great merits of Watts, it will perhaps be found that there is no doctrine of the great Christian creed and no great Christian emotion which does not find happy and frequently most faultless expression. His hymns of *Praise to God,* are frequently among the most noble in our language; for instance:

> Sing to the Lord who built the skies,
> The Lord that reared this stately frame;
> Let all the nation sound His praise,
> And lands unknown repeat His name.
>
> He formed the seas, He formed the hills,
> Made every drop, and every dust,
> Nature and time, with all her wheels,
> And pushed them into motion first.
>
> Now from His high imperial throne
> He looks far down upon the spheres;
> He bids the shining orbs roll on,
> And round He turns the hasty years.
>
> Thus shall this moving engine last
> Till all His saints are gathered in,
> Then for the trumpet's dreadful blast,
> To shake it all to dust again!

> Yet, when the sound shall tear the skies,
> And lightning burn the globe below,
> Saints, you may lift your joyful eyes,
> There's a new heaven and earth for you.

He was fond of singing *the uncreated glories of the Son of God,* His official and mediatorial Majesty, as in that complete and glowing hymn,

> Join all the glorious names.

Or,

> Go worship at Immanuel's feet.

He had to vindicate himself during his life for the use of doxologies, or hymns of *praise to the Holy Spirit,* as in

> Eternal Spirit, we confess
> And sing the wonders of Thy grace.

Or the invocation,

> Come, Holy Spirit, heavenly Dove!

There is an intense and immediate objectiveness about Watts' hymns; praise, like a clear and glowing firmament, encompasses them all, and the objects of adoration revolve, like the firmamental lights, clear and distinct to the vision; they are often interior and meditative, but they never indicate a merely morbid introspection; they seem to glow in the light of the objects of their adoration: again and again we are impressed by their reverent effulgence. They are not the singular rapture over the worshipper's own state of feeling, they are not even rapture so much on account of what is seen; they are praise and honour to the objects themselves, and they have indeed to be perverted before they can express any other sentiments than those they originally utter.

Few writers more affectingly set forth *the death of Christ :*

He dies! the Friend of sinners dies!
Lo! Salem's daughters weep around;
A solemn darkness veils the skies,
A sudden trembling shakes the ground.

Break off your tears, ye saints, and tell
How high our great Deliverer reigns;
Sing how He spoiled the hosts of hell,
And led the monster Death in chains.

Say, " Live for ever, wondrous King!
Born to redeem and strong to save;"
Then ask the monster, "Where's thy sting?"
And "Where's thy victory, boasting grave?"

The hymn, indeed, contains some weak lines, but the first
and the three last verses have even great dramatic vigour
and strength.

But hymns are not always to shine with splendid
lights, *they are to soothe and comfort;* hence such words
as—

Come hither, all ye weary souls.

We remember a venerable minister eighty-eight years
of age, who filled a conspicuous place in the Church of his
day; while he was dying his daughter said to him:

Jesus can make a dying bed
As soft as downy pillows are,
While on His breast I lean *my* head,
And breathe my life out sweetly there.

The old man listened as well as he could to the verse,
then turned his head on the pillow, repeated the words
" *my* head," and so died. Perhaps some critic would
remark that the versification is slightly inaccordant or
defective, but its tenderness has propitiated many a dying
pang.

Devotion is the eminent attribute of these hymns,—
ardent, inflamed rapture of holiness. Well has it been

said " to elevate to poetic altitudes ;" every truth in Christian experience and revealed religion needs the strength and sweep of an aquiline pinion ;" and this is what Isaac Watts has done ; he has taken almost every topic which exercises the understanding and the heart of the believer, and has not only given to it a devotional aspect, but has wedded it to immortal numbers ; and whilst there is little to which he has not shown himself equal, there is nothing he has done for mere effect. Rapt, yet adoring, sometimes up among the thunder-clouds, yet most reverential in his highest range, the "good matter" is in a song, and the sweet singer is upborne as on the wings of eagles ; but even from that triumphal car, and when nearest the home of the Seraphim, we are comforted to find descending lowly lamentations and confessions of sin—new music, no doubt, but the words with which we have been long familiar in the house of our pilgrimage.

> Religion never was designed
>   To make our pleasures less.

> Thou art the sea of love
>   Where all my pleasures roll,
> The circle where my passions move,
>   And centre of my soul.

> To Thee my spirits fly
>   With infinite desire,
> And yet how far from Thee I lie!
>   Dear Jesus, raise me higher.

> I cannot bear Thy absence, Lord,
> My life expires if Thou depart;
> Be thou, my heart, still near my God,
> And Thou, my God, be near my heart.

Such are the streams of devotion on which we are borne in the verses of Watts.

Some of his hymns are like *collects*, the compact, comforting little *watchwords and creeds of the Church*—

> Firm as the earth Thy Gospel stands.

Or—

> Our God, how firm His promise stands.

Sometimes we have a fine *bold trumpet-like tone of Faith* :

> Begin, my tongue, some heavenly theme,
>   And speak some boundless thing;
> The mighty works, or mightier name
>   Of our eternal King.
>
> His very word of grace is strong
>   As that which built the skies;
> The Voice that rolls the stars along
>   Speaks all the promises.
>
> He said, "Let the wide heaven be spread,"
>   And heaven was stretched abroad:
> "Abra'm, I'll be thy God," He said,
>   And He *was* Abra'm's God.

How well he has expressed the *depths of contrition* in his version of the 51st Psalm, what plaintive compassion—

> O Thou that hear'st when sinners cry!

And equally well he has depicted the *happiness* and *serenity* of "a heart sprinkled from an evil conscience :"

> O happy soul that lives on high!

Or—

> Lord, how secure and blest are they
> Who feel the joys of pardoned sin.

Then how vigorously his notes rouse and stir to the activities of the *Christian life* :

> Are we the soldiers of the cross,
> The followers of the Lamb?

Or—

> Stand up, my soul, shake off thy fears!

The *patriotic lyrics* and hymns of Watts have sounded,

how in his day they throbbed, with that pulse of prayer
for our country :

> Shine, mighty God! on Britain shine
>   With beams of heavenly grace;
> Reveal Thy power through all our coasts,
>   And show Thy smiling face.
>
> Amidst our isle, exalted high,
>   Do Thou our glory stand;
> And, like a wall of guardian fire,
>   Surround the favoured land.

And when the Americans held their great " Thanksgiving
Day," Watts' hymn, always sung to the venerable old
tune of St. Martin's, was, as Mrs. Stowe tells us, the
national hymn of the Puritans.*

> Let children hear the mighty deeds
>   Which God performed of old,
> Which in our younger years we saw,
>   And which our fathers told.
>
> Our lips shall tell them to our sons,
>   And they again to theirs,
> That generations yet unborn
>   May teach them to their heirs.

The extent to which the verses of Watts entered into
all the incidents of the social life of the United States
is well illustrated in the " Pearl of Orr's Island:" in a
very striking and pathetic manner the following stanzas
often interlace the conversations of that charming story :

> Our God, our help in ages past,
>   Our hope for years to come,
> Our shelter from the stormy blast,
>   And our eternal home.
>
> Under the shadow of Thy throne
>   Thy saints have dwelt secure:
> Sufficient is Thine arm alone,
>   And our defence is sure.

---

* " Old Town Folk," chap. iii.

Before the hills in order stood,
  Or earth received her frame,
From everlasting Thou art God,
  To endless years the same.

Thy word commands our flesh to dust—
  " Return, ye sons of men ; "
All nations rose from earth at first,
  And turn to earth again.

A thousand ages in Thy sight
  Are like an evening gone ;
Short as the watch that ends the night
  Before the rising sun.

The busy tribes of flesh and blood,
  With all their lives and cares,
Are carried downwards by the flood,
  And lost in following years.

Time, like an ever-rolling stream,
  Bears all its sons away ;
They fly, forgotten, as a dream
  Dies at the opening day.

Like flowery fields the nations stand,
  Pleased with the morning light ;
The flowers beneath the mower's hand
  Lie withering ere 'tis night.

Our God, our help in ages past,
  Our hope for years to come,
Be Thou our guard while troubles last,
  And our eternal home.

And we are reminded that this grand hymn, which we
have heard sung in barns and meeting-houses, in kirks
and cathedrals, also comes with tender pathos in one of
the affecting scenes of Charlotte Brontë.

What grand expressions of *personal faith* abound among
these verses, what a radiant casting back of the blunted
arrows of doubt and unbelief !

Questions and doubts are heard no more ;
Let Christ and joy be all our theme ;
His Spirit seals His Gospel sure,
To every soul that trusts in Him.

> Learning and wit may cease their strife,
> When miracles with glory shine;
> The Voice that calls the dead to life
> Must be almighty and Divine.

What faith in the *Saviour's glorious resurrection and second advent !*—

> With joy we tell this scoffing age,
> He that was dead hath left His tomb;
> He lives above their utmost rage,
> And we are waiting till He come.

Sabbath songs, songs for the social service at the close of the day, songs for every variety of Christian ordinance, songs especially for the Lord's Supper, songs of grief as the soul realises the death of the Redeemer, songs of rapture as the salvation becomes apprehensible—

> Salvation! O the joyful sound!

Or—

> Plunged in a gulf of dark despair.

The first *Elegies* in our language are among Watts' hymns. When early manhood has been smitten down in its green prime, how finely swells aloft that grand elegy with its triumphant close, the paraphrase of the text, " He weakened my strength in the way, He shortened my days : "

> It is the Lord our Saviour's hand
> Weakens our strength amidst the race:
> Disease and death at His command
> Arrest us and cut short our days.
>
> Spare us, O Lord, aloud we pray,
> Nor let our sun go down at noon;
> Thy years are one eternal day,
> And must Thy children die so soon?
>
> Yet in the midst of death and grief,
> This thought our sorrow shall assuage,
> " Our Father and our Saviour live;
> Christ is the same through every age."

Before Thy face Thy church shall live,
And on Thy throne Thy children reign:
This dying world shall they survive,
And the dead saints be raised again.

And when some form more than ordinarily venerable
or beautiful, holy or beloved, has been lowered into its
resting-place, while they laid wreaths of camellias and
evergreens on the coffin, uprose that wonderful elegy:

Hear what the Voice from heaven proclaims
For all the pious dead!
Sweet is the savour of their names,
And soft their sleeping bed.

And how often, in similar circumstances, that other
sweet requiem:

Why do we mourn departing friends?

Amidst trembling prayers, in the darkened room, in
the presence of some sweet shrouded and coffined form,
the memory of some soft sealed face and folded hands, and
spirit for ever at rest, has rose the hymn into pensive
rapture:

Are we not tending upward too,
As fast as time can move?
Nor would we wish the hours more slow
To keep us from our love.

Contrasting the evanescence of man, not merely with
the eternity of God, but with the eternity of Christ, and
the promised prevalence of His salvation everywhere, who
has not seen large meetings leap into hearty fervour at the
announcement of that noble prophecy:

Jesus shall reign where'er the sun
Does his successive journeys run.

Who has more triumphantly followed the spirit of the

believer into its glorious home and rest? Watts had a singularly bold and majestic manner in striking in the very first words of a hymn the key-note of the whole piece; indeed there was usually a singular fitness and force in the first line.

> Give me the wings of faith to rise
>   Within the veil, and see
> The saints above; how great their joys,
>   How vast their glories be!

Some critics have objected to what seems to us the sweet natural pathos of that verse:

> How we should scorn the clothes of flesh,
>   These fetters and this load,
> And long for evening to undress,
>   That we may rest with God.

Or that fine piece:

> Absent from flesh! O blissful thought!

And the following verses, not so often quoted, or so well known:

> And is this heaven? and am I there?
> How short the road! how swift the flight!
> I am all life, all eye, all ear;
> Jesus is here my soul's delight.
>
> Is this the heavenly Friend who hung
> In blood and anguish on the tree,
> Whom Paul proclaimed and David sung,
> Who died for them, who died for me?
>
> Creator-God, eternal light,
> Fountain of good, tremendous power,
> Oceans of wonders, blissful sight!
> Beauty and love unknown before.
>
> Thy grace, Thy nature, all unknown
> In yon dark region whence I came,
> Where languid glimpses from Thy throne
> And feeble whispers teach Thy name.

> I'm in a world where all is new,
> Myself, my God; O blest amaze!
> Not my best hopes or wishes knew
> To form a shadow of His grace.
>
> Fixed on my God, my heart, adore;
> My restless thoughts, forbear to rove;
> Ye meaner passions, stir no more;
> But all my powers be joy and love.

And one of the most touching of his funeral pieces is that magnificent funeral march for some departed saint, and worthy of the grand air to which it has often been sung—Handel's Dead March in "Saul:"

> Unveil thy bosom, faithful tomb!
> Take this new treasure to thy trust,
> And give these sacred relics room
> Awhile to slumber in the dust.
>
> Nor pain, nor grief, nor anxious fear
> Invade thy bounds: no mortal woes
> Can reach the forms which slumber here,
> And angels watch their soft repose.
>
> So Jesus slept! God's dying Son
> Passed through the grave and blessed the bed:
> Rest here, dear saint, till from His throne
> The morning break and pierce the shade!
>
> Break from His throne, illustrious morn!
> Attend, O earth, His sovereign word;
> Restore thy trust—a glorious form
> Called to ascend and meet the Lord.

A judicious and compendious arrangement in order of the hymns of Watts, would thus show that every form of expression apparently necessary for public service finds some adequate representation: worship, confession, prayer, expression of faith; and those churches which for nearly a century had no other volume to assist them in their public devotions, do not deserve so much pity as

has very frequently been expressed for them. Soon
after their publication they came to be used outside of
the communion for which they were designed. Ralph
Erskine, of Dunfermline, drew a great number of the
verses into his most remarkable volumes of divine
drollery, sometimes in a most remarkable manner debas-
ing the metre. Should the reader care to see an instance
of this he may find it in "Scripture Songs," Book III.,
Song III.; but there are many other instances.

Admirers of Wesley are fond of citing against Watts the
well-known saying attributed to him, that he would have
given all he had written for the credit of being the author
of Charles Wesley's hymn, "Come, O thou Traveller unknown." It has been truly said, his excessive modesty often
gloomed his greatness; Gibbons makes some such remark;
it, at any rate, kept all power and disposition to self-asser-
tion in the shade; but it is no reason why his admirers
now should imitate, with reference to himself, that virtue,
and be indifferent to his great powers as a sacred poet.

No hymn-writer has suffered so much from mutilation
as Watts. Sometimes the attempts at improvement have
been ludicrous. We remember a specimen of many:

> The little ants, for one poor grain
> *Exert themselves* and strive.

Instead of—

> Labour and tug and strive.

But such emendations are innocent when compared with
those in which the entire doctrine of the hymn has been
expelled.* Lord Selborne (Sir Roundell Palmer) has said,

* For illustrations of this, see " A Letter to the Rev. Mr. ————
or a Gnat destroying the Little Arian Foxes among the Vines," and
part of the " Remains of Dr. Watts' Clear'd from the Leaves and Rags
of Arianism."

" Watts altered some of Charles Wesley's hymns, much to his brother John's discontent, as he testifies in the preface to his Hymn Book." We have very little hesitation in assuring his lordship that he is mistaken, and that he will find no instance in which Watts altered, however slightly, Wesley's hymns. In two or three instances he altered and appropriated from Tate and Brady and Patrick, and acknowledged the extent of his alterations in notes, a courtesy never extended to himself.

Before Jehovah's awful throne,

is Watts altered, and admirably altered, by two words in the first line, but the entire hymn was appropriated; but indeed it was impossible that Watts could alter Wesley. Watts' work was all done, and had long been done, before Wesley appeared. Literary plagiarism we believe to be a much less common sin than many suppose. Minds on the same plane of thought and feeling are likely to discover the same images, and to indulge in the same expressions. Certainly Mr. Milner, in his " Life of Watts," is wrong when he says (page 276) that Watts' well-known lines :

The opening heavens around me shine
With beams of sacred bliss,

were probably suggested to Watts by Gray's—

The meanest flow'ret of the vale,
The simplest note that swells the gale,
The common sun, the air, the skies,
To him are opening paradise.

Watts' lines were published nine years before Gray was born !

Comparing the two great hymn-writers, Isaac Watts

and Charles Wesley, an adequate sense may be arrived at,
if the very important distinctions are noticed between the
work proposed in the verses of the two admirable men. It
is our conviction that while Watts has, in the stricter
term of the word poet, included in himself Charles Wesley,
the purpose of Wesley's verse was especially to describe
frames, feelings, and experiences, to set these to a sweet
strain of popular melody, such as might rouse the thousands for whom they were intended. Nothing is more
remarkable than the contrasted sense Watts and the
Wesleys entertained of their performances. The preface
published to the Wesleyan Hymn Book, in 1779, is one
of the most extravagant efforts of conceit in our language;
it is somewhat wonderful that the good taste of the
Wesleyan Conference does not omit it from the editions
now in the course of circulation. " Here," it says, " is no
doggerel, no botches, nothing put in to patch up the
rhyme, no feeble expletives; here is nothing tinged or
bombast, or low and creeping; here are no cant expressions, no words without meaning; those who impute this
to us know not what they say." " Here are," it continues,
" the purity, elegance, and strength of the English language, and the utmost simplicity and plainness suited to
every capacity." It goes on to assert that " in the following hymns is to be found the true spirit of poetry, such as
cannot be acquired by art or labour, but must be the gift
of nature. By labour a man may become a tolerable
imitation of Spenser, Shakespeare, or Milton, and may
heap together pretty compound epithets, such as pale-
eyed, meek-eyed, and the like; but unless he be born a
poet he will never attain to the genuine spirit of poetry."
How remarkably all this is in contrast to the spirit of
the writer whose hymns had been before the world nearly

half a century before this first collected edition of the Wesleys' hymns was published. John Wesley included many of Watts' hymns in his own hymn book, but their authorship was not acknowledged; and many others were vigorous translations from the German of Zinzendorf, Paul Gerhardt, etc.; Watts' hymn book was entirely and wholly his own.

It is ungracious work to bring into the rivalry of comparison or contrast two singers who have so sacredly served the Church. Yet we will dare to say it here, in the hymns of Watts there is that peculiar accent, that note of pain, that majesty and melody of the deep minor chord—that sounding of a deeper experience—that ineffable something which testifies to a capacity of agony, as well as to the assurance of ecstasy which is the true poet's prerogative and power. We would even say the very test of Watts' genius and experience is that many of his pieces, and some of his very highest, are unfitted for more than the select experience. Wesley's are more easy, common-place, and popular. The hymns of Watts, however, will stand a far higher test than that of the suffrages of large congregations or ecclesiastical communities—the sighs of the sick-room, the death-bed, the bereaved chamber, the private closet of heart devotion. With these verses on their lips refreshing their hearts, how many pilgrims have approached the

> Land of pure delight
> Where saints immortal reign.

Most of what has gone before applies to the hymns; but some especial reference should be made to the version of the Psalms. Palmer, in his " Life of Watts," says, " This is generally allowed to be his capital production in poetry, with which, in point of utility, none of his other pieces will bear comparison." From this verdict there will be many dissentients. It is certainly true that in some of the pieces he rises to the highest rendering of the evangelical sense of the Psalter. His object was to interpret the Psalms of Christ; it is not therefore very remarkable that when a young minister inquired of an elder which was the best commentary on the Psalms, he replied, "Watts' version of them." This judgment was not so singular as it seems.

Watts' may be called the Messianic version of the Psalms; he felt that without this construction they must be very greatly inexplicable. The unfolding this idea popularly was an immense boon to the churches. We are to remember that the Book of Psalms was the great Hebrew Psalter; it was the Book of Common Prayer and Praise, and when the Christian Church arose, it still continued the use of these divine airs for the expression of its experiences and its faith. Jerome says: "The labourer, while he holds the handle of the plough, sings Alleluia, the tired reaper employs himself on the Psalms, and the vine-dresser, while lopping the vines with his curved hook, sings something out of David; these are our ballads in this part of the world; these, to use the common expression, are our love songs." Chrysostom has a noble panegyric upon the use of the Psalms in the service of the Church. "If we keep vigil in the Church, David comes first, last, and midst. If early in the morning, David is first, last, and midst." Again, he goes on to declare how, "in the funeral solemnities for the dead, or when the girl sits at home spinning, and not in cities alone, and not alone in churches, but in the forum and in the wilderness, and even in the uninhabitable desert,

David excites to the praises of God." And this has
continued true ever since.

The case being so, why was it that, alike in Hebrew and
in Christian days, the Book of Psalms has had such a
sovereign power over holy souls? The personality of
David has even obscured the higher personality and the
Messianic symmetry; it is forgotten that in the Hebrew
language David signifies the beloved, the darling, the chosen
one, and that many of the Psalms, regarded as personal to
him, are rather to be apprehended in the *same manner*
in which his name occurs in Isaiah and Jeremiah and
Ezekiel, in which we have "the key of David," "David, a
leader and commander to the people," in "the sure mercies
of David," terms the fulness of which is lost sight of by
their being associated with the Hebrew prince, rather
than with Him who is the infinitely beloved of God and
man. Thus in numerous Psalms to which the prefix is
given, "A Psalm of, or by, David," a stricter reading
would be, "A Psalm to, or for, David;" in some instances
this sense comes out with great force, and thus they
illustrate that text in Ezekiel, penned hundreds of years
after David's death, "I will set one shepherd over them,
and he shall feed them, even my servant David (*i.e.* the
Beloved). He shall feed them and be their shepherd."
What a different fulness of meaning is given to such
innumerable passages as those in the 123rd Psalm, "For
thy servant David's sake turn not away the face of thine
anointed;" "The Lord hath sworn unto David, Of the
fruit of thy body will I set upon thy throne:" if we substitute the Beloved one for David in many such passages,
and what a rich meaning is unfolded! David was perhaps
the author of all these; but in that wonderful spirit of
the Hebrew playing upon words, just as he rose from his

own occupation to exclaim, " The Lord is my shepherd,"
so he rose from his own name, transforming it into a
Divine synonym, searching for its origin and filling it out
with divine and elevated ideas.* This was the spirit in
which Watts in his version restored the Psalms to Christ,
and removed them from the lower and more contracted
circle of human personality to the suffering and reigning
Messiah. Most readers were thankful for the noble restoration of the evangelical regalia to their rightful owner ;
and only here and there one or two, like the indecent and
insolent Bradbury, took exception to the performance as
" robbing them of their book of Praise," as that rash and
vehement man, referring to the version of Watts, said,
" David is no longer suffered to be our Psalmist."

This, then, is the spirit in which Watts translated the
Psalms, to the Christian sense preserving, as we have said,
the Messianic idea throughout, as in that stirring call to
Christian service :

> Arise, O King of Grace, arise
>   And enter to Thy rest!
> Lo! Thy church waits with longing eyes
>   Thus to be owned and blest.
>
> Enter with all Thy glorious train,
>   Thy Spirit and Thy word;
> All that the Ark did once contain
>   Could not such grace afford.

The aim of Watts in his Book of Psalms was to translate
the Old Testament phraseology into a New Testament
language and experience. James Hamilton has illustrated
this by an anecdote which it can scarcely be impertinent

---

* See this idea illustrated in " An Essay on the Book of Psalms," by
Mary Anne Schimmelpenninck, 1825, and " An Essay on the Literature
of the Book of Psalms," in the " Preachers' Lantern," vol. ii. p. 558.

to quote here ; he says : " I cannot tell it accurately, but I have heard of a godly couple whose child was sick and at the point of death.   It was unusual to pray together except at the hours of ' exercise ;' however, in her distress, the mother prevailed on her husband to kneel down at the bedside and offer a word of prayer.   The good man's prayers were chiefly taken from the best of liturgies, the book of Psalms ; and after a long and reverential introduction from the 90th and elsewhere, he proceeded, ' Lord, turn again the captivity of Zion ; then shall our mouth be filled with laughter and our tongue with singing.' And as he was proceeding, 'turn again our captivity,' the poor agonized mother interrupted him : ' Eh, man, you are aye drawn out for thae Jews, but it's our bairn that's deein',' at the same time clasping her hands and crying, ' Lord, help us ; oh, give us back our darling, if it be Thy holy will ; and if he is to be taken, oh take him to Thyself !'   And fond as I am," continues James Hamilton, " of scriptural phrases in prayer, I am fonder still of reality.   It is a striking fact that the prayers addressed to Christ in the Gospels are hardly one of them in Old Testament language ; just as New Testament songs embed in a language of their own Old Testament phrases ; " and, as we may add, just as the woman and her husband had the same purpose in their prayers.

   And it is in this way Watts seems to apologize for his attempts when he says, in his introduction to his version of the Psalms :

HEBREW MELODIES CHRISTIANIZED.

   " But since I believe that any Divine sentence, or Christian verse, agreeable to Scripture, may be sung, though it be composed by men uninspired, I have not been so curious and exact in striving everywhere to express the ancient sense and meaning of David, but have rather expressed myself as I may suppose David would have done, had he lived in the days of Christianity; and by this means, perhaps, I have sometimes hit upon the true intent of the Spirit of God in those verses farther and clearer than David himself could ever discover, as St. Peter encourages me to hope (1 Peter i. 11, 13) where he acknowledges that the ancient prophets, who foretold of the grace that should come to us, were, in some measure, ignorant of this great salvation; for though they testified of the sufferings of Christ and His glory, yet they were forced to search and inquire after the meaning of what they spake or wrote. In several other places I hope my reader will find a natural exposition of many a dark and doubtful text, and some new beauties and connections of thought discovered in the Jewish poet, though not in the language of a Jew. In all places I have kept my grand design in view, and that is to teach my author to speak like a Christian. For why should I now address God my Saviour in a song, with burnt sacrifices of fatlings, and with the fat of rams? Why should I pray to be sprinkled with hyssop, or recur to the blood of bullocks and goats? Why should I bind my sacrifice with cords to the horns of an altar, or sing the praises of God to high-sounding cymbals, when the Gospel has shown me a nobler atonement for sin, and appointed a purer and more spiritual worship? Why must I join with David in his legal or prophetic language to curse my enemies, when my Saviour in His sermons has taught me to love and bless them? Why may not a Christian omit all those passages of the Jewish psalmist that tend to fill the mind with overwhelming sorrows, despairing thoughts, or bitter personal resentments, none of which are well suited to the spirit of Christianity, which is a dispensation of hope and joy and love ?   What need is there that I should wrap up the shining honours of my Redeemer in the dark and shadowy language of a religion that is now for ever abolished, especially when Christians are so vehemently warned in the Epistles of St. Paul against a Judaizing spirit in their worship as well as doctrine ?   And what fault can there be in enlarging a little on the more useful subjects in the style of the Gospel, where the psalm gives any occasion, since the whole religion of the Jews is censured often in the New Testament as a defective and imperfect thing ? "

And, again, he says on the—

SPIRIT OF THE HEBREW PSALMS.

" Moses, Deborah, and the princes of Israel; David, Asaph, Habakkuk, and all the saints under the Jewish state, sung their own joys and victories, their own hopes, and fears, and deliverances, as I hinted before; and why must we, under the Gospel, sing nothing else but the joys, hopes, and fears of Asaph and David ? Why must Christians be forbid all other melody but what arises from the victories and deliverances of the Jews ?   David would have thought it very hard to be confined to the words of Moses, and sung nothing else on all his rejoicing days but the drowning of Pharaoh of the fifteenth of Exodus. He might have supposed it a little unreasonable, when he had peculiar occasions of mournful music, if he had been forced to keep close to Moses' prayer in the ninetieth Psalm, and always have sung over the shortness of human life, especially if he were not permitted the liberty of a para- phrase ; and yet the special concerns of David and Moses were much more akin to each other than ours are to either of them, and yet they were both of the same religion; but ours is very different. It is true that David has left us a richer variety of holy songs than all that went before him; but, rich as it is, it is still far short of the glorious things that we Christians have to sing before the Lord; we and our churches have our special affairs as well as they. Now, if by a little turn of their words, or by the change of a short sentence, we may express our own meditations, joys, and desires in the verse of those ancient psalmists, why should we be forbidden this sweet privilege? Why should we, under the Christian dispensation, be tied up to forms more than the Jews themselves were, and such as are much more improper for our age and state too? Let us remember that the very power of singing was given to human nature chiefly for this purpose, that our own warmest affections of soul might break out into natural or divine melody, and that the tongue of the worshipper might express his own heart."

The following well expresses his modest estimate of his work: "I must confess I have never yet seen any version or paraphrase of the Psalms, in their own Jewish sense, so perfect as to discourage all further attempts. But whoever undertakes the noble work, let him bring with him a soul devoted to piety, an exalted genius, and withal a studious application; for David's harp abhors a profane finger and disdains to answer to an unskilful or a careless touch. A meaner pen may imitate at a distance; but a complete translation or a just paraphrase demands a rich treasury of diction, an exalted fancy, a quick taste of devout passion, together with judgment, strict and severe, to retrench every luxuriant line, and to maintain a religious sovereignty over the whole work. Thus the psalmist of Israel might arise in Great Britain in all his Hebrew glory, and entertain the more knowing and polite Christians of our age. But still I am bold to maintain the general principle on which my present work is founded ; and that is, that if the brightest genius on earth, or an angel from heaven, should translate David and keep close to the sense and style of the inspired author, we should only obtain thereby a bright or heavenly copy of the devotions of the Jewish king; but it could never make the fittest psalm-book for a Christian people. It was not my design to exalt myself to the rank and glory of poets, but I was ambitious to be a servant to the Churches and a helper to the joy of the meanest Christian. Though there are many gone before me who have taught the Hebrew psalmist to speak English, yet I think I may assume this pleasure of being the first who hath brought down the royal author into the common affairs of the Christian life, and led the Psalmist of Israel into the Church of Christ, without anything of a Jew about him. And whensoever there shall appear any paraphrase of the Book of Psalms that retains more of the savour of David's piety, or discovers more of the style and spirit of the Gospel, with a superior dignity of verse, and yet the lines as easy and flowing and the sense and language as level to the lowest capacity, I shall congratulate the world, and consent to say, Let this attempt of mine be buried in silence."

This chapter must not be closed without some slight reference to the wonderful history and anecdote connected with these hymns; verses from them have been murmured from innumerable death-beds, have shone out as memorial lines on innumerable tombstones, and have proved, in how many instances, to be the converting word, the power of God unto salvation. When the great orator

and statesman of the United States, Daniel Webster, lay
dying, almost the last words which fell from those eloquent
lips which had so often moved in the Senate with thrilling
and overwhelming power, were those words of Watts'
51st Psalm; and he repeated them again and again:

> Show pity, Lord: O Lord, forgive;
> Let a repenting rebel live;
> Are not Thy mercies large and free?
> May not a sinner trust in Thee?

And the gravestone of the great shoemaker, scholar, linguist, and missionary, William Carey, in Bengal, contains
beside the name and date only that final confession of
faith:

> A guilty, weak, and helpless worm,
> On Thy kind arms I fall.

The late beautiful and beloved William Bunting used to
tell a story of a poor blind woman, in Liverpool, brought
to a sense of sin and salvation at a Wesleyan service held
in connection with the national fast upon the first visit of
cholera to this country. Her impressions had been stirred
by Watts' hymn—the 224th of the Wesleyan Selection—
"I'll praise my Maker while I've breath." The next
morning she called on the Rev. R. McOwen, and asked
if he could procure for her the book in which was the
hymn with those lines, also Watts',

> The Lord pours eyesight on the blind,
> The Lord supports the sinking mind.

It also was in the Wesleyan Hymn Book, which Mr.
McOwen placed in her hands. Her memory was soon
stored with the hymns which she delighted in repeating.
By her talent in shampooing she earned a respectable
livelihood. For this purpose she attended on the old

Earl of Derby, the grandfather to the present Earl. She repeated one of her hymns to him. The old Earl liked it, and encouraged her to repeat more. But one day, when repeating the hymn of Charles Wesley, "All ye that pass by," she came to the words:

> The Lord in the day of His anger did lay
> Your sins on the Lamb, and He bore them away,

he said, " Stop, Mrs. Brass, don't you think it should be—

> "The Lord in the day of His *mercy* did lay?"

She did not think his criticism valid; but it showed she was not repeating her verses to inattentive ears, and other indications showed that the blind woman was made a blessing to the dying nobleman. But such anecdotes might be multiplied and extended to many pages.

CHAPTER VIII.

A Circle of Friends.

THE friends of Watts, at almost any period of his life,
form an interesting and very memorable circle, a very
striking portrait gallery. Amongst them are some well-
known names, and some, comparatively unknown now,
famous then. We have said, about a mile from Theobalds,
within the parish of Cheshunt, lived RICHARD CROMWELL.
He was a member of Watts' church, although he removed
from Cheshunt some short time after Watts' settlement.

But a more remarkable person than Richard Cromwell
was Cromwell's niece, the granddaughter of the great
Protector, Mrs. BENDISH, in whom it was said the
very Protector himself lived again. Her husband was
Thomas Bendish, Esq., a descendant of Sir Thomas
Bendish, Baronet, ambassador from Charles I. to the
Court of Turkey. He died in 1707, but she survived
him till 1728, removing, however, in the latter years of
her life, to Yarmouth. She was a piece of astonishing
eccentricity. She had a great admiration for Owen as
a theologian and Watts as a poet; and very early in
his life Watts addressed to her his poem against tears.

She was a member of his church. Her admiration for
her grandfather was extraordinary, and no one was
permitted in her presence to express a doubt concerning
his legitimate sovereignty or essential greatness. What
she might have been as a man is beyond all power to
speculate; as a woman she certainly inherited much of
her grandfather's dreamy, musing, moody, and ruggedly
imperative character. Her character and her connections
both alike commanded for her great respect, but she was
an oddity. She was fond of night walks, even on lonely
roads. She would not suffer a servant to attend her,
saying God was a sufficient guard, and she would have no
other. Visiting at the houses of friends, she would
usually set off at about one in the morning in her chaise,
or on horseback, chanting as she went one of Watts'
hymns in a key, it is said, more loud than sweet. There
are pictures of her, word paintings, which bring her before
our eyes in the oddest light. Capable of comporting herself with dignity in the best society, she disdained no
menial employment, and very cheerfully turned her hand
to the pitch-fork or the spade among her labourers and
workmen, working herself with a right ready and forcible
good will, from the early morning to declining day, in an
attire as mean as the meanest of those with whom she was
toiling, giving no account, say some records, of either her
character or even her sex. It is a curious thing to find
the youthful Isaac Watts talking to this strong-minded
creature like a patriarch in his lines addressed to her in
1699, in which occurs the fine verse :

> If 'tis a rugged path you go,
> And thousand foes your steps surround,
> Tread the thorns down, charge through the foe;
> The hardest fight is highest crowned.

We could have liked a portrait of her from the pen of
Watts, or a record of some of his conversations with her
or with her uncle, but it does not appear to have been in
his way either to sketch the portraits of his friends or
to violate private confidences or conferences by putting
them on paper. Her son was another of Watts' inti-
mates, and with him the family of Bendish became
extinct. He died at Yarmouth, unmarried, in the year
1753.

Among the ministerial friends of Watts stands the
almost forgotten name of JOHN SHOWER, a very beautiful
and eminent man in his day, a man of large learning and
extensive travel. He had ministered for some time to an
English congregation at Rotterdam, and, returning to
England, he passed through the periods of trouble afflict-
ing the communion to which he belonged. Watts was on
terms of close intimacy with him, and they must have
been congenial in their lives of elevated and profoundly
cultured piety.

And there were men around Watts in the ministry
with whom he had great congeniality of sentiment.
Eminent among these was SAMUEL ROSEWELL, the son
of Thomas Rosewell, celebrated for his trial for high treason and unjust condemnation before the impious Jefferies.
Watts gives an interesting account of his visit to him on
his death-bed in one of his sermons preached at Bury
Street. "Come, my friends," says he, "come into the
chamber of a dying Christian; come, approach his pillow,
and hear his holy language : 'I am going up to heaven,
and I long to be gone, to be where my Saviour is.—Why
are His chariot-wheels so long in coming ?—I hope I am
a sincere Christian, but the meanest and the most unworthy.
—I know I am a great sinner, but did not Christ come to

save the chief of sinners ?—I have trusted in Him, and I
have strong consolation.—I love God, I love Christ.—I desire to love Him more, to be more like Him, and to serve
Him in heaven without sin.—Dear brother, I shall see you
at the right hand of Christ.—There I shall see all our
friends that are gone a little before (alluding to Sir T.
Abney).—I go to my God and to your God, to my Saviour
and to your Saviour.' These," observes Watts, "are some
of the dying words of the Rev. Mr. S. Rosewell, when,
with some other friends, I went to visit him two days
before his death, and which I transcribed as soon as I came
home, with their assistance." It was after this visit Watts
wrote to his friend the following note :

" DEAR BROTHER ROSEWELL,

"Your most agreeable and divine conversation,
two days ago, so sweetly overpowered my spirits, and the
most affectionate expressions which you so plentifully
bestowed on me awakened in me so many pleasing sensations, that I seemed a borderer on the heavenly world when
I saw you on the confines of heaven and conversed with
you there. Yet I can hardly forbear to ask for your stay
on earth, and wish your service in the sanctuary, after you
have been so much within view of the glorious invisi-
bilities which the Gospel reveals to us. But if that hope
fail, yet our better expectations can never fail us. Our
anchor enters within the veil, where Jesus, our forerunner,
is gone to take our places (Heb. vi. ult.). May your
pains decrease, or your divine joys overpower them ! May
you never lose sight of the blessed world, and of Jesus, the
Lord of it, till the storm is passed and you are safely
arrived. And may the same grace prepare me for the

same mansions, and give you the pleasure of welcoming to those bright regions

"Your affectionate and unworthy friend and brother,

"ISAAC WATTS.

'LIME STREET, *7th April*, 1722.

"Just going to Theobalds.

"P.S.—Our family salute you; they are much affected, pleased, and edified with their late visit.   Grace be with you and all your dear relations.   Amen."

And among his friends, as we have already seen, he kept up a considerable intimacy with his own fellow-townsman and fellow-student, SAMUEL SAY, son of Giles Say, who was ejected from the parish church of St. Michael's in Southampton, and one of the first ministers of the Non-conformist church of that town, and with which Watts' family was connected.   He was a kind of smaller Watts, a man of large and varied knowledge in the classics, mathematics, astronomy, and natural philosophy.   For forty-eight years he kept a journal of the alterations of the weather and of his observations of remarkable occurrences in nature.   Possessed of an extraordinary genius, it was veiled and shrouded by a modesty as extraordinary; but about two years before his death some of his papers were committed to the press, consisting of poems and essays on the "Harmony, Variety and Power of Numbers, whether in Prose or Verse."   He had a great admiration for Milton, and translated apparently with great elegance the introduction of "Paradise Lost" into Latin verse; and in the "Gentleman's Magazine," vol. xxxv., is an interesting paper by him, entitled, "The Resurrection Illustrated by

the Changes of the Silkworm." Watts thought highly of
his judgment, as the following, among other letters, indicates :

"*April* 11*th,* 1728.

" DEAR SIR,

"Your letter, dated from Feb. 10th to March 5th,
afforded me agreeable entertainment, and particularly your
notes on the 2nd Psalm, in which I think I concur in sentiment with you in every line, and thank you. The epi-
phonema to the 16th Psalm is also very acceptable, and, in
my opinion, the Psalms ought to be translated in such a
manner for Christian worship, in order to show the hidden
glories of that divine posey. I beg leave only to query
about the *Sheol* in Psalm 16, whether that phrase of 'not
seeing corruption' ought to be applied to David at all,
since Peter (Acts ii. 31) and Paul (Acts xiii. 36) seem to
exclude him. And though I will not say that your sense
of the *soul,* *i.e.,* the *life,* may answer the Hebrew manner
of the reduplication of the same thing in other words, yet,
as David sometimes speaks of the *soul* as a thing distinct
from the body, and may not the *soul* be taken in this
place and *Sheol* signify *Hades,* the state of the dead ?

"I am glad my little prayer-book is acceptable to you
and your daughter. I perceive you have been also (among
many others) uneasy to have no easier and plainer catechism for children than that of the Assembly. I had a
letter from Leicestershire the very same day when I
received yours on the same subject; and long after this a
multitude of requests have I had to set my thoughts at
work for this purpose. I have designed it these many
years. I have laid out some schemes for this purpose, and
I would have three or four series of catechisms, as I have

of prayers. I believe I shall do it ere long if God afford health. But, dear friend, forgive me if I cannot come into your scheme of ' bringing in the creed ; ' for it is, in my opinion, a most imperfect and immethodical composition, and deserves no great regard, unless it be put in at the end of the catechism for form's sake, together with the Lord's Prayer and Ten Commandments, as is done in the Assembly's Catechism. The history of the life and death of Christ is excessively long in so short a system ; and the design of the death of Christ (which is the glory of Christianity) is utterly omitted. Besides, the operations of the Spirit are not named. The practical articles are all excluded. In short, 'tis a very mean composure, and has nothing valuable—*præter mille annos.* My ideas of these matters run in another track, which, if ever I have the happiness to see you, may be matter for communication between us. I am sorry I forgot to put up the coronation ode in my pocket. I will count myself in debt till I have an occasion to send you something more valuable along with it. Two days (ago) I published a little essay on charity schools, my treatise of education growing so much longer in my hands than I designed. If it were worth while to send such a trifle you should have it. In the meantime I take leave, and with due saluations to yourself and yours,

" I am your affectionate brother and servant,

" I. WATTS."

WILLIAM COWARD is the name of one of Watts' intimate friends, an oddity in his way as great as Mrs. Bendish : he had been a merchant in the city ; he lived in retirement at Waltonstow ; his name is well known now in Nonconformist circles as the founder of " The Coward Trust," a useful fountain of benevolence for the education of young, and the assistance of poor decayed ministers. He was a type of man easily realised to the imagination, dogmatical and opinionated, a bundle of eccentricities. Among others, it was his whim to establish a rule that the doors of his house should never be opened, however pressing the emergency, after eight o'clock at night, to any person whatever, visitor or friend. The name of Hugh Farmer is still held in high and deserved respect for manifold attainments, one of Doddridge's most hopeful students, and who had probably been recommended to Mr. Coward by Doddridge, to whose academy Coward was a munificent helper. Farmer was the chaplain of the eccentric man, but he arrived one evening at the door too late; he found himself without lodging for the night, and was compelled to betake himself to the house of another, perhaps equally eminent, but more courteous friend, Mr. Snell, who not only took him in for that evening, but compelled him to stay with him for thirty years. ¡Nonconformist ministers appear to have possessed some singularly appreciative friends in those days. William Coward, however, was, if a man of singular eccentricity, one possessed of sterling virtues, and especially zealous in the maintenance of the more rigid articles of faith, and was constantly devising some plans of usefulness to assist both metropolitan and country ministers. Watts appears to have had great influence over him, and could comb his rugged asperities into smoothness. Watts it was to whom we are greatly indebted for the shape assumed by the " Coward Trust." He devoted £20,000, and by Watts' wise and most judicious advice it was left in such a manner that, unlike many other trusts, it has been saved from the consequence of diversion or litigation; and, largely and most respectably useful, it has furnished a most helpful hand in giving a thorough and most respectable education to many a young minister, and helping many a poor one, even to the present day. The "will" of William Coward is a curiosity, and may be studied, by those who have patience, on the walls of the library of the New College.

Among the friends of Watts, whose names ought to be mentioned, we must not omit that of JOHN SHUTE, LORD BARRINGTON, a person very interesting in his own times. He moved in that immediate circle of which Watts was a distinguished member; he was nearly of Watts' age, and his mother was a daughter of that Joseph Caryl who was one of Watts' early predecessors in the ministry at Mark Lane. He was a thoughtful, scholarly man, as the several works he published abundantly show.* His sixth and youngest son became the well-known Shute Barrington, Bishop of Durham. In the memoir prefixed to the three volumes of his father's works, the name of Dr. Watts is never even mentioned, although the verses from the lyrics, referring to the intimacy of Shute with John Locke, addressed to him by Watts, are quoted. He was a member of the Church meeting at Pinners' Hall, and had previously attended the ministry of Thomas Bradbury; but when that person behaved so indecently to Dr. Watts, and took so turbulent a part in the discussion with reference to the Trinity, Lord Barrington united himself with the Church at Pinners' Hall, then beneath the ministry of Dr. Jeremiah Hunt. It seems probable that an intimacy commenced early in life between Mr. Shute and Isaac Watts, perhaps before the settlement of Watts in the ministry. It was in 1718 that Swift writes of him, "One Mr. Shute is named for the secretary to Lord Wharton; he is a young man, but

* Lord Barrington's "Theological Works," 3 vols.

reckoned the shrewdest head in England, and the person in whom the Presbyterians chiefly confide; and if money be necessary toward the good work (that is, the repeal of the sacramental test) in Ireland, it is reckoned he can command as far as £100,000 from the body of Dissenters here.   As to his principles, he is a truly moderate man, frequenting the church and the meeting indifferently." He took the name of Barrington about the time this letter was written, a connection of his family, Francis Barrington, Esq., of Tofts, in Essex, leaving to him his estate conditionally upon his taking his name and adopting his arms.   The high favour in which he stood with George I. exposed him to the jealousy and enmity of Sir Robert Walpole.   He had an interview with the king on the first day after his arrival in London, apparently in order that he might decline certain offices of preferment which were made him, because the Schism and Conformity Bills were as yet unrepealed.   Upon this occasion he stated to the king the grievances beneath which Dissenters suffered, although they were amongst the most hearty and faithful friends of the House of Hanover.   In the fifth year of this reign he was created a peer.   He stood very high in the friendship of the king, and it seems that it was this very friendship which brought about the close of his political life when, in 1723, he was expelled from the House of Commons for his connection with the Harburgh lottery. This was a company formed for carrying on trade between England and the king's electoral dominions, and it had been proposed that it should be assisted by a lottery to defray the expenses in deepening the River Elbe near the port of Harburgh ; the project had not met with the appro-bation of Lord Barrington, but he received the king's personal commands to continue as sub-governor of the company, Prince Frederick being the governor. It furnished, however, the occasion which Sir Robert Walpole knew how to use for the removal from his path of a man dangerous to his own unscrupulous ambition. The project itself was simply a means, favoured by the king, for promoting trade between the two countries. But now, in his retirement, he betook himself to pursuits of a very different character, and the volumes of his theological works are most interesting, and show abundantly how he brought to bear upon the department of theology that clearness of judgment which had characterized his political life, united to a keen analytic power of criticism and discrimination very interesting to follow through the subjects he discusses; his essay " On the Dispensation of God to Mankind as revealed in Scripture " is especially entertaining and suggestive.

He was nephew, by his mother, of Sir Thomas Abney, and this would make his intimacy with the family in which Watts resided very natural; but at his house at Tofts he kept round about him much intellectual society, and sometimes even of persons widely differing in opinion from himself, such persons as Antony Collins,* the well-known sceptical writer of that day. The Greek Testament was frequently the subject of investigation and criticism, and on one occasion it is said Collins remarked concerning the apostle Paul, " I think so well of him as a man of sense and a gentleman, that if he had asserted he had worked miracles himself, I would have believed him."

Lord Barrington instantly produced a passage to that effect, when the disconcerted sceptic seized his hat and hastily retreated from the company. Upon another occasion his lordship inquired how it was that although he

* " Biog. Brit." Article, Barrington.

professed to have no religion himself, he was so careful
that his servants should attend regularly at church, when
he replied he did this to prevent them robbing and mur-
dering him.   This amiable nobleman, moderate, wise, and
well informed, if we may not rather speak of him as a man
of extensive and varied scholarship, was such a one as
could well appreciate and sympathize with Isaac Watts.
At the old house at Tofts, or Beckets, in Berkshire, where
Lord Barrington died, we may be sure that Watts was a
frequent visitor, and it was the frequency of the intercourse
probably which permits us so few letters between them,
and of those letters none before 1718.   We have already
quoted the high estimate he formed of Watts' " View of
Scripture History ;" his estimate of the " Logic " he rates so
highly that he says, " I shall not only recommend it to
others, but use it as the best manual of its kind myself,
and I intend, as some have done Erasmus or a piece of
Cicero, to read it over once a year."   The following note
sets every point of his friendship with Watts in a very
pleasing light :

"LONDON, *Jan.* 11, 1718.

" REV. SIR,

         " I cannot dispense with myself from taking the
first opportunity I have of acknowledging your great
favour in assisting me so readily to offer up the praise due
to Almighty God for His signal mercies vouchsafed me
on three several occasions, and of assuring you that it
was with the utmost concern I understood that I must
not flatter myself with the hopes of your being with us in
this last.   But how very obliging are you, who would give
yourself the trouble to let me know that, though you
could not give me the advantage of your company at

Hatton Garden, yet I should not want your assistance at a distance, where you would address such petitions to heaven to meet ours as tend to render me one of the best and happiest men alive. This they will influence to me in some measure, both by their prevalency at the throne of grace, and by instructing me in the most agreeable manner what I should aspire to. Whilst I read your letter, I found my blood fired with the greatest ambition to be what you wish me. I will, therefore, carefully preserve it, where it shall be least liable to accidents, and where it will be always most in my view. There, as I shall see what I ought to be, by keeping it always before me, I shall not only have the pleasure of observing the masterly strokes of the character you wish me, but, I hope, come in time to bear some resemblance to it. Whilst you were praying for us, we did not forget you ; nor shall I cease to beseech Almighty God to make you a bright example of passive virtue, till He shall see fit to restore you to that eminent degree of acceptableness and service you have once enjoyed.

"I am, sir, your most obliged humble servant,

"BARRINGTON.

" My wife is very much obliged by your civility. She has desired a copy of your letter, which, she says, will be as useful to her as it has been entertaining, if it be not her own fault. Both our humble services attend the good family where you are. I am sorry my lady's cold is like to deprive us of their company on Wednesday."

Yet another of the circle of friends, whose names occur to the mind when we think of Watts, is the saintly JAMES HERVEY. One of Watts' biographers speaks of " the

bloated effusions of Hervey which are now justly dis-
carded, then not only tolerated, but admired." It is an
unjust judgment; James Hamilton was much more fair
and faithful when he says of him that " he had a mind of
uncommon gorgeousness, his thoughts are marched to a
stately music, and were arrayed in the richest superla-
tives;" and he speaks of Hervey's "Theron and Aspasia"
as "one of our finest prose poems." James Hervey deserves
that his name should be mentioned with great affection
and respect. His life was perpetually stretched upon a
rack of infirmity and weakness. There is even a kind of
pathetic drollery in watching him at Weston Favell living
his bachelor's life, and, while stirring the saucepan which
held the gruel constituting his modest meal, turning aside
to derive some new fancy, fact, or image from the micro-
scope on his study table. As a writer, he indulged himself too freely in colour, but many of his works are very
pleasing ; he was not only passionately fond of natural
scenery, but in an equal degree delighted in the discoveries of natural history; his copious description of
the human frame is one of the most seductive disserta-
tions on anatomy and physiology in our language ;
and those subjects, not remarkable for being invested
with the charms of fancy, certainly do in his descriptions appear to be invested by the fascinations of poetry.
He was a friend of both Doddridge and Watts. He lived
ever in the neighbourhood of the grave, but his little
church of Weston Favell was filled with a loving congregation. It was a small flock, for it was a small
church : but the humble villagers felt a large amount of
affectionate regard for their feeble and yet famous friend.
Into his church he speedily introduced, after their publication, Dr. Watts' Hymns. So he tells Watts :

"To tell you, worthy Doctor, that your works have long been my delight and study, the favourite pattern by which I would form my conduct and model my style, would be only to echo back in the faintest accents what sounds in the general voice of the nation. Among other of your edifying compositions, I have reason to thank you for your 'Sacred Songs,' which I have introduced into the service of my church; so that in the solemnities of the Sabbath, and in a lecture on the week-day, your music lights up the incense of our praise, and furnishes our devotions with harmony. Our excellent friend, Dr. Doddridge, informs me of the infirm condition of your health, for which reason I humbly beseech the Father of spirits and the God of our life to renew your strength as the eagle's, and to recruit a lamp that has shone with distinguished lustre in His sanctuary; or, if this may not consist with the counsels of unerring wisdom, to make all your bed in your languishing, softly to untie the cords of animal existence, to enable your dislodging soul to pass triumphantly through the valley of death, leaning on your beloved Jesus, and rejoicing in the greatness of His salvation. You have a multitude of names to bear on your breast and mention with your lips, when you approach the throne of grace in the beneficent exercise of intercession; but none, I am sure, has more need of such an interest in your supplications than, dear sir, your obliged and humble and affectionate servant,

"JAMES HERVEY."

There could not be a very long intimacy between these two, or much knowledge of each other; they were both hermits, following, in the midst of much weakness, the calls of duty and the pursuits of a cultivated taste. The letter we have just quoted was written the year before Watts died; Hervey lived ten years longer, but died at the age of forty-seven. He forms one of a cluster of men singularly interesting to contemplate. With Doddridge, from their vicinity in the same county, he was on terms of the closest intimacy. He was a large scholar, a poet by natural temperament, and an intense lover of natural description. His works, once so famous, are almost forgotten, and have fallen into quite an undeserved neglect, partly arising, it may be, from the unfavourable estimate formed of them by those who have not read them, or who may have fixed their impressions from the scanning his " Contemplation of the Starry Heavens," or his " Reflections in a Flower Garden," or his " Descant on Creation." His portrait should be suspended in the gallery of those we are noticing as one, who, if not among Watts' most intimate friends, yet revered and loved him much.

But there is one name with which that of Watts is constantly united; it is the name of one whose nature in a marked and special manner seemed fitted to produce a perfect harmony and accord, it is the name of PHILIP DODDRIDGE. At what period the friendship commenced cannot be very exactly ascertained. Probably, had the life of Doddridge been spared to pen the biography of his venerable friend, the present biographer might have felt his work a superfluity of naughtiness; but, considerable as the distance was between the ages of the friends, Watts preceded his younger brother by only a short time to the grave. Like Watts, his name is especially associated with the hymnology of England; nor is there a collection of sacred songs which does not contain some strains from the pair of sweet singers. Doddridge is indeed rather known by a few pieces, very sweet and helpful, but limited in the range of their emotions, and never attempting the lofty and dazzling flight of Watts' nobler pieces.

Doddridge's life is full of interest; it has yet to be written, for there was a variety of incidents in his story which scarcely appears in the biography of Kippis, or the admirable memoir of Job Orton.   All things considered, it was a wonderful life : its activity was amazing, the variety of his literary acquirements and spoils was prodigious ; one would say he had much more of the poet's temperament than Watts ; he was impulsive, passionate, affectionate, yet we certainly miss in him that indefinable something which constitutes the poet, and which something, Watts assuredly possessed.

In some particulars both in his ancestry and earlier career Doddridge resembled Watts ; Philip, like Isaac, was the child (he was the twentieth) of a mother whom persecution had drifted to our shores ; at his birth his mother seemed so near to death that no attention was given to the almost lifeless little castaway, the infant, and the world almost lost Philip the moment he was born.

If Watts probably received his first lessons in biblical knowledge from his grandmother by the fireside of the old house in French Street, the Dutch tiles in the chimney constituting an illuminated and illustrated Bible, from which Doddridge's mother first initiated her own son into Bible lore, have become a famous tradition.   Like Isaac, Philip made so much progress in scholarship, that he had the offer of a training in either University if he would enter the Established Church ; it was made generously by the Duchess of Bedford.   Philip, like Isaac, declined the temptation, and so he found his *alma mater* beneath the more modest and obscure roof of a Dissenting academy at Kibworth, in Leicestershire.

Doddridge was born in the year when Watts first became the co-pastor of Dr. Chauncy, and he died in 1751, scarcely two years after the venerable friend whom he so much honoured and loved. Thus, when Watts died, Doddridge was on his way to the tomb, dying by the slow process of consumption. Great as was the difference in point of age, it is affecting to read the following letter from Watts to Doddridge—indeed, it simply expresses the truth they were " both going out of the world."

" Stoke Newington, *Oct.* 18, 1746, Saturday.

" Dear Sir,

" My much esteemed friend and brother,

" It was some trouble to me that you even fancied I had taken anything ill at your hands; it was only my own great indisposition and weakness which prevented the freedom and pleasure of *conversation;* and I am so low yet that I can neither study nor preach, nor have I any hope of better days in this world; but, blessed be God, we are moving onwards, I hope, to a state infinitely better. I should be glad of more Divine assistance from the Spirit of Consolation, to make me go cheerfully through the remaining days of my life. I am very sorry to find, by reports from friends, that you have met with so many vexations in these latter months of life; and yet I cannot find that your sentiments are altered, nor should your orthodoxy or charity be called in question. I shall take it a pleasure to have another letter from you, informing me that things are much easier, both with you and in the west country. As we are both going out of the world, we may commit each other to the care of our common Lord, who is, we hope, ours in an unchangeable covenant. I am glad to hear Mrs. Doddridge has her health better; and I heartily pray for your prosperity, peace, and success in your daily labours.

"I am yours affectionately, in our common Lord,

"I. WATTS.

"P.S.—I rejoice to hear so well of Mr. Ashworth: I hope my lady and I have set him up with commentators, for which he has given us both thanks. I trust I shall shortly see your third volume of the 'Family Expositor.'"

Watts' life was uniform; we can scarcely point to a period and say the man woke into life and being then and there; but Doddridge reached his period of interior life and labour when he became pastor and tutor at Northampton, and it would almost seem as if disappointment in love made a man of him.

The work accomplished by Doddridge in the academy of which he was tutor was enormous, and it exhibits the thoroughness of the training in the small unostentatious academy where the Dissenting ministers of that day gathered their stores of knowledge, and received their education for the ministry.

And he was great as a preacher—the peasants of the neighbourhood thought so—his usefulness among them was eminent; and Akenside, the poet, thought so. The variety of his correspondence is an amazing characteristic too; various, not only as to the personages with whom he corresponded, but the subjects upon which he corresponded with them. Like Watts, his sweet and gentle nature charmed the most obdurate—he had not even a Bradbury to ruffle the equanimity of his spirit—even the rough and savage Warburton became kind to him; he reviewed the

"Divine Legation," in the "Works of the Learned," a review of that day ; and it was to the English Bishop who quarrelled with everybody, the gentle Nonconformist was indebted for obtaining that easy passage in the sailing vessel, in which the captain gave up his cabin to him, that he might journey to the warm airs of Lisbon to lay aside his labours and to die. Doddridge is known by many of his works. His "Family Expositor" a long time held a place in the family and in the study ; but a far more extensive fame has followed the authorship of " The Rise and Progress of Religion in the Soul." This work, as its dedication to Dr. Watts shows, owes also its existence to him ; two letters exhibit, on either side, the sentiments these admirable men entertain for each other; the first is the dedication to which reference has been made :

" REV. AND DEAR SIR,

"With the most affectionate gratitude and re-spect I beg leave to present you a book, which owes its existence to your request, its copiousness to your plan, and much of its perspicuity to your review, and to the use I made of your remarks on that part of it which your health and leisure would permit you to examine. I address it to you, not to beg your patronage to it, for of that I am already well assured, and much less from any ambition of attempting your character, for which, if I were more equal to the subject, I should think this a very improper place, but chiefly from a secret delight which I find in the thought of being known to those whom this may reach as one whom you have honoured, not only with your friendship, but with so much of your esteem and approbation too, as must substantially appear

in your committing a work to me, which you had yourself projected, as one of the most considerable services
of your life.

"I have long thought the love of popular applause a
meanness which a philosophy far inferior to that of our
Divine Master, might have us to conquer.   But to be
esteemed by eminently great and good men, to whom we
are intimately known, appears to me not only one of
the most solid attestations of some real worth, but, next
to the approbation of God and our own consciences, one
of its most valuable rewards.   It will, I doubt not, be
found so in that world to which spirits like yours are
tending, and for which, through Divine grace, you have
obtained so uncommon a degree of ripeness.   And permit me, sir, while I write this, to refresh myself with the
hope that when that union of hearts which has so long
subsisted between us shall arrive to its full maturity and
endearment there, it will be matter of mutual delight to
recollect that you have assigned me, and that I have, in
some degree, executed a task which may, perhaps, under
the blessing of God, awaken and improve religious sentiments in the minds of those we leave behind us, and of
others that may arise after us in this vain, transitory, and
ensnaring world.

"Such is the improvement you have made of capacities for service that I am fully persuaded heaven has received very few in these latter ages who have done so much
to serve its interests here below ; few who have laboured
in this best of causes with equal zeal and success ; and
therefore I cannot but join with all who wish well to the
Christian interest among us, in acknowledging the goodness of Providence to you, and to the Church of Christ,
in prolonging a life, at once so valuable and so tender, to

such an advanced period. With them, sir, I rejoice that
God has given you to possess in so extraordinary a degree,
not only the consciousness of intending great benefit to the
world, but the satisfaction of having effected it, and seeing
such an harvest already springing up, I hope, as an earnest
of a more copious increase from thence. With multitudes
more I bless God that you are not in the evening of so
afflicted and so laborious a day rendered entirely incapable
of serving the public from the press and from the pulpit,
and that, amidst the pain your active spirit feels when
these pleasing services suffer long interruption from bodily
weakness, it may be so singularly refreshed by reflecting
on that sphere of extensive usefulness in which by your
writings you continually move.

"I congratulate you, dear sir, while you are in a multitude of families and schools of the lower class, condescending to the humble yet important work of forming
infant minds to the first rudiments of religious knowledge
and devout impressions, by your various catechisms and
divine songs, you are also daily reading lectures of logic
and other useful branches of philosophy to studious youth;
and this not only in private academies but in the most
public and celebrated seats of learning, not merely in
Scotland, and in our American colonies, where for some
peculiar considerations it might be most naturally expected, but, through the amiable candour of some excellent
men and accomplished tutors, in our English universities
too. I congratulate you that you are teaching no doubt
hundreds of ministers and private Christians by your
sermons, and other theological tracts, so happily calculated to diffuse through their minds that light of knowledge, and through their hearts that fervour of piety, which
God has been pleased to enkindle in your own. But

above all I congratulate you that by your sacred poetry, especially by your psalms and your hymns, you are leading the worship, and, I trust also, animating the devotions of myriads in our public assemblies every Sabbath, and in their families and closets every day. This, sir, at least so far as it relates to the service of the sanctuary, is an unparalleled favour by which God hath been pleased to distinguish you, I may boldly say it, beyond any of His servants now upon earth. Well may it be esteemed a glorious equivalent, and, indeed, much more than an equivalent, for all those views of ecclesiastical preferment to which such talents, learning, virtues, and interests might have entitled you in an establishment; and I doubt not but you joyfully accept it as such.

" Nor is it easy to conceive in what circumstances you could, on any supposition, have been easier and happier than in that pious and truly honourable family in which, as I verily believe in special indulgence both to you and to it, Providence has been pleased to appoint that you should spend so considerable a part of your life. It is my earnest prayer that all the remainder of it may be serene, useful, and pleasant. And as, to my certain knowledge, your compositions have been the singular comfort of many excellent Christians—some of them numbered among my dearest friends—on their dying beds, for I have heard stanzas of them repeated from the lips of several who were doubtless in a few hours to begin the 'Song of Moses and the Lamb,' so I hope and trust that, when God shall call you to that salvation, for which your faith and patience have so long been waiting, He will shed around you the choicest beams of His favour, and gladden your heart with consolations, like those which you have been the happy instrument of administering to others.

In the meantime, sir, be assured that I am not a little animated in the various labours to which Providence has called me, by reflecting that I have such a contemporary, and especially such a friend, whose single presence would be to me as that of a cloud of witnesses here below to awaken my alacrity in the race which is set before me. And I am persuaded that, while I say this, I speak the sentiment of many of my brethren, even of various denominations, a consideration which I hope will do something towards reconciling a heart so generous as yours, to a delay of that exceeding and eternal weight of glory which is now so nearly approaching. Yes, my honoured friend, you will, I hope, cheerfully endure a little longer continuance in life amidst all its infirmities from an assurance that, while God is pleased to maintain the exercise of your reason, it is hardly possible you should live in vain to the world or yourself. Every day and every trial is brightening your crown, and rendering you still more and more meet for an inheritance among the saints in light. Every word which you drop from the pulpit has now surely its peculiar weight. The eyes of many are on their ascending prophet, eagerly intent that they may catch, if not his mantle, at least some divine sentence from his lips, which may long guide their ways, and warm their hearts. This solicitude your friends bring in those happy moments when they are favoured with your converse in private, and, when you are retired from them, your prayers, I doubt not, largely contribute towards guarding your country, watering the Church, and blessing the world. Long may they continue to answer these great ends. And permit me, sir, to conclude with expressing my cheerful confidence that in these best moments you are often particularly mindful of one, who so highly

· esteems, so greatly needs, and so warmly returns that remembrance as,

"Reverend Sir, your most affectionate brother,

"And obliged humble servant,

"PHILIP DODDRIDGE.

"NORTHAMPTON, *Dec.* 13, 1744."

This dedication, of which Dr. Watts said, "It is the only thing in that book I can hardly permit myself to approve," may be appropriately followed by a letter to Mr. David Longueville, minister to the English church at Amsterdam, who had written to Dr. Watts asking his advice with reference to the translation of the works of Doddridge into the Dutch tongue; to this Watts replies:

"REV. SIR,

"It is a very agreeable employment to which you call me, and a very sensible honour you put upon me, when you desire me to give you my sentiments of that reverend and learned writer, Dr. Doddridge, to be prefixed to a translation of any of his works into the Dutch tongue. I have well known him for many years; I have enjoyed a constant intimacy and friendship with him ever since the providence of God called him to be a professor of human science, and a teacher of sacred theology to young men among us, who are trained up for the ministry of the Gospel. I have no need to give you a large account of his knowledge in the sciences, in which I confess him to be greatly my superior; and as to the doctrines of divinity and the Gospel of Christ, I know not of any man of greater skill than himself, and hardly sufficient to be his second. As he hath a most exact acquaintance with the things of

God and our holy religion, so far as we are let into the
knowledge of them by the light of nature and the reve-
lations of Scripture, so he hath a most happy manner of
teaching those who are younger. He hath a most skilful
and condescending way of instruction, nor is there any
person of my acquaintance with whom I am more entirely
agreed in all the sentiments of the doctrine of Christ. He
is a most hearty believer of the great articles and important principles of the Reformed Church, a most affectionate preacher and pathetic writer on the practical points
of religion, and, in one word, since I am now advanced in
age beyond my seventieth year, if there were any man to
whom Providence would permit me to commit a second
part of my life and usefulness in the Church of Christ,
Dr. Doddridge should be the man. If you have read that
excellent performance of his, ' The Rise and Progress of
Religion in the Soul,' etc., you will be of my mind ; his
dedication to me is the only thing in that book I could
hardly permit myself to approve. Besides all this, he
possesses a spirit of so much charity, love, and goodness
towards his fellow Christians, who may fall into some
lesser differences of opinion, as becomes a follower of the
blessed Jesus, his Master and mine. In the practical part
of his labours and ministry, he hath sufficiently shown
himself most happily furnished with all proper gifts and
talents to lead persons of all ranks and ages into serious
piety and strict religion. I esteem it a considerable
honour which the Providence of God hath done me, when
it makes use of me as an instrument in His hands to promote the usefulness of this great man in any part of the
world ; and it is my hearty prayer that our Lord Jesus, the
Head of the Church, may bless all his labours with most
glorious success, either read or heard, in my native lan-

guage or in any other tongue.   I am, reverend sir, with much sincerity your faithful humble servant, and affectionate brother in the Gospel of our common Lord,

" Isaac Watts."

" The Rise and Progress of Religion in the Soul " is still the best book of its kind; but, without doing any dishonour to its great merits, it may be said that it is built up too much upon a frame-work like that of Scupoli and A'Kempis, and we have known readers to whom it has rather been a message of despair than of mercy.   Salvation and spiritual happiness seem to be rather in the attainment of some subjective condition, than in the finished work of Christ ; the soul seems to be invited rather to brood over, or look in upon itself, than to look outward and upward to Christ.   Still it has been rendered into all the leading languages in Europe.   But it is in his hymns that the influence of Doddridge most resembles that of his friend.   His hymns have been spoken of as a kind of spiritual amber : but that term, appropriate as it is, is rather descriptive of hymns in general ; are they not all pieces of secreted spiritual electricity, rare and rich in spiritual emotion ? And many of Doddridge's have an ineffable beauty.   Logan, the Scotch poet, has the doubtful reputation of the authorship of several very sweet hymns ; we say doubtful, because the authorship turns rather ominously towards the more likely genius of Michael Bruce ; but, in any case, the famous hymn, so sanctified in almost every Scotch household, as it rises to the old tune of Martyrdom—

O God of Bethel, by whose hand,

ought not to be regarded as his.   It may not be uninteresting to notice together the variations in the two hymns :

LOGAN.

O God of Bethel! by Whose hand
  Thy people still are fed;
Who through this weary pilgrim-
    age
  Hast all our fathers led;

Our vows, our prayers, we now
    present
  Before Thy throne of grace.
God of our fathers! be the God
  Of their succeeding race.

Through each perplexing path of
    life,
  Our wandering footsteps guide:
Give us each day our daily bread,
  And raiment fit provide.

O spread Thy covering wings
    around,
  Till all our wanderings cease,
And at our Father's loved abode
  Our souls arrive in peace.

Such blessings from Thy gracious
    hand,
  Our humble prayers implore;
And Thou shalt be our chosen God
  And portion ever more.

DODDRIDGE.

O God of Jacob, by Whose hand
  Thine Israel still is fed,
Who through this weary pilgrim-
    age
  Hast all our fathers led;

To Thee our humble vows we
    raise,
  To Thee address our prayer,
And in Thy kind and faithful
    breast
  Deposit all our care.

If Thou through each perplexing
    path,
  Wilt be our constant guide:
If Thou wilt daily bread supply,
  And raiment will provide;

If Thou wilt spread Thy shield
    around,
  Till these our wanderings cease,
And at our Father's loved abode
  Our souls arrive in peace;

To Thee, as to our covenant-God,
  We'll our whole selves resign;
And count that not our tenth
    alone,
  But all we have is Thine.

It is not generally known that Doddridge pursued for many years the practice of Watts—perhaps he derived it from him—of writing a hymn after each or many of his sermons, so that the volume of his hymns is a tolerably large one, numbering three hundred and forty-seven. Many of them have great evangelical tenderness and beauty; we do not remember that they ever depart from a good and correct taste; they never soar up to Watts' daring heights, but they are often very sweet and exquisite; they are like the notes of a nightingale in the depths of evening shades, or sometimes like dove-like wings flashing near to the earth, but in the bright sunshine, " wings tipped with silver, or feathers of yellow gold." And, perhaps, we appreciate rather more the frequent ecstasy of his hymns in the memory of the fact that the story of his own life shows him not to have been incapable of human passion.

To Doddridge we are indebted for a pleasing illustration of the early reception of Watts' sacred verses ; Southey has quoted it in his life of Watts; the incident shows that the hymns, in spite of the sneers of Bradbury, were hailed with much delight, as supplying a very great want, not only in public but domestic service. The letter from Doddridge is dated 1731.

"Till heaven is enriched by your removal thither, I hope, sir, to find in you a counsellor and a friend, if God should continue my life, and I cannot but admire the goodness of Providence in honouring me with the friendship of such a person. I can truly say your name was in the number of those which were dearest to me long before I ever saw you. Yet, since I have known you, I cannot but find something of a more tender pleasure in the thought of your successful various services in the advancement of the best causes, that of real, vital, practical Christianity. What happened under my observation a few days ago gave me joy with regard to you, which is yet so warm in my mind that I hope, sir, you will pardon my relating the occasion of it. On Wednesday last I was preaching in a barn to a pretty large assembly of plain country people at a village a few miles off. After a sermon from Hebrews vi. 12, we sang one of your hymns (which, if I remember right, was the 140th of the second book). And in that part of the worship I had the satisfaction to observe tears in the eyes of several of the auditory, and after the service

was over, some of them told me that they were not able to
sing, so deeply were their minds affected with it, and the
clerk in particular told me he could hardly utter the words
of it.* These were most of them poor people who work for
their living. On the mention of your name, I found they
had read several of your books with great delight, and that
your hymns and psalms were almost their daily entertain-
ments. And when one of the company said, 'What if
Dr. Watts should come down to Northampton?' another
replied, with a remarkable warmth, 'The very sight of
him would be like an ordinance to me!' I mention the

---

* Dr. Southey, remarking on this incident, says: "The hymn,
indeed, was likely to have this effect upon an assembly whose minds
were under the immediate impression produced by a pathetic preacher."
They were those well-known words:

> Give me the wings of faith to rise
>   Within the veil, and see
> The saints above, how great their joys,
>   How bright their glories be.
>
> Once they were mourning here below,
>   And wet their couch with tears,
> They wrestled hard, as we do now,
>   With sins, and doubts, and fears.
>
> I ask them whence their victory came;
>   They with united breath
> Ascribe their conquest to the Lamb,
>   Their triumph to His death.
>
> They marked the footsteps that He trod,
>   His zeal inspired their breast;
> And, following their Incarnate God,
>   Possess the promised rest.
>
> Our glorious Leader claims our praise
>   For His own pattern given,
> While the long cloud of witnesses
>   Show the same path to heaven.

thing just as it was, and am persuaded it is but a familiar, natural specimen of what often occurs amongst a multitude of Christians who never saw your face. Nor do I by any means intend it as a compliment to a genius capable of entertaining by the same compositions the greatest and the meanest of mankind, but to remind you, dear sir (with all the deference and humility due to a superior character), how much you owe to Him who has honoured you as the instrument of such extensive service. Had Providence cast my lot near you, I should joyfully have embraced the most frequent opportunities of improving my understanding and warming my heart by conversing with you, which would surely have been greatly for my advantage as a tutor, a minister, and a Christian. As it is, I will omit none which may fall in my way; and when I regret that I can enjoy no more of you here, will comfort myself with the thoughts of that blessed state where I hope for ever to dwell with you, and to join with you in sweeter and sublimer songs than you have taught the Church below."

One of the most notable persons who crossed the life of Dr. Doddridge was Colonel James Gardiner: the stern soldier loved the gentle Doctor, and not less did the gentle spirit of the Doctor attach itself firmly to the stern soldier. Another instance of the singular hinges on which friendships are suspended. Doddridge wrote his life, and it created no little sensation, especially in those circles to which Colonel Gardiner belonged. One of the last letters of the Countess of Hertford to Dr. Watts refers so distinctly to this book and to the character of Doddridge, that it may appropriately find a place here:

" Reverend Sir,

"The last time I troubled you with a letter was to return you thanks for your work on the "Glory of Christ," a subject which can never be exhausted, or ever thought of without calling for all the praise which our hearts are capable of in our present imperfect state. My gratitude to you is again awakened by the obligation I am under (and, indeed, the whole Christian Church) to you for giving Dr. Doddridge the plan, and engaging him to write his excellent book of "The Rise and Progress of Religion in the Soul." I have read it with the utmost attention and pleasure, and, I would hope, with some advantage to myself, unless I should be so unhappy as to find the impression it has made on my heart wear off like the morning dew which passeth away, which God in His mercy avert. If you have a correspondence with him, I could wish you would convey my thanks to him, and the assurance that I shall frequently remember him in my humble (though weak) address to the throne of Almighty Grace (and which I know myself unworthy to look up to any otherwise than through the merits and sufferings of our blessed Saviour), that he may go on to spread the knowledge and practice of his doctrine, and that he may add numbers to the Church, and finally hear those blessed words, ' Well done, thou good and faithful servant, enter thou into thy Master's joy.'

"I cannot help mentioning to you the manner of this book falling into my hands, as I think there was something providential in it. About four months ago my poor lord had so totally lost his appetite that his physician thought it necessary for him to go to Bath. I was not a moment in doubt whether I should attend him there, because I knew

it was my duty, and, besides, I could not have been easy to
be absent when I hoped my care might be of some use.
Yet I undertook the journey with a weight upon my spirits,
and a reluctance which is not to be described, though I
concealed it from him. Since the great affliction with
which it pleased Almighty God to visit me by the death
of a most valuable and only son, I found myself happiest
in almost an entire retreat from the world, and being of a
sudden called into a place where I remembered to have
seen the utmost of its hurry and vanity exerted, terrified
my imagination to the last degree, and I shed tears every
time I was alone at the thought of what I expected to
encounter; yet this dreaded change has, by the goodness
of God, proved one of the happiest periods in my life, and
I can look back upon no part of it with greater thankfulness and satisfaction. I had the comfort to see my Lord
Hertford recovering his health by the use of those waters
as fast as I could hope for. I found it was no longer
necessary, as formerly, to avoid giving offence, to be always
or frequently in company ; I enjoyed the conversation of
two worthy old friends, whom I did not expect to meet
there, and had an opportunity of renewing my acquaintance
with Lady Huntingdon, and admiring that truly Christian
spirit which seems to animate the whole course of her life ;
and, as I seldom went out, I read a great deal, and Frederick,
the bookseller, used to send the new books which he received
on the waggon nights, of which I kept what I chose, and
sent back the rest. One night he sent me an account of
some remarkable passages relating to the life of Colonel
Gardiner ; as I had known this gentleman in his unconverted state, and often heard with admiration the sudden
and thorough change of his conduct for many years, it gave
me curiosity to read a book which seemed to promise me

some information upon that subject. I was so touched with
the account given of it that I could not help speaking of it
to almost everybody I saw; among others, the Dowager
Lady Hyndford came to make me a visit in the morning,
and as I knew she was of his country, and had lived much
in it, I began to talk to her of the book, and happened to
name the author. Upon which she said she would believe
whatever he wrote, for he was a truly good man, and had
wrote upon the ' Rise and Progress of Religion in the Soul'
in a manner which she was sure would please me. She
gave me the title in writing, and I bought the book the day
before I left Bath. I have now been at home three weeks,
and have already had the pleasure to engage several others
to read it, who, I hope, will think of it as I do. I would
not wish to trouble you to write to me yourself, but a letter
from your amanuensis to let me know how you enjoy your
health, and whether you are still carrying on some work of
your pen to the glory of our great Master, would be a very
sincere pleasure to me. Let me beg to be remembered in
your prayers, for I am every day more sensible of the im-
perfection of my own, and yet, I hope, my heart is sincere
in its desires, that it may be brought to a perfect conformity
and submission to the will of my heavenly Father. My
Lord Hertford always mentions you with regard, and will
be glad of your acceptance of the assurance of his friendship.

" I am, with an affectionate esteem, Sir,

" Your most faithful and obliged humble servant,

" F. HERTFORD."

It is impossible not to feel that, viewed from many
aspects, Philip Doddridge must have been Watts' most

congenial friend. The largest portion of Watts' work was
done before they knew each other, but friendships founded
in sympathy ripen very rapidly, and the difference of years
is very slightly felt where there is a great and happy congeniality of hearts. Watts was not a glowing correspondent, but none of his letters are so tender as those to
Doddridge, to whom he writes as his " dear and valuable
friend," and always his "affectionate brother and fellow
servant," and the letters warm greatly as the correspondence increases. Doddridge always looked up to, and spoke
of, Watts in terms of extraordinary reverence and affection;
in their work they were very similar ; Doddridge's nature
was smaller than his friend's, but in its measure it was
very harmonious and perfect. Watts had a fine metaphysical sagacity, and the keenness with which he analyzed
never interfered for a moment with the clearness of visions
by which he stepped from the discrete to the concrete, and
from parts to the whole ; hence, notwithstanding his fair
and catholic nature, he appears to have been much more
absolutely dogmatic than Doddridge, and it was perhaps
the defect of this great man's teaching that from the fatal
facility which brought him into contact with every class and
shade of opinion, the lines of his more absolute creed were
not fixed with sufficient distinctness : but from his tutorship
there passed forth a variety of men who all delighted to
confess their obligations to Doddridge,—Hugh Farmer,
Andrew Kippis, Job Orton, Benjamin Fawcett, and, if not
the most scholarly, that beautiful and well-known teacher,
who realized perhaps beyond any his tutor's spirit and his
tutor's peculiar power, Risdon Darracott. Such was Doddridge, without some notice and knowledge of whom a
review of the life and times, the friends and labours of
Watts would be incomplete.

One hundred and twenty years have passed away since Philip Doddridge died, but his name and many of his works are still as sweet and fragrant as ever. His " Life of Colonel Gardiner " is still one of the most interesting of religious biographies ; his " Family Expositor " still holds its place in the family ; his theological lectures are still an invaluable curriculum ; his correspondence is full of entertainment and interest ; his hymns are still sung in all our churches, and that to which we have referred, which ought assuredly to be spoken of as his, " O God of Bethel," sounded the other day down the aisles of Westminster, as the body of Livingstone was lowered into the grave. Doddridge's body, of course, was denied a resting-place at Lisbon by the civil and ecclesiastical authorities, but it was permitted to repose in the burying-ground of the English Factory. The great earthquake, which occurred shortly after, left his grave undisturbed, and it is a spot of holy ground unto this day.*

* See an admirable and interesting summary of Doddridge's Life and Character,—" Philip Doddridge : " " North British Review."

CHAPTER IX.

The Countess of Hertford and Mrs. Rowe.

ONE of the most considerable of Watts' correspondents and apparently intimate friends, was Frances, Countess of Hertford, afterwards Duchess of Somerset. This lady was the daughter of the Honourable Mr. Thynne, brother to Lord Weymouth; she married Algernon, Earl of Hertford, son of Charles Seymour, Duke of Somerset, who succeeded to the honours and estates of his father on December 2nd, 1748, *i.e.* about a week after the death of Dr. Watts. The Countess appears to have been a woman of great piety, amiability, and accomplishments. Thomson, in his " Seasons," addresses her:

> " O Hertford, fitted or to shine in courts
>   With unaffected grace, or walk the plain
>   With innocence and meditation joined
>   In soft assemblage, listen to my song,
>   Which thy own season paints; when Nature all
>   Is blooming, and benevolent like thee."

A collection of select letters, published by Mr. Hull, in two volumes, includes eleven written by the Duchess, and

they have been well characterized as exhibiting rectitude of
heart, delicacy of sentiment, and a truly classic ease and
elegance of style ; tinged with an air of melancholy, occasioned by the loss of her only son, Lord Beauchamp, to
whom she so frequently refers in her letters to Dr. Watts.
His death at Bologna, in 1744, cast a settled gloom over
her mind, for he was a youth who seemed to give evidences
of superiority and worth of character calculated to confer
honour on the exalted station to which he was destined,
had his life been spared.   Her letters all breathe the spirit
of unaffected simple piety and resignation ; and from the
time of her husband's elevation to the dukedom, her life
was subjected to the experience of intense troubles, first, in
the death of her own son, and very shortly after, in 1750,
the death of the Duke, her husband ; and it is with reference to these occasions of grief that she writes to Lady
Luxbrough, September 9th, 1750: "You are very obliging
in the concern you express for the scenes of sorrow I have
passed through.   I have indeed suffered deeply, but, when
I consider it is the will of God, who never chastises His
poor creatures but for their good, and reflect at the same
time how unworthy I was of these blessings, which I now
lament the loss of, I lay my hand upon my mouth, and dare
not repine, but hope I can with truth appeal to Him in
the following words : ' Such sorrow is sent that none may
oppose His holy will.   Let me sigh and offer up all my
sighs to Him !   Let me mourn, and in the meantime bless
His name in the midst of my sorrow.' "

She did not herself long survive, only till July 7th,
1754, leaving an only daughter, who subsequently became
Duchess of Northumberland.   The Countess herself was
the great and intimate friend likewise of Mrs. Rowe ; and
when this lady died, to the Countess and to Dr. Watts she

left those confidential letters to which reference may be
made in subsequent pages of the present volume.   How far
she drew the Doctor from his retreat, how often he visited
the lady at her various houses, we have no means of knowing ; the friendship continued certainly from 1729 to the
close of Watts' life, and it was probably commenced some
time before this date, for the terms of the first letters are
those of warm friendship.   In 1731 she refers to her children, especially to the son, who was to be in after years a
source of such grief to the mother's heart, and she says,
"My young people send their services to you ; I assure you
my little boy has grown a great proficient in your 'Songs
for Children,' and sings them with great pleasure."   The
lady herself secretly cultivated the recreation of verse, and
sometimes forwarded her fancies in this way to the Doctor,
but she says, "I beg the favour of you not to give any
copy of the enclosed verses, for I would wish my excursions of this kind to be a secret from everybody but you,
and a friend or two more, who know that I do not aim at
the character of a genius by any attempt of this nature,
but am led to them merely to amuse a leisure hour, and
speak the sentiments of my heart."   She wrote, however,
an elegy on Mrs. Rowe, which called forth an epigram from
the Doctor, which was published in his posthumous volume
of Miscellanies, "Remnants of Time, employed in Prose
and Verse":

> Struck with a sight of Philomela's urn,
> Eusebia weeps and calls the Muse to mourn ;
> While from her lips the tuneful sorrows fell,
> The groves confess a rising Philomel.

Writing from the Hermitage on St. Leonard's Hill, she
says : "I return you thanks for the epigram you were so
good as to send me, and should think myself very happy if

anything of mine could deserve to show the joy I should feel in being able to imitate Mrs. Rowe in the smallest instance. I have only two meditations of hers, which she gave me with the strongest injunctions not to let anybody see them, lest they should be thought too rapturous; but as I conclude she would not have included *you* among those from whom she meant they should be concealed, I will have them copied if you desire it." There are in her letters very pleasing indications of an amiable mind and heart: she writes to him of the books which have met her in the course of her reading, and her remarks are characterized by a quiet wisdom and judgment: "My Lord and Betty (the future Duchess of Northumberland) are in London, so that my son and his governor are my only companions at present; but we pass our time agreeably enough between reading, walking, and such other amusements as this place in which we are and the season of the year afford us; we have been lately reading 'Leonidas,'* in which I think there are many fine thoughts; but I hear the town are much divided in their sentiments about it, since one part are for preferring it to Milton, and others for levelling it to the lowest rank of poetry. I confess neither of these appear to me a just representation of it. If you have read it, I shall be glad to know your thoughts of it." In another letter she remarks upon the poet Pope: " I think everybody must wish a muse like Mr. Pope's were more inclined to exert itself on Divine and good-natured subjects; but I am afraid satire is his highest talent, for I think his 'Universal Prayer' is by no means equal to some other of his works, and I think his tenth stanza:

* Glover's " Leonidas," a poem scarcely ever read or referred to now, but which created considerable interest on its publication, and for some time held a conspicuous place in English poetry.

> Teach me to feel another's woe,
>   To hide the faults I see ;
> That mercy I to others show,
>   That mercy show to me :

an instance how blind the wisest men may be to the errors of their own hearts, for he certainly did not mean to imprecate such a proportion of vengeance on himself as he is too apt to load those with whom he dislikes ; nor would he wish to have his own failings exposed to the eye of the world with all the invective and ridicule with which he publishes those of his fellow creatures." The following is one of the most interesting and favourable letters from the many which Dr. Gibbons has preserved of the correspondence extending over so many years :

"*Jan.* 17, 1739.

" SIR,

" I am truly sorry to find you complain of any decay, but I am sure if you have any it must be bodily, and has no other effect than that which both Mr. Waller* and yourself have so happily described as letting in light upon the soul. I never read anything in life that pleased me better than your meditations on Revelation x., and I hope I shall not only delight in reading the words, but lay the substance

---

* Mr. Waller's lines, to which her ladyship refers, are at the conclusion of his Divine Poems :

> The soul's dark cottage, battered and decayed,
> Lets in new light through chinks that time has made :
> Stronger by weakness wiser men become,
> As they draw near to their eternal home :
> Leaving the old, both worlds at once they view,
> That stand upon the threshold of the new.

The verses of Dr. Watts which her ladyship intends is the poem in his " Horæ Lyricæ," entitled " A Sight of Heaven in Sickness."

of it to my heart, to which end allow me to beg your prayers as an assistance.

"My lord's state of suffering—for he is again confined to his bed by the gout—gives me little opportunity and less inclination to lose much time in the gay amusements which are apt to divert other people from the thoughts of their dissolution ; but I am not sure that a life of care and anxiety has not as bad an effect by fixing the mind too attentively on the present gloom, which obscures every cheerful ray which would otherwise enliven one's spirits. I wish I had anything to send more worth your reading than the following verses, but I have so little leisure that I can scarce get time to write letters to the few friends I correspond with. These lines were written one morning in October as I was sitting in a bow-window in my chamber at St. Leonard's Hill, which looks on a little grove in the garden, and beyond was an extensive view of the forest :

> How lately was yon russet grove
> The seat of harmony and love !
> How beauteous all the sylvan scene !
> The flowers how gay, the trees how green !
> But now it no such charms can boast,
> Its music gone, its verdure lost ;
> The changing leaves fall fast away,
> And all its pride is in decay ;
> Where blossoms deckt the pointed thorn
> Now hangs the wintry drop forlorn ;
> No longer from the fragrant bush
> Odours exhale, nor roses blush.
> Along the late enamelled mead
> No golden cowslip lifts its head,
> Scarce can the grass its spires sustain,
> Chilled by the frost, or drenched with rain.
> Alas ! just thus with life it fares.
> Our youth like smiling spring appears,
> Allied to joy, unbroke with cares ;
> But swiftly fly those cheerful hours,
> Like falling leaves, or fading flowers ;

We quickly hasten to decline,
And ev'ry sprightly joy resign:
Then be our heart prepared to leave
Those joys, nor at their absence grieve;
Sublimer pleasures let us prove,
And fix our thoughts on those above,
By the bright eye of sacred truth
Review the dangers of our youth,
Think how by turns wild passions raged,
By calm reflection now assuaged,
And bless the gentle ev'ning hour,
When reason best exerts its power,
And drives those tyrants from our breast,
Whose empire they too long possest:
Devotion comes with grace divine,
Around them heavenly glories shine,
While ev'ry gloom their rays dispel,
And banish the deceits of hell;
Ambition now no more aspires,
Contentment mod'rates our desires,
From envy free we can behold
Another's honours, or his gold,
Nor jealousy our rest alarms,
No longer slaves to mortal charms.
With prudence, patience comes along,
Who smiles beneath oppressive wrong:
If then such peaceful heav'nly guests
Age introduces to our breasts,
Can we his soft approaches fear,
Or heave a sigh, or drop a tear,
Because our outward forms decay,
And time our vigour steals away?
Should we regret our short-lived bloom,
Which, could it last us to the tomb,
Must quickly there to dust consume?
If thus life's progress we survey,
View what it gives, what takes away,
We shall with thankful hearts declare,
It leaves us all that's worth our care.

" I am importuned by a very valuable old woman, who is declining apace, to beg your prayers. She took me from my nurse, and if I have any good in me I owe it to her.

She was trusted by my mother with the care both of my sister and myself, and has lived with me ever since. But now, though past seventy, she cannot meet death without terror, and yet I believe I may venture to answer that she has always lived under the strictest sense of religion; but lowness of spirit, joined to many bodily infirmities, will shed darkness on the most cheerful minds, and hers never was of that cast. I fear she has very few months, if weeks, to come on earth, and a notice that you will grant her request would make her, I believe, pass them with some comfort. I am forced to take another page to assure you of my lord's compliments, and those of my young people ; the two latter are very well. I have no other view in sending the above verses but to prove that my confidence in your friendship has received no alteration from the length of time which has passed since I had an opportunity of assuring you in person with how true a regard

"I am, Sir,

"Your most faithful humble servant,

"F. HERTFORD."

It is pleasant in these letters to notice the indications of a quiet and retreating spirit. Upon her return, after a considerable absence, to the family seat near Marlborough, she says : " I have the pleasure of finding my garden extremely improved in the two years I have been absent from it, some little alterations I had ordered are completed; the trees which I left small ones are grown to form an agreeable shade, and I have reason to bless God for the pleasantness of the place which is allotted me to pass many of my retired hours in ; may I make use of them to fit me for my last, and that I may do so, allow me to beg the continuation

of your prayers." She several times refers to her " dear old
nurse," the " very valuable old woman" mentioned in the
lengthy letter quoted above : " Your good prayers for poor
Rothery have met with unexpected success, she is so much
recovered that I begin to think she will get entirely well,
and if she does I think nothing of that kind has since I
can remember looked more like a miraculous operation of
the healing power of the Almighty. I hope the same Divine
mercy will long preserve you a blessing to the age, and that
you will find your strength return with the warm weather."
This was written from Windsor Forest; the next month she
writes from Marlborough : " My poor old woman has got
hither, contrary to her own and all our expectations ; she
has the deepest gratitude for your goodness to her, and begs
you will accept her thanks; she is still very weak, and I
fancy will hardly get over the autumn."

This lady's letters exhibit a vein of intelligence and
interesting reading in pleasant contrast to the frivolity of
most of the courtly ladies of that age. " I have just had
the oddest pamphlet sent me I ever saw in my life, called
' Amusemens Philosophiques sur le Language des Bêtes.'
It was burnt by the hands of the common executioner at
Paris, and the priest who wrote it banished till he made a
formal retraction of it, and yet I think it very plain by the
style that the man was either in jest or crazed. It is by no
means wanting of wit, but extremely far from a system of
probability." Again, in another letter : " I have forgotten
whether in any of my later letters I ever named to you a
little book newly translated from the Italian, by the same
Mrs. Carter who has a copy of verses printed in the beginning of Mrs. Rowe's works, occasioned by her death.
The book she has now translated is Sir Isaac Newton's
' Doctrine of Light and Colours made easy for the Ladies.'

My daughter and I have both read it with great pleasure, and flatter ourselves that we at least understand some parts of it." It would be interesting to know who was the lady referred to in the following letter—it was probably Mrs. Elizabeth Carter; the work of the Doctor's to which so marked a reference is made was undoubtedly his discourses "On the World to Come," which had only just been published, a copy of which he had forwarded to her, and which had been acknowledged two or three weeks before in a letter from his "faithfully affectionate servant, F. Hertford."

"MARLBOROUGH, *July* 30, 1739.

" SIR,

" I would much sooner have written to you to thank you for the favour of your last letter, had I enjoyed more leisure; but I have had a friend with me this last month who has engrossed a good many of those hours which I used to employ in writing to my correspondents. She is a very pious and religious, as well as agreeable woman, and has seen enough of the world in her younger years to teach her to value its enjoyments and fear its vexations no more than they deserve, by which happy knowledge she has brought her mind and spirits to the most perfect state of calmness I ever saw ; and her conversation seems to impart the blessing to all who partake of her discourse. By this you will judge that I have passed my time very much to my satisfaction while she was with me ; and, though I have not written to you, you have shared my time with her, for almost all the hours I passed alone I have employed in reading your works, which for ever represent to my imagination the idea of a ladder or flight of steps, since every volume seems to rise a step nearer the language of heaven, and there is a visible progression toward that better country through every page; so that, though all breathe piety and just reason, the last seems to crown the whole, till you shall again publish something to enlighten a dark and obstinate age, for I must believe that the manner in which you treat Divine subjects is more likely to reform and work upon the affections of your readers than that of any other writer now living. I hope God will in mercy to many thousands, myself in particular, prolong your life many years. I own this does not seem a kind wish to you, but I think you will be content to bear the infirmities of flesh some years longer to be an instrument in the hands of God toward the salvation of your weak and distressed brethren. The joys of heaven cannot fade, but will be as glorious millions of ages to come as they are now, and what a moment will the longest life appear when it comes to be compared with eternity!"

Upon the death of Mrs. Rowe, as she had left her meditations for the hands of Dr. Watts, when he proposed to publish the volume with his preface, he also very naturally proposed to dedicate it to their friend the Countess. With extraordinary modesty, however, she shrunk from this. She writes: "The sincere esteem I have for you makes it very difficult for me to oppose anything you desire, and it is doubly so in an instance where I might have an opportunity of indulging so justifiable a pride as I should feel in letting the public see this fresh mark of your partiality to me, but as I am apprehensive that the envy such a distinction would raise against me might draw some vexation with it, I hope you will have the goodness to change the dedication into a letter to a friend, without giving me any such appellation." In another letter, with characteristic modesty, she says: "I can, with the strictest truth, affirm that I do not know any distinction upon earth that I could feel a truer pleasure in receiving were I deserving of it, but as I am forced to see how much I fall below the idea which the benevolence of your nature has formed of me, it teaches me to humble myself by that very incident which might administer a laudable pride to a more worthy person.   If I am constrained to acknowledge this mortifying truth, you may believe there are many people in the world who look upon me with more impartial eyes than self-love will allow me to do ; and others, who perhaps think I enjoy more of this world's goods than I either merit or than falls to the common lot, look at me with envious and malignant views, and are glad of every opportunity to debase me or those who they believe entertain a favourable opinion of me.   I would hope that I have never done anything, wilfully I am sure I have not, to raise any such sentiments in the breast of the meanest person upon earth, but yet experience has convinced me that I have not been happy enough to escape them.   For these reasons, sir, I must deny myself the pleasure and the pride I should have in so public a mark of your friendship and candour, and beg that if you will design me the honour of joining any address to me with those valuable remains of Mrs. Rowe, that you will either retrench the favourable expressions you intended to insert, or else give me no other title at the top of it than that of a friend of yours and hers, an appellation which, in the sincerity of my soul, I am prouder of than I could be of the most pompous name that human grandeur can lay claim to."

She shrunk from all observation, and in another letter says, " I will trespass so far on your good nature as to beg you will leave out whatever will imply my attempting to write poetry ; but if there be any among the things you have of mine which you think worth placing among yours

I shall have just cause to be pleased at seeing them come abroad in such company, if you will have the goodness to conceal my name, either under that of Eusebia or A Friend, a title which I shall think myself happy to deserve." This letter enables us to identify four poetical pieces, entitled " A Rural Meditation," " A Penitential Thought," " A Midnight Hymn," and the " Dying Christian's Hope," inserted in Watts' Miscellanies, and attributed to Eusebia, as the compositions of the Countess.   It may not be unpleasant to the reader to have brought before him some of these verses, which will show that the modesty of the Countess need not have been dictated by the poverty of her expression :

A RURAL MEDITATION.

Here in the tuneful groves and flow'ry fields,
Nature a thousand various beauties yields :
The daisy and tall cowslip we behold
Arrayed in snowy white, or freckled gold.
The verdant prospect cherishes our sight,
Affording joy unmixed, and calm delight
The forest-walk, and venerable shade,
Wide-spreading lawns, bright rills, and silent glade,
With a religious awe our souls inspire,
And to the heav'ns our raptured thoughts aspire,
To Him who sits in majesty on high,
Who turned the starry arches of the sky ;
Whose word ordained the silver Thames to flow,
Raised all the hills, and laid the valleys low ;
Who taught the nightingale in shades to sing,
And bade the skylark warble on the wing ;
Makes the young steer obedient till the land,
And lowing heifers own the milker's hand ;
Calms the rough sea, and stills the raging wind,
And rules the passions of the human mind.

This correspondence sets in a very beautiful light the character of this amiable and excellent lady, no doubt one of Watts' attached friends, and intercourse with whom, through the long period of twenty years, must have been to him a frequent source of rest and enjoyment. When their intimacy commenced she was in immediate attendance on the Queen Caroline, wife of George I. In those days the attempts which subsequently were made by the Countess of Huntingdon to create a feeling of piety and purity in the neighbourhood of the court had not been commenced, the manners of the great were not favourable to goodness and virtue, and the general spirit of the time brings out into strong relief the character of this gentle and noble lady; seldom apparently free from illness, her thoughts usually move round those loftiest sources of consolation in which the highest or the humblest equally find the surest and most abiding alleviation and repose.

In 1737 Watts sustained a loss in the innermost and most intimate circle of his acquaintance by the death of Mrs. Rowe. His early relations with this lady have round them some traditions of a tender mystery; it is generally supposed that upon his side at one time his feelings for Miss Singer, her maiden name, were something more than those of mere friendship. The charms of the lady appear to have been considerable, and procured her previous to marriage many admirers, among others Prior, the poet, who sought the lady's hand in vain, and in his poem on " Love and Friendship " expresses himself after the most approved fashion of the disconsolate Werthers of that day, informing her that—

> He dies in woe, that thou mayst live in peace.

It would seem that Watts' attachment was some time talked about extensively, for Young refers to it in one of his satires :

What angels would those be, who thus excel
In theologics, could they sew as well!
Yet why should not the fair her text pursue?
Can she more decently the Doctor woo?
Isaac, a brother of the canting strain,
When he has knocked at his own skull in vain,
To beauteous Marcia often will repair,
With a dark text to light it at the fair.
Oh how his pious soul exults to find
Such love for holy men in womankind!
Charmed with her learning, with what rapture he
Hangs on her bloom, like an industrious bee;
Hums round about her, and with all his power,
Extracts sweet wisdom from so fair a flower.

More respectfully, Mrs. Barbauld appears to allude to the circumstance when addressing Mrs. Rowe, she says:

Thynne, Carteret, Blackmore, Orrery approved,
And Prior praised, and noble Hertford loved,
Seraphic Ken, and tuneful Watts were thine,
And virtue's noblest champions filled the line.

But there is no reason, beyond the idle chatter of the town, to suppose that there was more than ardent friendship between the two; Watts was not a man ever likely to have been refused in marriage, and the talk appears only to have originated from the fact that people in general suppose that there can be no community of taste, and intellectual intercourse, and high and even ardent friendship between opposite sexes without its pointing to marriage. That it was not so in this instance appears certain, not only from the very high regard Mrs. Rowe always entertained for Watts, but from the terms of the letter addressed to him to be delivered after her death; we would rather suppose it possible, although we do not assert it, that Elizabeth Singer might have been not indisposed to a relationship the idea of which was not encouraged by the Doctor, and which he deferred to the calmer communion of intimate friendship and high esteem. The proofs that this was the case are not very clear if the circumstance is probable. However it might be, it never interfered with their friendship which continued not only unbroken to death, but beyond death.

Mrs. Rowe was a lady quite famous in her own time; to an elevated piety she united in her style of composition many of the faults of the age in which she lived; her works were tinctured by an ardent mode of expression little in harmony with the more frigid expressions of our own day. For Dr. Watts she entertained the highest esteem. She died suddenly, but in her cabinet were found letters for two or three of the friends who held the highest place in her affections, especially for the Countess of Hertford and Dr. Watts; the letter to the Doctor was accompanied by the manuscript of her "Devout Exercises," which she requested him to publish after a complete and thorough revision. A portion of his correspondence with the Countess upon this we have already quoted; the volume is dedicated to the Countess as Mrs. Rowe's intimate friend, and Watts, whose mind and heart were now in a state of quiet and holy calm, dispassionately reviews the merits of her various works; he does not altogether vindicate her ardent style, on the other hand, he is far from severely reprehending it; he remarks how in former years even grave divines had expressed the fervours of devout love to the Saviour much in the style of the Song of Solomon, and says, " I must confess that several of my compositions in verse written in younger life were led by those examples unwarily into this track." Indeed, many of his hymns, especially those which are paraphrases of the Song of Solomon, are quite as ardent as anything we meet with in the writings of Mrs. Rowe. The love of Christ is a principle, but we should be sorry to think that in the heart of the believer it may not glow with all the fervour and force of a great passion ; the language of the Apostle Paul shows us that it may, but his language is not coloured by the singular ecstasy of the Oriental mind ; it is fervid, but the line is very distinctly marked between the expressions of a merely human passion, which, however pure upon the heart which utters them, may by hearts less holy and elevated seem to be almost the utterance of license, and even to colder though not less holy natures may seem to border on profanity. There are Christians still who delight in this doubtful method of expressing and setting forth the holiest affections. Watts in all his religious works had at all times the ardent and fervent words of a poetic and imaginative nature, but he considerably pruned both thought and speech as the years passed in study and seclusion brought a riper wisdom ; he did not repress the ardours of the heart, but he gave to their expression a chastened and colder form ; he was not satisfied indeed by light without love, but he clothed that love with a more sacred reticence. Mrs. Rowe's writings have all an exceedingly unreticent character, but she lived apparently a holy life, realizing very greatly the ardours which gushed so glowingly from her pen, and it says much for all that she was in herself, that through so many long years she retained a close and intimate friendship with a judgment so wisely balanced, and a nature so simple and domestic, as that which evidently shines in the character of the Countess of Hertford.

CHAPTER X.

Shimei Bradbury.

THERE was living in London contemporary with Watts one of those ungentle, unbeautiful spirits, from whose malignant jealousy few men of eminence entirely escape; he appears to have been to Watts what Alexander the coppersmith was to Paul, he did him much evil and sought to do more. Bradbury was one of the most vehement and virulent spirits of the times, he was infected with the prevalent spirit of railing long before he began to cast about his Shimei and Rabshakeh pleasantries upon Watts; he was well known for his capabilities in this way, and in 1715 Daniel Defoe reproved him in a pamphlet entitled, " A Friendly Epistle by way of Reproof, from one of the people called Quakers to Thomas Bradbury, a dealer in many words." The following paragraph illustrates the character of the man the pamphlet is intended to represent: " Men, especially, Thomas, preaching men, as thou art, ought much rather to move their people and their brethren to forbear and forgive one another, than to move and excite them to severities, and to executing revenge upon one another, lest the day come when that which they call justice may be deemed injustice. I counsel thee, therefore, that thou forbear to excite thy sons of Belial to do

wickedly, but rather that thou preach to them that they
repent, for the Kingdom of Heaven is at hand; which I
meekly advertise thee is the proper duty of thy employment,
whereas the other is the work of darkness and tendeth to
blood."

Again, he says: "I must lead thee by the hand, not
by the nose, Thomas—others have done thee that office
already—that thou mayst be convinced, yea, even confounded, for those whom thou hast, with so great confidence, taken on thee to recommend as good men, and men
fearing God. I do thee justice, Thomas, and therefore
observe in thy behalf that thy modesty would not permit
thee to say, ' They were men hating covetousness.' " *

Bradbury was one of those men who, pursuing politics
in the pulpit with vehement and intolerant pertinacity,
degrade the standard of the minister of the Gospel; he
was even charged with desiring the blood of the ministers
of Queen Anne in the pamphlets of the day, especially in
" Burnet and Bradbury; or, the Confederacy of the Press
and the Pulpit for the Blood of the last Ministry."†

A life of Watts would be quite incomplete which did
not give some account of his very eminent but now almost
forgotten assailant and enemy, Thomas Bradbury. Born
at Wakefield, in Yorkshire, he had all the characteristics
of a typical Yorkshireman; he was a bold and hearty, and
possibly, whatever that may be worth, well-meaning man;
he possessed a considerable amount of natural genius,
especially for doubtful drollery and expletive. It is a
wonder that his name has not found a record in such

---

* " Daniel Defoe, His Life and Recently Discovered Writings." By
William Lee. 3 vols.

† See " Memoirs of the Life and Times of Daniel Defoe," etc. By
Walter Wilson, Esq.

histories as Macaulay's and Stanhope's, for it has a semi-historical interest. He was probably the most representative political Nonconformist among the ministers in the City of London of his day, and a well-known anecdote tells that he was the first to proclaim, as he did from his pulpit, the accession of George I. to the throne. It is said that he was walking through Smithfield in a very pensive and thoughtful mood on Sunday, August 1st, 1714, when the great "Schism Bill" was about to take effect, when Bishop Burnet happened to pass in his carriage; the Bishop called to his friend, and inquired into the cause of his great thoughtfulness. "I am thinking," replied Bradbury, "whether I shall have the constancy and courage of the noble army of martyrs whose ashes are deposited in this place, for I most assuredly expect to see similar times of violence and persecution, and that I shall be caused to suffer in a like cause."

The Bishop was himself equally zealous with Bradbury for the cause of Protestantism; he told him that the Queen was very ill, that she was given over by her physicians, who expected every hour to be her last; and he further said, that he was even then on his way to the Palace to inquire the particulars, and that he would despatch a messenger to Mr. Bradbury with the earliest intelligence of the Queen's death, and that if he should be in the pulpit when the messenger arrived, he should drop a handkerchief from the gallery as a token of that event. The messenger employed was Mr. John Bradbury, a brother of the preacher, and one in the medical profession. The Queen died while Bradbury was preaching, and the intelligence was conveyed to him by the signal agreed upon; perhaps the preacher may be forgiven if his heart was filled with joy; he indeed suppressed his feelings during the sermon, but in his prayer gave thanks to God who had again delivered the nation from the power of evil counsels, and implored a Divine blessing upon his majesty King George and the House of Hanover. He always gloried in being the first who proclaimed King George the First.

This anecdote gives a fair idea of the character of the man; one more utterly unlike Isaac Watts it is impossible to conceive; he was a man whose learning was limited, he had neither taste nor capacity for those refined subtleties either of argument or imagination into which Watts was forced by the necessities of controversy in his times; also, Bradbury was a rugged, rough-and-ready speaker and thinker, possessed of a dangerous prompt wit, not always free from a coarse disregard of the feelings of others; nor can we fail to see that there mingled, perhaps unconsciously to himself, a considerable amount of jealousy of his more eminent and illustrious brother. Before Watts had received his invitation to become the co-pastor or successor of Dr. Chauncy, the congregation had heard Mr. Bradbury; it is easily understood that the courtly, polished, and perhaps fastidious people would scarcely appreciate an eloquence like that of " bold Bradbury "—a term by which Queen Anne designated him. Then, at the first signal of his hostility to Watts, one of his own most distinguished people, Watts' friend, Lord Barrington, forsook him; it was perhaps not likely to improve his temper, and Watts, although exceedingly firm in his own convictions, as he had not the strength so neither had he the disposition for any vehement political action, and if he stepped aside slightly to use his influence in political partisanship, it was unfortunately not to aid the particular persons espoused by Bradbury. And so it was that in the sermons of this free-spoken man there are handed down to us perhaps the

most harsh and unjust words which ever assailed the ministry of Isaac Watts. It was at a later period of life, when
Watts was very infirm, that, at a meeting of the ministers
in the Redcross Street Library, he rose to propose some
resolution, and, with his weakly constitution and feeble
voice, he found considerable difficulty in making himself
heard, when Bradbury called out to him in the meeting,
" Brother Watts, shall I speak for you ? " The quiet little
Doctor turned to him and said, " Why, Brother Bradbury,
you have often spoken *against* me." At first he had encouraged the idea of Watts' publication of his Paraphrase
of the Psalms and of his Hymns, but when they came
forth, although they proved so acceptable to congregations
in general, he continued to use the dull version of Dr.
Patrick until his dying day in his own place, New-court
Chapel, and prevented their introduction into the service at
Pinners' Hall. There, however, on one occasion the clerk
happened unluckily to give out one of Watts' pieces ; up
rose Bradbury immediately, exclaiming, " Let us have none
of Watts' *(w)hims.*"

In all this, and in other such instances, a faithful
biographer must see the traces of a good deal of mere
jealousy. It is quite an exceptional instance in the life of
Watts, and it must seem singular that so sweet and gentle
a nature should have suffered from the misrepresentations
of any, and Bradbury has perhaps, even in his grave, been
the most abiding enemy to Watts' reputation. It seems
scarcely probable that the Unitarians could have so auda-
ciously claimed our writer as their own, had not Bradbury
set them a wicked example in his sermons. One of the
most affecting and earnest passages in the correspondence
of Watts is his remonstrance with his unjust brother
against unseemly attacks upon him, and misrepresenta-

tions of his opinions. Watts, so far as we can see, was never either discourteous or unjust; but he bitterly felt it that while, by his hymns and his treatises, he was attempting to shake the ground of the Arian heresy, his name was, from the pulpit and the pen, covered with obloquy as injuring and shaking the foundations of the most exalted faith in Christ. Bradbury was not concerned to reply to arguments, but in a right-down vehement manner to denounce those from whom he differed. He was no metaphysician. Turning over the many volumes of his sermons, we find them all characterized by strong evangelical statement, a very happy arrangement of thoughts, and great lucidity and apt readiness of expression. He never passed beyond the sense or culture of an ordinary audience; it must also be said that he never put the bridle on his wit. He was a man who could never find himself in the wrong, and who must always have the last word, and that word a disagreeable one. In a most extraordinary manner he could write and say the most abusive and bitter things, and seem quite surprised that the person to whom they were addressed did not take them as expressions of kindness. He tells Watts that he is " profane, conceited, impudent, and pragmatical; " he says: " You are mistaken if you think I ever knew, and much less admired, your mangling, garbling, transforming, etc., so many of your Songs of Zion; your notions about psalmody, and your satirical flourishes in which you express them, are fitter for one who pays no regard to inspiration, than for a Gospel minister, as I may hereafter show in a more public way." And when Watts mildly demurred to this as a personal reflection, he says, in reply: "Should any one take the liberty of burlesquing your poetry, as you have done that of the Most High God, you might call it personal reflection indeed;

when I consider that most of those expressions are adopted
either by the New Testament or the evangelical prophets,
I tremble at your mowing them together, as you were
resolved to make the Songs of Zion ridiculous." Again he
says : " Do you think that the ministers of London are to
stand still while you tear in pieces eight great Articles
of their faith ? And must every one who answers your
arguments be accused of personal reflections ? " Such is
the vein in which this noisy man writes. Watts replies in
a spirit of singular meekness ; Bradbury, while indulging
in the coarsest invective, professes a large amount of
respect and honour, and Watts says : " I am always ready
to acknowledge whatsoever personal respect Mr. Bradbury
has conceived for one of so little merit as I can pretend to ;
but I know not how to reconcile the profession of so much
respect with so many and so severe censures, and with
such angry modes of expression, as you have been pleased
to use both in print and in writing." Vindicating himself
for attempting to set the Psalms of David to the service of
song, he says :

"You tell me that 'I rival it with David, whether
he or I be the sweet psalmist of Israel. I abhor the
thought; while yet, at the same time, I am fully persuaded that the Jewish psalm-book was never designed to
be the only psalter for the Christian Church ; and though
we may borrow many parts of the prayers of Ezra, Job, and
Daniel, as well as of David, yet if we take them entire as
they stand, and join nothing of the Gospel with them, I
think there are few of them will be found proper prayers
for a Christian Church ; and yet, I think, it would be very
unjust to say 'we rival it with Ezra, Job, etc.' Surely
their prayers are not best for us, since we are commanded
to ask everything in the name of Christ. Now, I know no

reason why the glorious discoveries of the New Testament should not be mingled with our songs and praises, as well as with our prayers.   I give solemn thanks to my Saviour, with all my soul, that He hath honoured me so far as to bring His name and Gospel in a more evident and express manner into Christian psalmody.

"And since I find you have been pleased to make my hymns and imitations of the Psalms, together with their prefaces, the object of your frequent and harsh censures, give me leave to ask you whether I did not consult with you while I was translating the Psalms in this manner, fourteen or fifteen years ago ?   Whether I was not encouraged by you in this work, even when you fully knew my design, by what I had printed, as well as by conversation ?   Did you not send me a note, under your own hand, by my brother, with a request that I would form the fiftieth and the hundred and twenty-second Psalms into their proper old metre ?   And in that note you told me too that one was six lines of heroic verse, or ten syllables, and the other six lines of shorter metre; by following those directions precisely, I confess I committed a mistake in both of them, or at least in the last; nor had I ever thought of putting in those metres, nor considered the number of the lines, nor the measure of them, but by your direction, and at your request.   I allow, sir, with great freedom, that you may have changed your opinion since, and you have a right to do it without the least blame from me ; but I do declare it, that at that time you were one of my encouragers, and therefore your present censures should be lighter and softer.

" You desire me at the end ' to remember former friendships,' but you will give me leave to ask which of us has forgot them most ; and I am well assured that I have more effectually proved myself all that which you are pleased to subscribe, viz., your steady, hearty, and real friend, your obedient and devoted servant,

"I. WATTS."

And the following letter is a very fair illustration of the temper and spirit of Watts' replies to his censorious and abusive brother:

"LIME STREET, *Nov.* 1, 1725.

"REVEREND SIR,

"On Friday night last my worthy friend and neighbour, Mr. Caleb Wroe, called on me at Theobalds, and desired me to convey the enclosed paper to you, with his humble thanks for the share you have given him in the late legacy intrusted with you, and he intreats that you would please to pay the money into the hands of this messenger, that I may return it to him; and I cannot but join my unfeigned thanks with his, that you are pleased to remember so valuable and pious a man in your distributions, whose circumstances are by no means above the receipt of such charitable bequests, though his modesty is so great as to prevent him from sueing for an interest in them.

"But while I am acknowledging your unexpected goodness to my friend, permit me, sir, to inquire into the reason of your unexpected conduct towards myself in so different a manner. It is true I live much in the country, but I am not unacquainted with what passes in town. I would now look no further backward than your letter to the Board at Lime Street, about six months ago, where I was present. I cannot imagine, sir, what occasion I had given to such sort of censures as you pass upon me there among others, which you are pleased to cast upon our worthy brethren; nor can I think how a more pious and Christian return could have been made by that Board at that time than to vote a silence and burial of all past contests, and even of this last letter of yours, and to desire your company amongst us as in times past. I had designed, sir, to have never taken any further notice of this letter, if I had not been abundantly informed that your conduct since is of the same kind, and that you have persisted in your public reflections on many of my writings in such a manner as makes it sufficiently appear that you design reproach to the man, as much as to show your zeal against his supposed errors. The particular instances of this kind I need not rehearse to you; yourself are best acquainted with them. And yet, after all this, I had been silent still; but as I acknowledge God and seek Him in all my ways, so I am convinced it is my duty to give you a private admonition, and, as a brother, I intreat you to consider whether all this wrath of man can work the righteousness of God? Let me intreat you, sir, to ask yourself what degrees of passion and personal resentment may join and mingle themselves with your supposed zeal for the Gospel? Jesus, the searcher of hearts, He knows with what daily labour and study, and with what constant addresses to the throne of grace, I seek to support the doctrine of His Deity as well as you, and to defend it in the best manner I am capable of. And shall I tell you also, sir, that it was your urgent request, among many others, that engaged me so much further in this study than I at first intended. If I am fallen into mistakes, your private and friendly notice had done much more toward the correction of them than public reproaches. I am not conscious to myself that either my former or latter conduct towards you has merited such indignities as these; nor can I think that our blessed Lord, who has given you so rich a furniture of imagination, and such sprightly talents for public service, will approve such employment of them in the personal disgrace of your brethren that own the same faith, that preach the same Saviour, and attempt to spread abroad the same doctrines of salvation.

"I wish, sir, it were but possible for you to look upon your own conduct, abstracted from that fondness which we all naturally bear to self, and see whether there be no occasion for some humbling and penitent thoughts in the sight of God. It is not the design of this writing to carry on a quarrel with you. It has been my frequent prayer, and it will be my joy, to see your temper suited to your work, and to hear that you employ your studies and your style for the support of truth and godliness in the spirit of the Gospel, that is, in the spirit of meekness and love. And I conclude with a hearty request to Heaven that your wit may be all sanctified, that you may minister holy things with honour and purity and great success, and you may become as eminent and public an example of piety, meekness, heavenly-mindedness, and love to all the saints, as your own soul wishes and desires. Farewell, sir, and forgive this freedom of your humble servant and fellow labourer in the Gospel of Christ,

"I. WATTS."

It is very satisfactory, however, throughout the correspondence to feel that Watts, the only one of the two names in which we now feel much interest, preserves a spirit of quietness and candour; the correspondence was forced upon him by the noisy Bradbury, and as he commenced it so he was determined to have the last of it. Watts had quietly implored him to silence, saying: "Let us examine what is past, and take care for the time to come what we write or print with regard to our brethren be expressed in such language as may dare appear and be read by the light of the last conflagration, and the splendour of the tribunal of our returning Lord." This produced a tempest of a letter, in which Bradbury says : " I learn no such passive obedience to an unreasonable adversary, but rather the contrary ; you should have left off contention before it was meddled with, for I doubt not to open to the world your shame."

The correspondence is very lengthy ; it is not probable that it will ever be reprinted ; it is not worth the patience of perusal, unless to add to the esteem of the subject of these memoirs. Bradbury's turbulent nature in the course of it seems to be utterly ungoverned, and raves along in a manner quite fatal to any respect with which a desire to think well of the man might possess the reader's mind. It had perhaps been better if the wave of this correspondence had, like most of Watts' letters, been lost to the eye, but, by some fatality, it is the only complete piece of correspondence in our author's life published. Walter Wilson remarks upon it that " the letters are of that personal nature as do but little credit to the writers." This is very unjust ; if Mr. Wilson had read, he must have known that there is not one word in the letters of Watts which does not reflect the quiet holiness of a spirit at perfect peace with itself, only desirous of healing the heart of his antagonist. Bradbury even censures him because, after his attacks on Watts in print, he did not reply in print, but referred to them in private letters to him ! Watts had expressed his desire in seeking the truth, and says :

" I acknowledge with respect and thankfulness the kind opinions you have entertained of me, and I really ' value all the care you have shown not to grieve my spirit,' whensoever

I see it practised. I easily believe, indeed, that your natural talent of wit is richly sufficient to have taken occasions from an hundred passages in my writings to have filled your pages with much severer censures. In the vivacity of wit, in the copiousness of style, in readiness of Scripture phrases, and other useful talents, I freely own you for my superior, and will never pretend to become your rival. But it is only calm and sedate argument that weighs with me in matters of controversy, nor will I be displeased with any man for showing me my mistakes by force of argument, and in a spirit of meekness; it is only in this manner truth must be searched out, and not by wit and raillery."

To this came back the following:

" Your profession of ' seeking the truth ' is very popular, and I do not wonder to find it so often in all your writings; but then there is such a thing as ' ever learning, and not being able to come to the knowledge of the truth.' And it is pity, after you have been more than thirty years a teacher of others, you are yet to learn the first principles of the oracles of God. What will our hearers think of us when we succeed the greatest men of our last age in nothing else but their pulpits? Is there no certainty in the words of truth? Was Dr. Owen's church to be taught another Jesus, that the Son and Holy Spirit were only two powers in the Divine nature? Shall the men who planted and watered so happy a part of the vineyard have all their labours rendered in vain? Shall a fountain in the same place send forth sweet water and bitter? What need is there of a charge?"*

On the whole, it is well to refer to this controversy. It is a painful, important item in Watts' life, and brings out

* See the whole of this in the "Posthumous Works of the late learned and Rev. Isaac Watts," 1779.

very clearly how singularly he was removed from irritable passions, and it sadly reveals how impossible it seems even for the most gentle natures to escape the venom and the vileness of the "perils of false brethren."

Bradbury unquestionably was firmly attached to evangelical truth, so far as he knew it, and his discourses in the two volumes called "The Mystery of Godliness, Considered in Sixty-one Sermons," are certainly interesting, suggestive, and even admirable specimens of preaching ; but, we have said, he was chiefly known as a political preacher. His printed discourses contain few intimations of that wit which was a favourite weapon with him in the pulpit, and of which we have some indications in the sermon entitled "The Ass and the Serpent,"a comparison between the tribes of Issachar and Dan in their regard for civil liberty—a sermon, like all those in the volume which contains it, devoted to rousing the spirit of the times in which he lived. Regularly as the fifth of November came round, he commemorated the day in a sermon, and afterwards adjourned with his friends to dine at a tavern, where, it is said, he always sung the national song, "The Roast Beef of Old England ;" there, no doubt, jest and joke passed round pretty freely, for, as we have intimated, he had a sprightly wit and a copious flow of eloquence. Watts gently remonstrated with him for these displays, to which he replied in his vehement and peppery style. George Whitefield, at a later period, more strongly remonstrated with him on his conduct in this particular, but not apparently with much effect. It is said that upon the death of Queen Anne, an incident to which we have already referred, he took for his text on the occasion of her funeral sermon, "Go, see now this cursed woman and bury her, for she is a king's daughter." The story is exceedingly likely, for he belonged to a race of men not

indisposed to misuse Scripture after that unbecoming
fashion; and we may surely say, notwithstanding the
ominous shadows which brooded over the closing years
of a reign commenced with so much promise, the anecdote, even the possibility that it may be true, testifies
to the cruel coarseness, the low profane jocularity, and
ungrateful injustice of the man. He was a hearty politician, to whom all refinements of speech or sentiment
were unknown, and, right or wrong, he plunged on in
a reckless kind of fashion. He adopted as his motto,
Pro Christo et patriâ, For Christ and my country.
Charity may be permitted to hope that he, at any rate,
thought the motto did not unworthily represent the
man, if sometimes in his conduct he seems somewhat unworthily to represent the motto. And while Watts was
pursuing his studies in scholarly seclusion, never knowing
the happiness of robust health, and, although a firm Nonconformist, on good terms with bishops and ministers of
the Church of England, and ministers and members of
many communions of Christians, Bradbury mixed with
freedom with the moving parties in the City, and was ever
ready to lift up his voice loudly about all the political
circumstances of the passing hours. Thus the two men,
although ministers of the same order, within a very short
distance of each other, were in their sympathies wide apart ;
they desired, indeed, the same great ends, but the roads they
took to their attainment were widely different. It is still
singular and unaccountable, but for the personal motives
we have assigned above, that Bradbury should have expressed himself with so much bitterness and hostility concerning his old friend, whose principles, neither in religion
nor politics, could ever have been at any very great remove
from his own ; but so it is, that amidst the multitude of

friends that honoured and esteemed Watts highly for his work's sake, we find Bradbury standing aside like a very Shimei pouring upon him his perpetually reiterated torrent of contempt, obloquy, and scorn, and no motive appears but the dangerous one which influences three-fourths of all the evil and hatred in the world, jealousy of a rank for which he was unfit, and genius to which he could not attain. On the whole, it may be said of Bradbury, in the language of an old English poet, he was " like a pair of snuffers, he snips the filth in other men, and retains it in himself ; " it could not be said of him " the snuffers were of pure gold." As Archbishop Abbott says of Jonah, in his sermons on the prophet : " Some drams and grains of gold appear in him and his action, but dross is there by pounds ; little wine, but store of water ; some wheat, but chaff enough."

CHAPTER XI.

His Times.

TAKE the life of almost any man who has stood in any relation to the thought and intelligence of his times, in any period of English history, and it is interesting to regard him by the light of the events flowing on around him. Watts was almost a literary solitary; he cannot be referred to as greatly influencing the times in which he lived, but an outline of his life is incomplete if we give no reference to the events of his time. From the last years of the reign of Charles II. to the closing years of George II. constitutes the era of Watts. Every age seems eminently important to its actors—sometimes even to spectators—and yet that age stands out with singular distinctness. How different the times of Watts' birth and those of his death : the infant in the arms of a weeping mother, beneath the bars of the dungeon of the imprisoned Nonconformist, and the old man, that same infant, passing away, with the great Methodist movement rising into activity over the whole nation. A little room, scarcely tolerated in Southampton, where a few persecuted Nonconformists assembled together, and large chapels, capable of holding thousands, rising amidst the far-off wastes of Northern Yorkshire and Western Cornwall, and a sudden burst of religious vitality finding vent in hymns and meetings over the whole country.

If the change in the aspect of religious life was remarkable, not less remarkable was the change, or rather perhaps we ought to say the changes, which had been brought about in the political. The period of Watts' childhood was the most ominous, unhappy, and unsettled in English story; men knew not what to expect, they knew not whither they were drifting. Those were the days of the great Monmouth Rebellion and Jeffreys' " Bloody Assize;" the days of the execution of Algernon Sidney and Lord William Russell, the days of Titus Oates. The mind of England was full of plots, and the fear and the shadow of plots, succeeded by internal discords, and a disunited front to possible external foes. Well has it been said, " It was high time that James should go; it was time that William should come."

The closing years of Watts' life Mr. Hallam ventures to speak of, and Earl Stanhope confirms the verdict, as nationally the happiest period of all England's history, a brief period during which plenty and comfort seemed everywhere to abound. We do not refer to the moral state of the people; that appears to have been low enough, but the nation had reached, and the people were experiencing, the blessedness of a lull of peace after that great storm which had shaken every timber of the national vessel. The period of George II. appears to be that ideal time upon which many look back under the designations of " Happy England " and " Merry England." Between these two periods how many intervening chapters occur! and it is not a little distressing to a biographer that it seems

impossible to lay the hand upon scarcely a letter of the
many multitudes of letters which Watts must have
written, and many, one cannot but think, illustrating some
of the circumstances and the characters of the times, and
his interest in them.*

Thus, for instance, he was an intimate friend of that
David Polhill who was one of the foremost men in the
affair of the great " Kentish Petition," a circumstance
which shines brightly among the gallant actions of those
who, with daring intrepidity, supported William III. It
was at a time when pusillanimity and fear of France would
have been fatal. The House of Commons, rent by faction,
was very slow in vindicating the king; five Kentish gentlemen, magistrates, interpreting the opinion of their county,
signed as deputies a petition calling upon the House to lay
aside their own personal differences, to attend better to
public affairs, and especially to vote sufficient supplies to
sustain the king and his allies. It was a daring step; the
five gentlemen who bore the petition to the House all presented themselves as responsible for it; the House instantly
voted that it was scandalous, infamous, and seditious, calculated to destroy the constitution of Parliament, and to
subvert the established government of the realm. The five
gentlemen, of whom David Polhill was one, were, amidst
the acclamations of the nation, committed to prison, and
there for some time they continued. The pen of Defoe
sprang into eloquence on their hehalf, and when they
were liberated, as they were shortly, one of those demon-
strations—not of the mob—but of the strong middle
classes of England, greeted them on Blackheath on their
way home, bells clanging, bonfires burning, and Kent

* See an interesting table of " Memorable Affairs in my Life and
Coincidents," in Watts' writing, in Appendix to this volume.

altogether in such a state as it had not been in since the Restoration of Charles II.

1703—one wonders if Watts went down into the City on the 31st of July that year, to see one whom he must very well have known, who, as we have seen, studied some years before Watts was there, at the Dissenting Academy in Stoke Newington—Daniel Defoe, standing in the pillory; for Defoe's great and even intimate friend, William III, was dead, and the men who had long winced beneath his wit, and had longed for the time of their reprisals, fancied the time had come at last; but, indeed, the sentence which was intended for punishment turned into a painful kind of triumph. It cannot be a pleasant position for the head and the hands to be fixtures in that fashion for an hour; but if the sentence has to be borne, then it is pleasant to find the rude machine adorned with flowers and garlands, and the odium of the punishment transferred from the sufferer to his judges. However, they ruined Defoe.

This was the year in which, as Watts mentions in his slight autobiographic memoranda, occurred the great storm, one of the most fearful England has ever known. Whole buildings were hurled down, two hundred and fifty thousand timber trees torn up by the roots, spires beaten from the churches, and the lead from the roofs of more than one hundred churches rolled up like scrolls. Eight thousand persons perished by drowning; the Severn overflowed its banks, and fifteen thousand sheep besides other cattle perished; eight hundred dwelling-houses, four hundred windmills, and barns without number, were thrown down. Some people were killed in their beds, among others Dr. Kidder, Bishop of Bath and Wells, and his wife. The damage done in London amounted to about a million of pounds sterling, in Bristol to £150,000. The damage on

the sea was still more considerable, many ships of the royal
navy were cast away, and innumerable merchant vessels.
Imagination quite fails to realize the horrors of that
tremendous night; it was as one has said of it, "As if the
destroying angel hurried by shrouded in his very gloomiest
apparel."

And side by side with such great national calamities
went our great national rejoicings. This was the moment
in our history when the genius of Marlborough was rising,
and the victories of Blenheim and Ramillies were taking
place, holding in check, beyond any question, the audacity
of Louis XIV., and exhibiting the power and influence of
England in the foreign affairs of Europe in a manner
never so remarkably exhibited before.

Such were "the times that went over him." Watts lived
through all those curious transactions round the Court of
Queen Anne; lived also through the great Sacheverell riots
—and a curious time that was for Dissenters, as he bears
testimony again in his little outline of coincidences with
his autobiographical memoranda. "March 1st, 1710. The
mob rose and pulled down the pews and galleries of six
meeting-houses, that is, Mr. Burgess, Mr. Bradbury, Mr.
Earle, Mr. Wright, Mr. Hamilton, and Mr. Charles Taylor,
but were dispersed by the guards under Captain Horsey,
at one or two in the morning." He passed through all
that excitement of public feeling arising from the introduction of the "Schism Bill," which, beyond anything, covered
with gloom the last days of the reign of Queen Anne.
When she ascended the throne, Watts wrote a lyric in
honour of her happy accession; there was no inconsistency
in his expressing almost a burst of gladness and joy at her
decease. The "Schism Bill" was worthy of the very
worst days of the Stuarts; it was intended to crush all

Nonconformist schools, and all Dissenting academies; any Nonconformist teacher was to be imprisoned three months, every schoolmaster was to receive the sacrament and take the oaths, and if afterwards guilty of being present at a conventicle, to be incapacitated and imprisoned. Earl Stanhope, in his quiet, very interesting, and, on the whole, impartial history, speaks of "this tyrannical act," and well remarks: "It is singular that some of the most plain and simple notions, such as that of religious toleration, should be the slowest and most difficult to be impressed upon the human mind."* It is interesting to notice that this measure was greatly the creation of Lord Bolingbroke, a man who, while "he thought it," as Earl Stanhope says, "necessary to crush Dissenters," was himself altogether independent and incapable of any religious faith or conviction. Infidelity has never found its interests on the side of true freedom, but only of lawlessness and licentiousness, to which it is ever fond of applying the glorious term. In the midst of the panic created by this measure the Queen died, died on the very day the Schism Act was to have taken effect, and George I. succeeded to the English throne. He commenced his reign with a noble declaration of liberty of conscience. At his first appearing in council he said, " I take this occasion to express to you my firm purpose to do all that is in my power for the supporting and maintaining the Churches of England and Scotland as they are by law established, which I am of opinion may be effectually done without the least impairing the toleration allowed by law to her Protestant Dissenters, so agreeable to Christian charity."

Watts lived through that great agitation which consigned

* See " History of England," by Earl Stanhope, vol. i. chap. 1.

Francis Atterbury, the Bishop of Rochester, first to the Tower, and then to exile, for his complicity with the Pretender, and attempts to bring back the Stuarts. Atterbury was sworn by many oaths to maintain the Protestant succession, but his guilt was soon manifest beyond any doubt, even to the most lenient and doubtful mind. It was greatly to men of Watts' order of religious conviction that the reigning family owed the stability of its power; and when the fury of the clergy, especially the High Church clergy, was excited by the arrest of the Bishop, one of their own order, and attempts even made to set him forth in the light of a martyr, it is interesting to notice that it was Bishop Gibson, the friend and correspondent of Watts, who allayed the storm.*

The intense antipathy to Rome and the Papacy, so manifest in the writings of Watts, and in the wild passions of the times, was not without a cause, and a cause which would make itself especially felt in the City of London. When Watts was ordained over the church in Mark Lane, only fifteen years had elapsed since the Revocation of the Edict of Nantes; that dreadful act of persecution had poured over many parts of England and of America the noble refugees of freedom and Protestantism; multitudes found their way to the neighbourhood of London; not far from the neighbourhood of Watts' church, there sprung up a Protestant French colony. They did no harm to this nation by their exile hither,—they brought character, and piety, and invention, and wit; where they rested they reared the unadorned and humble temples of their simple

---

* Lord Macaulay says: " There was considerable excitement, but it was allayed by a temperate and artful letter to the clergy, the work, in all probability, of Bishop Gibson, who stood high in the favour of Walpole, and shortly after became minister for ecclesiastical affairs."

Protestant service. Possessed themselves of the hymns of Clement Marot, they probably suggested a psalmody, sweeter and more elevated than our churches at that time possessed—but in many instances their sufferings in the course of their expatriation had been dreadful. From year to year they still escaped to our shores, and found their way to London; the people and their pastors were aided by the government of William and Mary, and by the succeeding governments. It was not possible but that the dread of honest and quiet thinkers, and the more turbulent passions of the people, should be awakened against that fearful system which seemed so recklessly to strike at all national happiness and prosperity; and in England the Papacy had its agents almost ubiquitous, crafty, cunning, powerful, cruel, and remorseless; it was no time for the indulgence of a mere philosophical calm and dreams of generous toleration. There were frequent wild outbreaks of madness and wrath in heated and excited mobs, and the language indulged by writers, usually so clear and wise, became intense in hatred to Rome; but let the reader transfer his feelings to that time, and interpret his feelings by natural fear, and he will scarcely be able to visit either manifestation with very severe reprehension.

The times through which Watts lived were indeed very remarkable, regarded from many points of view. Well might the nation shudder at the idea of any approach to Popery on the part of our own government; for if the villages and towns of our coast opposite to France, and the neighbourhoods of the little suburban villages of Shoreditch and Spitalfields, were thronged with the refugees of persecution from France, refugees of a similar persecution from Austria also, at a later period, poured into Prussia, into New England, and into some parts of our own country, and especially into London. The Church of Rome did not, in those days, permit many years to pass without refreshing the memory of Protestants as to her power and disposition to persecute. Watts interested himself on behalf of the poor Saltzburgers (£33,000 was raised in London for their relief). Multitudes settled at Ebenezer, in Georgia. The Rev. F. M. Ziegenhagen writes to Watts that " any old rag thrown away in Europe is of service to them, old shoes, stockings, shirts, or anything of wearing apparel from men and women, grown people or children. Wherefore, dear sir, if Baron Oxie's supposition be true, perhaps you might, by the blessing of God, be the happy instrument to get here and there something of old clothes for them to cover their nakedness." To this application Watts appears to have responded, as Mr. Ziegenhagen again replies : " The readiness you show in assisting the poor Saltzburgers, nay, your well receiving the mentioning them and their circumstances in my last letter, gave me great satisfaction." Those of these persecuted ones who passed over to the American plantations appear to have settled surprisingly, aided by England ; George Whitefield bears testimony to the great blessings which rested upon them. England made a parliamentary grant of £10,000 to relieve their sufferings. Our readers know the amazing story, the mighty exodus, the march of the exiles, amounting to 20,678, in the depth of winter. The pathos of that story is immortalized in one of the sweetest poems of Goethe, and for us in the prose of Thomas Carlyle. Prussia threw her arms open to receive them ; but many perished on the march for want of food, having been obliged to leave their goods behind them. The Count of Warnigrode gave a substantial dinner to 900 of them ; the Duke of Brunswick liberally entertained others ; the clergy of Leipsic met a number of the wanderers on their

way, and led them into the city through the gates, singing
Luther's hymn as they passed in. The Revocation of the
Edict of Nantes, to which we have referred, happened a
short time before Watts commenced his ministry; this rousing event happened when it was drawing towards its close.

As we turn over some of the hymns of Watts, and some
pages of his and other writings of the day, it seems as if
the denunciations of Rome were wanting in good taste, and
tender charitableness of feeling. The sentiments Watts
expressed and indulged in never appear to go beyond the
bounds of propriety; his sentiments towards Rome are
shared by John Milton, who wrote while the valleys
of Piedmont were flaming with burning villages, and
covered with the bodies of the slaughtered saints of God.
In those years Rome had the power to get up every now
and then some such startling *spectacle* to astonish Europe
and mankind.   Papists are still surprised that such enter-
tainments were not taken in good part, and that, on the
contrary, fervid expressions of indignation were uttered,
and loud prayers put up that God would save England from
the dominancy of Rome again in the politics of our nation.
Men like Watts judged such expressions to be neither
unnatural, unholy, nor unwise : they had not reached that
stoical calm which contemplates either the insolent out-
rage and persecution of a hierarchy trampling under foot
the holiest rights of men, or the groans of protracted
suffering, with indifference ; they lived in the neighbourhood of danger, and did not affect a calmness of feeling
as they beheld, even in their own neighbourhood, infidelity and priestism working together, as they so often
work, forging fetters for a nation.

In several pages of this volume glances have been given
at the aspects of the age and its manners, so far as they

affected, or were affected by, the subject of this memoir. A large portion of that time may be spoken of as the most dissolute age of England, and even in the later period it was a rude, rough time. In those regions in which vice did not abound, a thick, dark night of ignorance " covered the people." However we may boast of a few splendid names in literature, and however some character or incident gives effect and pomp to the scenery, still it is only worthy of the apt description of John Foster* that " we are only gazing with delight at a fine public bonfire, while in all the cottages round the people are shivering for want of fuel." It was a time along whose way romance loves to loiter; when the lanthorn lighted the sedan on the neighbourly visit in town as well as country; when, also, no home was exempted from the housebreaker, and every suburb was haunted by highwaymen.

We need not dwell at greater length on the literary characteristics of the age; incidentally we may remind our readers that to Watts, in the later years of his life, we owe the introduction to the world of a poem which has not long ceased to be a very popular one, " The Grave," by Robert Blair, the minister of the parish of Athelstanford, in Scotland. Blair sent his poem to Watts, and Watts thought so well of it that he sent it to Doddridge, and both advised its author to publish it, and appear to have been able to render him some valuable assistance in making it known. Almost forgotten now, it immediately took the popular taste. It is not wonderful that it did so, for it has all the gloomy magnificence of a body lying in state ; but it is gloomy without vulgarity, and has the gorgeousness of the silver shieldings and splendid heraldry on the black velvet. It is short ;

* **Essay on " Popular Ignorance."**

it perhaps seems to us now almost a sentimental piece
of commonplace; but it instantly took possession of the
public mind, and is still included in most respectable
collections of English poets. It belonged to a class of
pieces which appear to have been great favourites with
people in those days, and which have furnished abundant
materials for sermons ever since—Hervey's "Meditations
among the Tombs," and Young's "Night Thoughts,"—
although the last is a very far superior piece of work, and
may deserve to be spoken of as one of the finest of purely
didactic poems. Blair, in his far-off home among the East
Lothians, had everything which to such a nature as his
would be likely to press home with a pensive force upon
the mind; and the deep reality of James Hervey's nature,
every one at all acquainted with his biography well knows.
Edward Young, it may without much indignity to charity
be believed, was a man of a very different order, in whom
unrealized sentiment considerably dominated the character.
He was a man of unquestionable genius, and he so far laid
his genius on the altar of religion that he produced not
only the poem to which we are referring, but many others,
which, if not of equal eminence, had a decided religious
influence. But he was a constant haunter of the abodes of
fashion, a hanger-on of Courts, and not at all indisposed to
avail himself of every kind of help in seeking to further his
purposes in life. He was not below the average of men, but
the "other-worldliness" of his poem contrasts strangely
enough with the worldliness of the author; if, when he
wrote of the other world, he wrote like a saint, we cannot
forget that, when he wrote of this, he wrote as a keen
satirist. In fact, all this belongs to the character of the
poetry of the period; it was not real, it was stiff and
stilted; it was poetry in brocade; nothing about it looks

very real. Of course there are beautiful lines and beautiful passages to be quoted, but its men and women are not real. The poetry of our own times, as compared with those, has gained immeasurably in this, in reality, and a large proportion of the things which were said and admired then would be regarded as simply ridiculous now.

No reference has been made to the States of America. The United States had no existence in Watts' day— America was regarded then much as we regard Australia now. Watts had many friends there, and much interesting correspondence exists between them; especially interesting it is to find in the history of Harvard University that Watts' name occurs as one of its early benefactors.

CHAPTER XII.

Return to Stoke Newington.

IT would be a very difficult thing to realize now in the
suburb of Stoke Newington, the Stoke Newington of
Isaac Watts' day. The mighty city has absorbed it; the
lanes, the fields, the woods, the old bridge, the old church,
and the very river have vanished. It must have been a
very pretty little rural village, comprised in a small cluster
of houses; it may even be spoken of as a kind of sequestered
hermitage, amidst whose shades those who desired it might
find, if the stillness of nature could give it, perfect peace.
Even more than forty years after Watts' death there were
only one hundred and ninety-five houses; within the
memory of old inhabitants it was still but a village. In
Watts' day it was probably surrounded by trees; a short
time before he took up his residence there, there were
seventy-seven acres of woodland in demesne, part of the
ancient forest of Middlesex, so justifying its name from
Stoke, a wood (*Stoke Newington*, the new little town in the
wood). A very pleasant retreat, the like of which we
should have to look a long way from any London suburb
to discover now. The ancient houses have disappeared

from the present vicinity, and two of the last, and those in which Watts passed his early and his later age, the houses of Hartopp and Abney, have only just been pulled down. We have noticed the history of Fleetwood's house, built in the reign of Queen Elizabeth ; but tradition assigns to some old houses in the village, called the "Bishop's Place," the frequent visits of Henry VIII., and here, on a part of these premises, was born Samuel Rogers, the poet ; and it is a singular and noticeable thing, that as the father of the poet died in 1793, and had lived the greater part of his life at Stoke Newington, those who knew the poet talked with a man who was the child of one who had probably not only seen but talked with Isaac Watts.   There is a spot in Stoke Newington still called "King Henry's Walk," and when the premises supposed to be his retreat were taken down, parts of the old wainscot were found to be richly gilt and ornamented with paintings, although, indeed, almost obliterated.

Stoke Newington, about the period when Watts resided there, was the residence and retreat of many celebrities. Here, as we have seen, Defoe was educated, and for some time resided ; and here, a little later, resided another whose name has been a charm over childhood, Thomas Day, the author of "Sandford and Merton." Watts had only been dead two years when John Howard came to reside in the village. The place seems especially to have been the retreat of retired statesmen or merchants, but all ranks seem to mingle memories in the little village. Queen Elizabeth's Walk is founded on the tradition that in the Manor House the Princess Elizabeth was concealed during a part of the reign of Queen Mary. London suburbs were wont to retain the flavour of a peculiar kind of society, and not less really than Twickenham retained its literary eminence; not less renowned than Clapham for its "Sect," was Stoke Newington eminent as the home and haunt of Nonconformist celebrities.* The interest of the place, however, gathers greatly round the memories of the houses of the Hartopp and the Abney families, for Watts is the greatest name connected with Stoke Newington, and in both these houses he found his home.

Watts' biographers have hitherto not nicely discriminated the periods of his residence; reading Southey, it might be supposed he had passed all his life at Stoke Newington; reading Milner, it might be supposed he not only passed the greater part of his life, but closed his days at Theobalds. The truth is, that Thomas Gunston, the brother of Lady Abney, purchased a house and twenty-five acres of land with the Manor of Stoke Newington. He pulled the house down, and commenced the erection of a very large and elegant house on the site of the old one, but he died in 1700, just before the completion of the building. He was a young man, and Watts was young, and between the two there appears to have been a bond of exceedingly close and tender friendship. When Thomas Gunston died he left the house to his sister, then residing at Theobalds with her husband, Sir Thomas Abney, and there Watts resided with them; but many years after, probably when time had softened the stroke which seems to have been felt very keenly, Lady Abney left Theobalds and came to her house in Stoke Newington. Watts came with the family, and in this house were passed the last thirteen years of his life, and there, shortly after the death of her revered friend, Lady Abney died. The house then became the property of the eldest daughter,

---

* See the "Clapham Sect." Sir James Stephen's Essays in "Ecclesiastical Biography."

Miss Elizabeth Abney, who never married, and whose name occurs as a considerable benefactor to the neighbourhood. Upon her death, she directed by her will the lease and estate to be sold, and after the payment of certain legacies, the residue to be distributed to poor Dissenting ministers, to their widows, and other objects of charity; the sale realized £13,000.

This, then, was the spot associated with some of Watts' earliest, happiest days, and was the scene of their quiet close. His friendship with Thomas Gunston was evidently founded on moral and intellectual relationship, and when he died, he poured out his grief in a long elegy, published in the Lyrics. It is noticeable in the poetry of Watts, and of that day, that so many of the subjects are devoted to the memory of friends. If a friend died, or if any other circumstance happened in life, it seemed necessary to embody the impressions in verse, and we need not, perhaps, regard this as altogether artificial and unnatural; in Watts' instance, we may be sure it was not so, although many of the expressions sound extravagant; those to which most exception is taken have scarcely more of this characteristic than some of the similar poems of Milton; we may, for instance, remember Lycidas :

> Mourn, ye young gardens, ye unfinished gates,
> Ye green enclosures and ye growing sweets
> Lament; for ye our midnight hours have known,
> And watched us walking by the silent moon
> In conference divine, while heavenly fire,
> Kindling our breasts, did all our thoughts inspire
> With joys almost immortal.

And again—

> Oft have I laid the awful Calvin by,
> And the sweet Cowley, with impatient eye
> To see these walls, pay the sad visit here,
> And drop the tribute of an hourly tear.

Still I behold some melancholy scene,
With many a pensive thought and many a sigh between.
Two days ago we took the evening air,
I and my grief.

Amidst the exaggerations, however, which a prosaic age
may fancy it detects, there is no reason for including expressions which it would certainly be impossible to appropriately
use now; the poet calls upon the dusky woods and echoing
hills, the flowery vales overgrown with thorns, the brook
that runs warbling by, the lowing herd, and the moaning
turtle, the curling vine with its amorous folds, and the
stately elms, the reverent growth of ancient years, standing
tall and naked to the blustering rage of the mad winds.
These are images which must have been simply natural and
appropriate when the piece was written; all is changed,
entirely changed now, unless some exception be made for
the elms which are, or were, recently standing. The death
of this amiable, excellent, and promising young man stands
out as probably the most intense grief of Watts' life. As
there was a community of taste, leisure for the indulgence
of the pursuits of the intellect and the heart, and the
strong wish to gratify the instincts of a noble nature, it is
not wonderful that Watts poured out his feelings in so
lengthy a poem.

The young man appears to have come of a high-spirited
family; his father, John Gunston, befriended many of the
ministers when they fell beneath the arm of persecution;
and when the eminent Dr. Manton was imprisoned in the
Gate House for refusing the Oxford Oath, the Lady
Broughton, his keeper, placing the keys at his disposal,
allowed him an opportunity of visiting his friend, Mr.
Gunston, at Newington. Thus we have the early and
tender connection of Watts with this village. And not

long since the old house was standing. An amiable and accomplished man of our time writes, in a letter dated May, 1840: "On my return to town I stopped at Stoke Newington, and paid a promised visit to an old friend and colleague at Abney House, where he has charge of the literary education of some twenty candidates for the ministry. The house—that in which Dr. Watts lived for more than a generation, composed his precious hymns, and at last died —afforded me, in its noble antique apartments, in its still rich embellishments, its surrounding grounds (said to contain the bones of Oliver Cromwell), and, above all, its sacred associations, more delight than I can express." *

On the spot where the house stood, with its beautiful grounds, gardens, and trees extending round, is now laid out the Abney Park Cemetery, amongst whose forests of tombs may be detected innumerable names very dear to the memories of modern Nonconformists: since the closing of Bunhill Fields, Abney Park Cemetery has become what it was, a sort of *santa croce,* or *campo santo* of revered and hallowed dust.

Though now within a short walk of the great city, it seemed a sequestered village when Watts resided there. The roads were probably not of the best, and there were no lights upon them. The woods intervening and in the neighbourhood, would furnish shelter for many social annoyances, and even dangers. But it was nearer to London than the more stately and palace-like abode of Theobalds, and, noble as it was, it was altogether a plainer habitation. Watts was probably, after the death of Sir Thomas Abney, very much the modest master of both abodes. Until within a short period of its dissolution the house contained such memories of Watts as adorned the

* " Memorials, etc. etc. of the late W. M. Bunting."

walls of Theobalds. We have seen that he was a painter, and the fashion at that time was to adorn the wainscoting and walls and panels. There were noble rooms in the mansion, and thus were they relieved, mostly by subjects of a classical, mythical, and allegorical character. He painted four characters of Youth and Age, Mirth and Grief, for two of the parlours, "where," says Dr. Robinson, "they are at this present day." To the time of its fall the mansion testified to the taste and elegance with which it was fitted up, the painted room displaying costly ornaments, and altogether a fine specimen of the age in which it was arranged; the mouldings gilt, and the whole of the panels and sides painted with subjects from " Ovid," and on the window-shutters pictorial decorations, supposed to have been the production of the pencil of Watts, emblematical of Death and Grief, and evidently alluding to the decease of Mr. Gunston. The elms, to which reference has been already made, continued to excite attention to the last. Planted long before the building was commenced, they continued to wave their widowed branches after it had passed away. Dr. Robinson mentions a portrait of Watts which long continued in the house, an indifferent portrait of him when a young man, in a blue night-gown, wig and band, and three or four duplicate mezzotinto prints of him when older by G. White, 1727, clerically habited, with a Bible in his right hand, and under him in capitals :

ISAAC WATTS

" In Christo mea vita latet, mea gloria Christus, hunc lingua, hunc calamus celebrat nec magis, tacebit. In uno Jesu omnia."

And on the upper corner " To live is Christ, to die is gain."

Here his last days were passed; Dr. Gibbons does not mention in what year the family left Theobalds to return to Stoke Newington, but it must have been about thirteen years before his death; and during this time, although his life was clouded by many pains and infirmities, he still continued the active operations of his pen, and, as we shall have occasion to see, the active operations of his mind, employing himself especially in attempting to solve what seems to many the insolvable question of the Trinity of Persons in the Godhead. But as he descended towards the closing years it seems that he suffered greatly from some members of his own family. In a letter from the Rev. John Barker to Dr. Doddridge, written nearly two years before Watts' death, we read: "The behaviour of Dr. Watts and the wretch Buckston towards Dr. Isaac is a most marvellous, infamous, enormous wickedness; Lady Abney, with inimitable steadiness and prudence, keeps our friend in peaceful ignorance, and his enemies at a becoming distance, so that in the midst of the persecution of that righteous man he lives comfortably; and when a friend asks him how he does, answers, 'Waiting God's leave to die.'"*

* Doddridge's "Life and Correspondence," vol. iv. p. 520.

CHAPTER XIII.

The World to Come.

" THE World to Come " was for a long time one of those
favourite pieces which occupied a place upon our
forefathers' book-shelves, and especially charmed the
dwellers at home in those times and places when and where
there were no Sabbath evening services ; it belongs to that
era when Christian people found their spiritual pleasure
and refreshment in Baxter's "Saint's Everlasting Rest,"
to which work it bears no inconsiderable resemblance.
Southey, in his "Life of Watts," in which, like Johnson,
he lays aside all his acerbity against Watts and Dissenters,
appears to dwell with much pleasure on this book. Probably most of our readers are now unacquainted with it ;
and, if so, they have to learn how much there is in these
two volumes of suggestion and instruction. Watts was
fond of dwelling in imagination upon, and dilating with
his pen over, the conditions of the world to come. The
work first appeared in two volumes, although the second
was not published until the year 1745, when Watts was
drawing near to the period of his own entrance into that
kingdom, upon whose conditions he had speculated so

largely and interestingly. Some portions of this work
soon found their way into other languages; his piece
on "The End of Time" was translated, as a tract, into
most of the tongues of Europe; an edition is now cir-
culating, or was a short time since, in modern Greek, on
the shores of the Levant; and none of the prose works of
Watts have perhaps obtained so large an acceptance, or
produced, on the one hand, more serious impressions, and,
on the other, more quieting and comfortable consolation.

The work has the characteristic of the times in which
it was written—diffuseness; but here, if sometimes there
is an indulgence in those fancies and colourings of speech
of which we become impatient now, we find some of the
best illustrations of that happy power of illumination and
imagination which we should expect to abound in the
works and sermons of such a poet as Watts. The poet and
the metaphysician meet, and mutually aid each other in
the attempt to enter upon the mysteries of the unseen
world; his ideas, perhaps, do not differ greatly from those
which are ordinarily entertained amongst us. Franke, the
well-known German pietist, was the means of the translation of a portion of the work in Geneva, and the translator said, in introducing the work, that "the preacher
had taken occasion of flying with his thoughts into the
blessed mansions of the just, and had given not only a
very probable and beautiful idea of the glory of a future
life in general, but also an enumeration of the many sorts
of enjoyments and pleasures that are to be met with there."

But Watts' "World to Come" is not limited to the
work that bears that title. His thoughts perpetually
hovered round that fascinating theme. He was constantly,
as we find in many of his pieces, engaged in attempts
to understand the nature of metaphysical substance.

Though from Revelation we can only gather that " we
know not what we shall be," yet there are precious hints
from which we may obtain all that is sufficient for comfort and for light, especially in the Great Teacher's promise that " where I am there shall also My servant be,"
and the assurance of His apostle that " we shall see Him
as He is."

It would not be uninteresting to group together all
Watts' words from his various works illustrating his conception of " The World to Come," his conjectures concerning
the mode of our immortality ; thus he presents to us—

THE BRAIN BOOK.

" We may try to illustrate this matter by the similitude
of the union of a human soul to a body. Suppose a
learned philosopher be also a skilful divine and a great
linguist, we may reasonably conclude that there are some
millions of words and phrases, if taken together with all
the various senses of them, which are deposited in his
brain as in a repository, by means of some correspondent
traces or signatures ; we may suppose also millions of
ideas of things, human and divine, treasured up in various
traces or signatures in the same brain. Nay, each organ
of sense may impress on the brain millions of traces
belonging to the particular objects of that sense ; especially the two senses of discipline, the eye and the ear ; the
pictures, the images, the colours, and the sounds, that are
reserved in this repository of the brain, by some correspondent impressions or traces, are little less than infinite ;
now, the human soul of the philosopher, by being united
to this brain, this well-furnished repository, knows all

these names, words, sounds, images, lines, figures, colours, notions, and sensations. It receives all these ideas; and is, as it were, mistress of them all. The very opening of the eye impresses thousands of ideas at once upon such a soul united to a human brain; and what unknown millions of ideas may be impressed on it, or conveyed to it in successive seasons, whensoever she stands in need of them, and that by the means of this union to the brain, is beyond our capacity to think or number. Let us now conceive the Divine Mind or Wisdom as a repository stored with infinite ideas of things present, past, and future: suppose a created spirit, of most extensive capacity, intimately united to this Divine Mind or Wisdom : may it not by this means, by Divine appointment, become capable of receiving so many of those ideas, and so much knowledge, as are necessary for the government and the judgment of all nations ? And this may be done two ways, viz., either by the immediate application of itself, as it were by inquiry, to the Divine Mind, to which it is thus united, or by the immediate actual influences and impressions which the Divine Mind may make of these ideas on the human soul, as fast as ever it can stand in need of them for these glorious purposes. Since a human brain, which is mere matter, and which contains only some strokes and traces, and corporeal signatures of ideas, can convey to a human soul united to it many millions of ideas, as fast as it needs them for any purposes of human life; how much more may the infinite God, or Divine Mind or Wisdom, which hath actually all real and possible ideas in it in the most perfect manner, communicate to a human soul united to this Divine Wisdom, a far greater number of ideas than a human brain can receive ; even as many as the affairs of governing and judging this world

may require.   This may be represented and illustrated by
another similitude, thus : suppose there were a spherical
looking-glass or mirror vast as this earth is ; on which
millions of corporeal objects appeared in miniature on all
sides of it impressed or represented there, by a thousand
planetary and starry worlds surrounding this vast mirror ;
suppose a capacious human spirit united to this mirror, as
the soul is to the body : what an unknown multitude of
ideas would this mirror convey to that human spirit in
successive seasons !   Or, perhaps, this spirit might receive
all these ideas at once, and be conscious of the millions of
things represented all round the mirror.   This mirror may
represent the Deity ; the human spirit taken in these ideas
successively, or conscious of them all at once, may represent to us the soul of Christ receiving, either in a simultaneous view, or in a successive way, unknown myriads of
ideas, by its union to Godhead ; though, it must be owned,
it can never receive all these ideas which are in the Divine
Mind."

And thus he endeavours to image to his mind the worlds :

EARTH, HEAVEN, AND HELL.

" I have often tried to strip death of its frightful colours,
and make all the terrible airs of it vanish into softness
and delight ; to this end, among other rovings of thought,
I have sometimes illustrated to myself the whole creation
as one immense building, with different apartments, all
under the immediate possession and government of the
great Creator.   One sort of these mansions are little,
narrow, dark, damp rooms, where there is much confinement, very little good company, and such a clog upon
one's natural spirits, that a man cannot think or talk with

freedom, nor exert his understanding, or any of his intellectual powers with glory or pleasure. This is the Earth in which we dwell. A second sort are spacious, lightsome, airy, and serene courts open to the summer sky, or at least admitting all the valuable qualities of sun and air, without the inconveniences; where there are thousands of most delightful companions, and everything that can give one pleasure, and make one capable and fit to give pleasure to others. This is the Heaven we hope for. A third sort of apartments are open and spacious too, but under a wintry sky, with perpetual storms of hail, rain, and wind, thunder, lightning, and everything that is painful and offensive; and all this among millions of wretched companions cursing the place, tormenting one another, and each endeavouring to increase the public and the universal misery. This is Hell.

"Now what a dreadful thing it is to be driven out of one of the first narrow dusky cells into the third sort of apartment, where the change of the room is infinitely the worst! No wonder that sinners are afraid to die. But why should a soul that has good hope, through grace, of entering into the serene apartment, be unwilling to leave the narrow smoky prison he has dwelt in so long, and under such loads of inconvenience? Death to a good man is but passing through a death entry, out of one little dusky room of his Father's house into another that is fair and large, lightsome and glorious, and divinely entertaining. Oh may the rays and splendours of my heavenly apartment shoot far downward, and gild the dark entry with such a cheerful beam as to banish every fear, when I shall be called to pass through."

He teaches and very much elaborates, as Southey says, the doctrine of Milton:

—What, if earth
Be but the shadow of Heaven, and things therein
Each to other like, more than on earth is thought?

Southey somewhat naturally finds an occasion for humour
in that Milton beheld in heaven a place for armies, the
review of bright brigades, and illustrious cohorts with keen
swords and long bright spears, and so he remarks, " The
Heaven of Watts' imagination was coloured by his earthly
pursuits, and whether there were to be reviews of armies
or not there were to be sermons." " For," says Watts,
" not only is there the service of thanksgiving here and of
prayer, but such entertainment as lectures and sermons
also, and there all the worship that is paid is the established worship of the whole country." But the conceptions
formed by Watts of the heavenly state are majestic in the
main. " For the Church," he says, " on earth is but a
training school for the church on high, and is, as it were,
a tiring-room in which we are dressed in proper habit for
our appearance and our places in that bright assembly."
Thus he beholds " Boyle and Ray pursuing the philosophy
in which they delighted on earth, contemplating the wisdom
of God in His works; and Henry More and Howe continuing
their metaphysical researches with brightened and refined
powers of mind." It is singular that Watts, who speculated so keenly and clearly into the nature of metaphysical
substance, should have thus somewhat embarrassed his
views of the heavenly state by discriminating so much the
pursuits of a pure and perfect soul, by characteristics which
partake of the faulty views of an earthly understanding ;
but we are to remember that he wrote for useful purposes,
and we may believe that some of those excursions of the
fancy, while scarcely consistent even with his own meta-
physics, added not a little to the pleasant horizon spread

out before the view of those readers unable or indisposed to follow him into more abstract and pure regions of thought. Interestingly and curiously he seeks to trace the progress of the soul from the visible to the invisible world; we know this world by Space and Substance, the solution of these in connection with our existence in that future world to come is not less a trouble to Watts than it has been to the rest of us. Space he endeavoured to annihilate, Substance also, and he argues, as Isaac Taylor has argued since in his " Physical Theory of Another Life," that as dis-embodied spirits cannot exist *everywhere,* and do not pro-bably exist *anywhere,* philosophically they may be said to exist *nowhere.** The question then is whither does the soul depart when it is separated from the body ? Perhaps it may be furnished with some new vehicle of a more refined matter, which will remind readers of Abraham Tucker's singular chapters in his " Light of Nature," on the " Vehicular State ;" and it is very suggestive to find him intimating that it may abide where death finds it, not changing its place, but only its manner of thinking and acting, and its mode of existence, and without removal finding itself in heaven or in hell according to its own consciousness, and that is, according to its own previous training or education, and then he says, " I may illustrate this by two similitudes, and especially apply them to the case of holy souls departing." They may remind the reader of Henry Vaughan's beautiful verse :

> If a star were confined in a tomb,
>   Its captive light would e'en shine there ;
> But when it bursts it dissipates the gloom,
>   And shines through all the sphere.

---

* " Without question we must affirm that Body is the necessary means of bringing Mind into relationship with space and extension, and so of giving it *Place*, very plainly a disembodied spirit, or we ought

" Suppose a torch enclosed in a cell of earth, in the midst
of ten thousand thousand torches that shine at large in a
spacious amphitheatre. While it is enclosed, its beams
strike only on the walls of its own cell, and it has no communion with those without. But let this cell fall down at
once, and the torch that moment has full communion with
all those ten thousands; it shines as freely as they do, and
receives and gives assistance to all of them, and joins to
add glory to that illustrious place.

" Or suppose a man born or brought up in a dark prison,
in the midst of a fair and populous city. He lives there
in a close confinement; perhaps he enjoys only the twinkling light of a lamp, with thick air and much ignorance;
though he has some distant hints and reports of the
surrounding city and its affairs, yet he sees and knows
nothing immediately but what is done in his own prison,
till in some happy minute the walls fall down; then he
finds himself at once in a large and populous town, en-
compassed with a thousand blessings. With surprise he
beholds the king in all his glory, and holds converse with
the sprightly inhabitants. He can speak their language,
and finds his nature suited to such communion. He
breathes free air, stands in the open light; he shakes himself, and exults in his own liberty."

The gentle spirit of Watts trembled before hell; he expressed his belief in eternal punishment in the strongest
and most unequivocal terms, not because he found it
plainly in his understanding, but because he found it
plainly declared in the New Testament, while yet, like
other fathers in the Church, he expresses within himself a
latent hope that God has some secret and mitigating

rather to say, an unembodied spirit, or sheer mind, is NOWHERE."—Isaac
Taylor's " Physical Theory of Another Life," chap. ii.

decree, and that although we neither dare preach nor speculate upon it, bowing to the word, we yet may hope that Infinite Love will find out a way.*

Some readers will be surprised to find that among his proofs of a separate state, Watts does not hesitate, although very modestly, to avow some belief in Apparitions. It was the age of superstition and supernatural visitations. Joseph Addison indeed was aiming at a sweeping reform, and attempting to lay all the ghosts in the country. Watts says—

CONCERNING THE POSSIBILITY OF APPARITIONS.

" At the conclusion of this chapter I cannot help taking notice, though I shall but just mention it, that the multitude of narratives, which we have heard of in all ages, of the apparition of the spirits or ghosts of persons departed from this life, can hardly be all delusion and falsehood. Some of them have been affirmed to appear upon such great and important occasions as may be equal to such an unusual event; and several of these accounts have been attested by such witnesses of wisdom, and prudence, and sagacity, under no distempers of imagination, that they may justly demand a belief; and the effects of these apparitions, in the discovery of murders and things unknown, have been so considerable and useful, that a fair disputant should hardly venture to run directly counter to such a cloud of witnesses without some good assurance on the contrary side. He must be a shrewd philosopher indeed who, upon any other hypothesis, can give a tolerable account of all the narratives in Glanvil's ' Sadducisimus Triumphatus,' or

---

* See Preface to the second vol. of " World to Come," Octavo edition.

Baxter's 'World of Spirits and Apparitions,' etc. Though I will grant some of these stories have but insufficient proof, yet if there be but one real apparition of a departed spirit, then the point is gained that there is a separate state.

" And, indeed, the Scripture itself seems to mention such sort of ghosts or appearances of souls departed (Matt. xiv. 26). When the disciples saw Jesus walking on the water they 'thought it had been a spirit.' And (Luke xxiv. 37) after His resurrection they saw Him at once appearing in the midst of them, 'and they supposed they had seen a spirit;' and our Saviour doth not contradict their notion, but argues with them upon the supposition of the truth of it, 'a spirit hath not flesh and bones as ye see Me to have." And, Acts xxiii. 8, 9, the word 'spirit' seems to signify 'the apparition of a departed soul,' where it is said, 'The Sadducees say there is no resurrection, neither angel nor spirit;' and, verse 9, 'If a spirit or an angel hath spoken to this man,' etc. A spirit here is plainly distinct from an angel; and what can it mean but an apparition of a human soul which has left the body ? "

An acquaintance with the " World to Come " will take away even now from the reader any surprise at the popularity it once enjoyed during years when printed sermons were not very abundant, and when readers received without questioning the doctrines and statements of such books as bore the imprint of the names of eminent men. Many passages are fraught with a most pleasing eloquence, and, read by a serious mind, are well calculated to convey not only passing, but permanent impressions. Shall we take two or three ?

ALL THINGS PREACH THE END OF TIME.

" Time, hastening to its period, will furnish us with perpetual new occasions of holy meditation. Do I observe the declining day, and the setting sun sinking into darkness? So declines the day of life, the hours of labour, and the seasons of grace ; oh may I finish my appointed work with honour ere the light is fled ! May I improve the shining hours of grace ere the shadows of the evening overtake me, and my time of working is no more ! Do I see the moon gliding along through midnight, and fulfilling her stages in the dusky sky ? This planet also is measuring out my life, and bringing the number of my months to their end. May I be prepared to take leave of the sun and moon, and bid adieu to these visible heavens, and all the twinkling glories of them ! These are all but the measures of my time, and hasten me on towards eternity. Am I walking in a garden, and stand still to observe the slow motion of the shadow upon a dial there ? It passes over the hour lines with an imperceptible progress, yet it will touch the last line of daylight shortly : so my hours and my moments move onward with a silent pace ; but they will arrive with certainty at the last limit, how heedless soever I am of their motion, and how thoughtless soever I may be of the improvement of time, or the end of it. Does a new year commence, and the first morning of it dawn upon me ? Let me remember that the last year was finished, and gone over my head, in order to make way for the entrance of the present : I have one year the less to travel through the world, and to fulfil the various services of a travelling state : may my diligence in duty be doubled, since the number of my appointed years is diminished !

Do I find a new birth-day in my survey of the calendar, the day wherein I entered upon the stage of mortality, and was born into this world of sins, frailties, and sorrows, in order to my probation for a better state ? Blessed Lord, how much have I spent already of this mortal life, this season of my probation, and how little am I prepared for that happier world! How unready for my dying moment! I am hastening hourly to the end of the life of man, which began at my nativity : am I yet born of God ? Have I begun the life of a saint ? Am I prepared for that awful day which shall determine the number of my months on earth ? Am I fit to be born into the world of spirits through the strait gate of death ? Am I renewed in all the powers of my nature, and made meet to enter into that unseen world, where there shall be no more of these revolutions of days and years, but one eternal day fills up all the space with Divine pleasure, or one eternal night with long and deplorable distress and darkness ? When I see a friend expiring, or the corpse of my neighbour conveyed to the grave : alas ! their months and minutes are all determined, and the seasons of their trial are finished for ever ; they are gone to their eternal home, and the estate of their souls is fixed unchangeably : the angel that has sworn their 'time shall be no longer' has concluded their hopes, or has finished their fears, and, according to the rules of righteous judgment, has decided their misery or happiness for a long immortality. Take this warning, oh my soul, and think of thine own removal! Are we standing in the churchyard, paying the last honours to the relics of our friends ? What a number of hillocks of death appear all round us ! What are the tombstones but memorials of the inhabitants of that town, to inform us of the period of all their lives, and to point out the day when it was said to each of them, your 'time shall be no longer.' Oh may I readily learn this important lesson, that my turn is hastening too ! Such a little hillock shall shortly arise for me on some unknown spot of ground ; it shall cover this flesh and these bones of mine in darkness, and shall hide them from the light of the sun, and from the sight of man, 'till the heavens be no more.' Perhaps some kind surviving friend may engrave my name, with the number of my days, upon a plain funeral stone, without ornament and below envy ; there shall my tomb stand, among the rest, as a fresh monument of the frailty of nature and the end of time. It is possible some friendly foot may, now and then, visit the place of my repose, and some tender eye may bedew the cold memorial with a tear : one or another of my old acquaintance may possibly attend there to learn the silent lecture of mortality from my grave-stone, which my lips are now preaching aloud to the world : and if love and sorrow should reach so far, perhaps, while his soul is melting in his eye-lids, and his voice scarce find an utterance, he will point with his finger and show his companion the month and day of my decease. Oh that solemn, that awful day, which shall finish my appointed time on earth, and put a full period to all the designs of my heart and all the labours of my tongue and pen. Think, oh my soul ! that while friends or strangers are engaged on that spot, and reading the date of my departure hence, thou wilt be fixed under a decisive and unchangeable sentence, rejoicing in the rewards of time well improved, or suffering the long sorrows which shall attend the abuse of it in an unknown world of happiness or misery."

And we should think that many a believer has read the following with sentiments of delight :

CHRIST ADMIRED AND GLORIFIED IN HIS SAINTS.

" Astonishing spectacle ! When the dark and savage
inhabitants of Africa, and our forefathers, the rugged and
warlike Britons, from the ends of the earth, shall appear
in that assembly, with some of the polite nations of Greece
and Rome, and each of them shall glory in having been
taught to renounce the gods of their ancestors, and the
demons which they once worshipped, and shall rejoice in
Jesus the King of Israel, and in Jehovah the everlasting
God. The conversion of the Gentile world to Christianity is
a matter of glorious wonder, and shall appear to be so in
that great day : that those who had been educated to believe in many gods, or no god at all, should renounce
atheism and idolatry, and adore the true God only ; and
those who were taught to sacrifice to idols, and to atone
for their own sins with the blood of beasts, should trust in
one sacrifice, and the atoning blood of the Son of God.
Here shall stand a believing atheist, and there a converted
idolater, as monuments of the almighty power of grace.
There shall shine also in that assembly here and there a
prince and a philosopher, though ' not many wise, not
many noble, not many mighty are called.'*   And they
shall be matter of wonder and glory : that princes, who
loved no control, should bow their sceptres and their
souls to the royalty and Godhead of the poor Man of Naza-
reth : that the heathen philosophers, who had been used to
yield only to reason, should submit their understandings to
Divine revelation, even when it has something above the
powers and discoveries of reason in it.

" Come, all ye saints of these latter ages, 'upon whom the

* 1 Cor. i. 26.

end of the world is come,' raise your heads with me, and
look far backwards, even to the beginning of time, and the
days of Adam ; for the believers of all ages, as well as of
all nations, shall appear together in that day, and acknowledge Jesus the Saviour : according to the brighter or
darker discoveries of the age in which they lived, He has
been the common object of their faith. Ever since He
was called ' the Seed of the woman,' till the time of His
appearance in the flesh, all the chosen of God have lived
upon His grace, though multitudes of them never knew
His name. It is true, the greater part of that illustrious
company on the right hand of Christ lived since the time
of His incarnation, for the ' great multitude which no man
could number ' is derived from the Gentile nations. Yet
the ancient patriarchs, with the Jewish prophets and saints,
shall make a splendid appearance there : ' one hundred
and forty-four thousand are sealed among the tribes of
Israel ;' these of old embraced the Gospel in types and
shadows ; but now their eyes behold Jesus Christ, the
substance and the truth. In the days of their flesh they
read His name in dark lines, and looked through the long
glasses of prophecy to distant ages, and a Saviour to come ;
and now, behold, they find complete and certain salvation
and glory in Him. ' These all died in faith, not having
received the promises, but having seen them afar off, and
were persuaded of them, and embraced them.' They died
in the hope of this salvation, and they shall rise in the
blessed possession of it.

"Behold Abraham appearing there, the father of the faithful, ' who saw the day of Christ, and rejoiced to see it ;'
who trusted in his Son Jesus, two thousand years before
He was born ; his elder family, the pious Jews, surround
him there, and we, his younger children among the Gentiles,

shall stand with him as the followers of his faith, who trust in
the same Jesus almost two thousand years after He is dead.
How shall we both rejoice to see this brightest day of the
Son of Man, and congratulate each other's faith, while our
eyes meet and centre in Him, and our souls triumph in
the sight, love, and enjoyment of Him in whom we have
believed !   How admirable and divinely glorious shall our
Lord Himself appear, on whom every life is fixed with
unutterable delight, in whom the faith of distant countries
and ages is centered and reconciled, and in whom 'all the
nations of the earth appear to be blessed,' according to
the ancient word of promise.

"Then one shall say : ' I was a sensual sinner, drenched in
liquor and unclean lusts, and wicked in all the forms of
lewdness and intemperance ; the grace of God my Saviour
appeared to me, and taught me to deny worldly lusts,
which I once thought I could never have parted with.   I
loved my sins as my life, but He has persuaded and constrained me to cut off a right hand, and to pluck out a
right eye, and to part with my darling vices ; and behold
me here a monument of His saving mercy.'

"' I was envious against my neighbour,' shall another
say, ' and my temper was malice and wrath ; revenge was
mingled with my constitution, and I thought it no iniquity ;
but I bless the name of Christ my Redeemer, who, in the
day of His grace, turned my wrath into meekness ; He
inclined me to love even my enemies, and to pray for them
that cursed me ; He taught me all this by His own example, and He made me learn it by the sovereign influences
of His Spirit.   I am a wonder to myself, when I think
what once I was.   Amazing change, and Almighty grace !'

"Then a third shall confess : ' I was a profane wretch, a
swearer, a blasphemer ; I hoped for no heaven, and I feared

no hell; but the Lord seized me in the midst of my rebellions, and sent His arrows into my soul; He made me feel the stings of an awakened conscience, and constrained me to believe there was a God and a hell, till I cried out astonished, " What shall I do to be saved ? " Then He led me to partake of His own salvation, and, from a proud, rebellious infidel, He has made me a penitent and a humble believer, and here I stand to show forth the wonders of His grace, and a boundless extent of His forgiveness.'

" A fourth shall stand up and acknowledge in that day : ' And I was a poor carnal, covetous creature, who made this world my god, and abundance of money was my heaven ; but He cured me of this vile idolatry of gold, taught me how to obtain treasures in the heavenly world, and to forsake all on earth, that I might have an inheritance there ; and, behold, He has not disappointed my hopes : I am now made rich indeed, and I must for ever sing His praises.'

" There shall be no doubt or dispute in that day whether it was the power of our own will, or the superior power of Divine grace, that wrought the blessed change, that turned the lion into a lamb, a grovelling earthworm into a bird of paradise, and of a covetous or malicious sinner made a meek and a heavenly saint. The grace of Christ shall be so conspicuous in every glorified believer in that assembly, that, with one voice, they shall all shout to the praise and glory of His grace, ' Not to us, O Lord, not to us, but to Thy name be all the honour !'

" Behold that noble army with palms in their hands ; once they were weak warriors, yet they overcame mighty enemies, and have gained the victory and the prize ; enemies rising from earth and from hell to tempt and to accuse them, but they overcame ' by the blood of the

Lamb.' What a Divine honour it shall be to our Lord Jesus Christ, ' the Captain of our salvation,' that weak Christians should subdue their strong corruptions, and get safe to heaven through a thousand oppositions within and without ! It is all owing to the grace of Christ, that grace which is all-sufficient for every saint. They are made ' more than conquerors through Him that has loved them.' Then shall the faith and courage and patience of the saints have a blessed review ; and it shall be told before the whole creation what strife and wrestlings a poor believer has passed through in a dark cottage, a chamber of lone sickness, or perhaps in a dungeon ; how he has there combated with ' powers of darkness,' how he has struggled with huge sorrows, and has borne, and has not fainted, though he has been often ' in heaviness through manifold temptations.' Then shall appear the bright scene which St. Peter represents as the event of sore trials (1 Peter i. 6, 7). ' When our faith has been tried in the fire of tribulation, and is found more precious than gold,' it shall shine to the praise, honour, and glory of the suffering saints, and of Christ Himself at His appearance.

"Behold that illustrious troop of martyrs, and some among them of the feebler sex and of tender age. Now, that women should grow bold in faith, even in the sight of torments, and children, with a manly courage, should profess the name of Christ in the face of angry and threatening rulers ; that some of these should become undaunted confessors of the truth, and others triumph in fires and torture, these things shall be matter of glory to Christ in that day ; it was His power that gave them courage and victory in martyrdom and death. Every Christian there, every soldier in that triumphing army, shall ascribe his conquest to the grace of his Lord, his Leader, and lay down all their trophies at the feet of his Saviour, with humble acknowledgments, and shouts of honour.

" Almost all the saved number were, at some part of their lives, weak in faith, and yet, by the grace of Christ, they held out to the end, and are crowned; ' I was a poor trembling creature,' shall one say, ' but I was confirmed in my faith and holiness by the Gospel of Christ; or, I rested on a naked promise, and found support, because Christ was there, and He shall have the glory of it.' ' In Him are all the promises yea, and in Him amen, to the glory of the Father;' and the Son shall share in this glory; for He died to ratify these promises, and He lives to fulfil them.

" ' Oh, what an almighty arm is this,' shall the believer say, ' that has borne up so many thousands of poor sinking creatures, and lifted their heads above the waves!' The spark of grace that lived many years in a flood of temptations, and was not quenched, shall then shine bright to the glory of Christ, who kindled and maintained it. When we have been brought through all the storms and the threatening seas, and yet the raging waves have been forbid to swallow us up, we shall cry out in raptures of joy and wonder: ' What manner of Man is this, that the winds and the seas have obeyed him?' Then shall it be gloriously evident that He has conquered Satan, and kept the hosts of hell in chains; when it shall appear that He has made poor, mean, trembling believers victorious over all the powers of darkness, for the Prince of Peace has bruised him under their feet."

CHAPTER XIV.

𝔗𝔥𝔢 𝔐𝔞𝔫.

WATTS, as we have seen, lived so much in retirement and retreat, and was so constant a sufferer from the infirmities of health, that little is known in the way of incident and anecdote of his life. In a sense, indeed, he lived constantly before the eyes of men, for his industry, when he was capable of industry, must have been immense; he must have read extensively, he thought deeply, and he possessed not only an active but a facile pen, which appears to have served him very readily when he desired to translate his thoughts into language. His life belongs to that order we represent by such names as Richard Hooker, Jeremy Taylor, and John Howe : we do not here compare or contrast the finer details of their character, but, like them, he appears to have been essentially a man of contemplation; his activity was only the reflection of a contemplative life. In height ·he was quite beneath the common standard; Dr. Gibbons says not above five feet, or, at most, five feet two inches; we are not accustomed to associate so small a stature with any commanding presence in the pulpit; yet his preaching was greatly admired, and Dr. Jennings says that it was not only weighty and powerful, " but there was a certain dignity and respect in his very aspect which commanded attention and awe, and when he spoke, such strains of truly Christian eloquence flowed from his lips as one thinks could not be easily slighted, if resisted." He was altogether a very slight figure—thin, an oval face, an aquiline nose, his complexion fair and pale, and, Gibbons says, his forehead low ; but this does not appear in his portrait, nor does that which it usually indicates, a want of generosity, mark his character. When unable to preach, it was with difficulty he could be persuaded to accept the stipend of the church of which he was the pastor, saying that, as he could not preach, he had no title to any salary. His refusal was not accepted, but the delicate sense of honour marks the character of the man ; while, from the time he lived in the Abney family, he devoted a third part of his income to charitable purposes. His eyes appear to have lighted up his face ; they are described as singularly small and grey, and are said to have been amazingly piercing and expressive. His voice was very fine and slender, but regular, audible, and pleasant. The anecdote is well known of him that when he was in one of those coffee-houses—then the haunts of men who knew what company they might expect to find, for every particular coterie had its own place of rendezvous—he overheard his name given by one person to another, who said in surprise, " What ! is that the great Dr. Watts ?" Whereupon he wrote down a verse and handed it to him :

> Were I so tall to reach the pole,
>   And grasp the ocean in a span,
> I must be measured by my soul,—
>   The mind's the standard of the man.

We have never thought the anecdote a very likely one ; Watts was altogether too quiet, and we may use the word, majestic in his manner to make it possible he would do this. The verse is indeed his, but it occurs in a lengthy poem, and it is possible that it was fitted into a fabulous incident which some inventor of scenic situations thought might be, or ought to be, true. There is another anecdote which has been related of him, although we have seen it attributed to others, how, when once in a coffee-house, and somewhat in the way of a tall giant of a man, he said to Watts, " Let me pass, O giant !" and Watts replied, " Pass on, O pigmy !" " I only referred to your mind," said the giant; " I also to yours," replied Watts.

Whatever impression such anecdotes may convey, one of his chief characteristics was a very modest appreciation of himself. " His humility," said Dr. Jennings, " like a deep shade, set off his other graces and virtues, and made them shine with greater lustre." And of those attributes of his character of which others thought most highly, he thought very inconsiderably. And to such a character is often allied that which is very noticeable in him, a very grateful sense of all favours conferred upon him. There was nothing narrow in his mind, he had a great width of thought and a great width of love : although, as we have seen, a Nonconformist by strong conviction, judging the communion to which he belonged as favourable to civil and religious freedom, and regarding the service as most in harmony with what he considered the simplicity of the Gospel, he was on terms of friendship with many other communions, and especially with several of the prelates, ministers, and members of the Established Church. It would be expected, although this is not invariably the case, that a mind so richly stored, united to so ready an

eloquence, would shine in conversation, and this was the
case. It is said that in conversation his wit sparkled;
his biographer says, "It was like an ethereal flame, ever
vivid and penetrating;" but he had an aversion to satire.
Referring to the pictures he sometimes introduces, illustrating the vices and follies of his age, he utterly disclaims
the idea that in them he has attempted to portray any personal character. "I would not," he says, "willingly create
needless pain or uneasiness to the most despicable figure
among mankind; there are vexations enough among the
beings of my species without my adding to the heap. When
a reflecting glass shows the deformity of a face so plain as
to point to the person, he will sooner be tempted to break
the glass than reform his blemishes; but if I can find any
error of my own happily described in some general
character, I am then awakened to reform it in silence,
without the public notice of the world, and the moral
writer attains his noblest end." He was not happy in the
friendship of listeners, who took down with any accuracy
the sayings which fell from him; and it is probable that
in conversation, although rich and full, wide and wise, it
was rather remarkable for these characteristics than for
either its gaiety or its force.

There were few waste moments for which he had to give
an account; he acted like a miser by his time, and permitted few moments to pass without their being garnered
and compelled to pay interest. We read of his writing
on horseback, and whithersoever he travelled the objects
which entered either the eye or the ear seem to have left
abiding impressions. It seems even the injustice of his
opponents in disputation did not make him angry. Such
injustice we know he had to experience; and when, in his
later years, he offended on both sides, one writer complain-

ing of him that he had gone too far, and another that he had not gone far enough, he contented himself by saying, " Moderation must expect a box on both ears." A character like that of Watts inspires confidence in almost all that proceeds from his pen : the men, indeed, who carry what Chalmers called " weight in life," are usually the tall, the self-assertive, and the strong ; none of these attributes mark him, and yet he appears to have carried great weight. It was not by vehemence, but by wisdom ; he did not win by the forcible striking of the ball, but by prescience and a judicious calculation.

Watts, like so many of the great wits, poets, and authors of his time, was what we should now consider very slightly versed in the accomplishments of travel : a few places in the neighbourhood of London and Southampton and Tunbridge Wells seem almost to exhaust his excursions. Indeed, England was for the most part an unknown country, and as to the continent of Europe, men of wealth and fashion were expected to perfect their education by the grand tour, but to persons even in Watts' circle of society, France, Switzerland, and Italy, with their cities, memories, forests, and mountains, were unknown. Gray had not yet discovered Cumberland and Westmoreland, and when discovered, there were no facilities to make travel thither very easy ; Yorkshire and Lancashire were almost equally unknown. The place to which we frequently find Watts retreating for the benefit of his health was Tunbridge Wells, and a singular place it must have been for a retreat, judging from the description Macaulay has given us of it in his history ; but it furnishes us with a singular sense of the simple things which excited the imagination, to read how Watts regarded it. Many a modern reader is struck with surprise at Shakespeare's description of the cliffs of Dover—a description of terror and fear arising from precipitous heights, which we could scarcely now persuade ourselves to be just of Helvellyn and Pendle. The rocks of Tunbridge seemed to Watts so wild and fearful that they furnish him with a subject for a sermon, " On the vain Refuge of Sinners," from the text reciting the condition of those who said to the mountains and rocks, " Fall on us, and hide us from the face of Him that sitteth upon the throne." The sermon is expressly called "A Meditation upon the Rocks near Tunbridge Wells," and he says :

" When I see such awful appearances in nature, huge and lofty rocks hanging over my head, and at every step of my approach they seem to nod upon me with overwhelming ruin; when my curiosity searches far into hollow clefts, their dark and deep caverns of solitude and desolation, methinks, whilst I stand amongst them, I can hardly think myself in safety, and, at best, they give a sort of solemn and dreadful delight. Let me improve the scene to religious purposes, and raise a Divine meditation. Am I one of those wretches who shall call to these huge impending rocks to fall upon me ? "

When Watts first visited Tunbridge Wells in search of health and refreshment, it must have been to our modern sense an uncomfortable place ; even at the close of his life and in his later visits, it was only just rising into importance as the retreat of the coteries of fashion and letters ; it is almost the only spot left now which we may be sure, from some points of view, looks much as it did in the day when Watts, Richardson, or Johnson walked along the Pantiles, and inhaled the breezes from the neighbouring rocks and grounds. Such as it was at the close of the seventeenth and the eighteenth centuries, we find described in the pages of Macaulay and some of the novelists and

poets. The waters possessed some real, and acquired an artificial, fame; there was no town, only a few neat and rustic
cottages, some of these moveable; moveable cabins and
huts were drawn on sledges from one part of the common
to another. Fashionable London tradespeople went down
and spread out their bazaars under the trees, and near the
spring; a fair was daily held, in which were booths where
the man of letters and the politician might find his cup of
coffee, his newspaper, and his friend; and others, in which
the gambler might find his vice and his victim. On the
whole, it was a merry place for sated and wearied fashionable loungers, where they might believe that they were
becoming rural, and charm themselves into the persuasion
that they were the spectators of a poetry of nature, which
they would have been indisposed to experience too long
or too deeply; but a place where we cannot suppose
that Watts found himself for any length of time at
home. He was, however, frequently there, and upon
one occasion he was guilty of one of the few of what
may be called the vanities of verse which fell from his
pen. The atmosphere of watering-places is favourable to
every kind of literary as well as other lounging. Watts
was not altogether insensible, we should suppose, to the
charms of female beauty, and certainly a man may well be
moved to express himself in verse concerning it, when
feeble verses have been erroneously attributed to him.
It was in the summer of 1712, when at Tunbridge Wells,
that he wrote the following lines in honour of Lady
Sunderland, one of the daughters of the Duke of Marlborough; her husband had just been dismissed from the
councils of the queen, and she had just withdrawn from
the court. We may suppose the little clusters of various
loungers and talkers would be surprised to see them in

some one of the little local flying " Mercury's " of the day
where these verses appeared and were attributed to Watts;
he appears to have felt it was an occasion for some apology
for stepping into such a by-way ; he does so in the following note, upon which fancy may a little divert itself as to
the life he and others led at Tunbridge Wells :

TO AMYNTAS.

" Perhaps you were not a little surprised, my friend, when
you saw some stanzas on the Lady Sunderland at Tunbridge Wells, and were told that I wrote them ; but when
I give you a full account of the occasion your wonder will
cease. The Duke of Marlborough's three daughters, namely,
the Lady Godolphin, the Lady Sunderland, and the Lady
Bridgewater, had been at the Wells some time when I
came there ; nor had I the honour of any more acquaintance with any of them than what was common to all the
company in the Wells, that is, to be told who they were
when they passed by. A few days afterwards they left
that place, and the next morning there was found a copy
of verses in the coffee-house, called the ' Three Shining
Sisters ;' but, the author being unknown, some persons
were ready to attribute them to me, knowing that I had
heretofore dealt in rhyme. I confess I was ashamed of
several lines in that copy. Some were very dull, and
others, as I remember, bordered upon profaneness.

" That afternoon I rode abroad as usual for my health,
and it came into my head to let my friends see that, if I
would choose such a theme, I would write in another
manner than that nameless author had done. Accordingly,
as I was on horseback, I began a stanza on the ' Three

Shining Sisters,' but my ideas, my rhyme, and the metre would not hit well while the words ran in the plural number ; and this slight occurrence was the real occasion of turning my thoughts to the singular ; and then, because the Lady Sunderland was counted much the finest woman of the three, I addressed the verses to her name. Afterwards when I came to the coffee-house, I entertained some of my friends with these lines, and they, imagining it would be no disagreeable thing to the company, persuaded me to permit them to pass through the press."

But here are the verses—

ODE TO LADY SUNDERLAND, 1712.

Fair nymph, ascend to Beauty's throne,
And rule that radiant world alone ;
Let favourites take thy lower sphere,
No monarchs are thy rivals here.

The court of Beauty built sublime,
Defies all pow'rs but heaven and time ;
Envy, that clouds the hero's sky,
Aims but in vain her shafts so high.

Not Blenheim's field, nor Ister's flood,
Nor standards dyed in Gallic blood,
Torn from the foe, add nobler grace
To Churchill's house than Spenser's face.

The warlike thunder of his arms
Is less commanding than her charms :
His lightning strikes with less surprise
Than sudden glances from her eyes.

His captives feel their limbs confined
In iron ; she enslaves the mind :
We follow with a pleasing pain,
And bless the conqueror and the chain.

The Muse that dares in numbers do
What paint and pencil never knew,
Faints at her presence in despair,
And owns th' inimitable fair.

Presently appeared the following epigram or *impromptu* composed by some divine, of which it has been truly remarked that it is difficult to say whether the author or the lady has the greater compliment !—

> While numerous bards have sounded Spenser's name,
> And made her beauties heirs to lasting fame,
> Her memory still to their united lays
> Stands less indebted than to Watts's praise.
> What wondrous charms must to that fair be given,
> Who moved a mind that dwelt so near to heaven!

Tunbridge Wells is still the pleasant resort of those who seek the mild and quiet attractions of charming scenery, refreshing breezes, and crags and downs ; but the romantic season of Tunbridge Wells is to be sought for about the period when Watts and his contemporaries were visitors there, scenes open to the fancy which it would be difficult to realize now amidst its splendid palatial residences ; even Nature must look less like Nature than it did then, while the superior auxiliaries of comfort and accommodation have, as in almost all such instances, been purchased at the expense of dissipating the charms and rural beauties of a place which still retains so many of them as to make one of the most attractive and satisfying haunts for a sick heart among the sanatories of England.

The life of Dr. Watts must be illustrated rather from his works than from its incidents.   It is remarkable that so little is recorded of him ; his powers of conversation seem to have been considerable, and his reputation for wit was what we might naturally suppose from the liveliness of many of his prose writings.   But he was certainly unfortunate in his first biographer.   Dr. Gibbons was an accomplished man, a correct and fine scholar, but surely the last thing for which he was ever intended, either by nature or

by grace, was to write a biography. *His* contains many
noticeable and acute remarks, and some passages which
almost dilate into beauty ; but it is strange that, constant
as was his intercourse with his friend, he has preserved
scarcely anything either of anecdote, conversation, or description illustrating their intercourse ; and it seems certain
that Watts' life would have well repaid the assiduity of a
Boswell.   His mind was remarkably full, and Gibbons
testifies how, on any and every occasion, he was able to
express himself at once with great force, propriety, and
elegance.   But his biographer only tells us how his life,
from the time of his earliest studies, afforded little variety,
and consequently has few subjects for narration—it "flowed
along in an even, uniform tenor ; one year, one month, one
week, one day being, in a manner, a repetition of the
former."   Like some other eminent men, it somewhat
appears as if he finished the furnishing of his mind when
in his youngest years, and devoted all the after period of his
life to the unfolding, amplifying, expounding, and popular-
izing the stores he had amassed and acquired.   Dr. Gibbons
refers to the fact that his "Treatise on Astronomy and
Geography" was most probably prepared for the tuition of
Mr.—afterwards Sir John—Hartopp ; when published in
1725, in the dedication to Mr. Eames, he says that : "The
papers had lain by him in silence above twenty years ;" and
as to his "Logic," we have already referred to it ; and the
dedication in which he tells his former pupil that "it was
fit that the public should receive, through his hands, what
was originally written for the assistance of his younger
studies, and was thus presented to him."   And thus we are
assured that the work which met with so large a reception
and distinguished applause was prepared in days when he
was himself little more than a youth, to serve his own

purposes of tuition. Such was the life of this interesting man—it was a fountain of life and power. In the spacious chapel-walk in Southampton there is a pavement-stone marked with the letter W—it stands for Watts; but, as Mr. Carlyle says in his interesting paper on Watts, it might stand for Watts' Well; it was once the property of Isaac Watts, and the well has a long story, well authenticated in the church records of the Above Bar congregation. That well of clear, beautiful water was purchased by old Isaac Watts from his friend, Robert Thorner, the founder of the Southampton Charity. It was on, and constituted a part of, the tenement known by the name of the Meeting-house; then it was leased to the church, then it was purchased by the church. It was known in Southampton two hundred years ago. It is now a fountain sealed, but still it is known, and proudly the pastor says, "Our father Isaac gave us this well, and drank thereof, himself and his children."* Watts' Well is no inapt symbol or emblem of Watts' life and labours. Even lost to sight, sealed over, its springs still pour along their refreshing, cooling, and transparent streams; nor have the crowds who hurry thoughtlessly by power to interfere with the useful freshness of its pure blessings.

"The last days are the best witnesses for a man." "Blessed," says old Robert Harris, "shall he be that so lived that he was desired, and so died that he was missed." Isaac Watts illustrated in a remarkable manner power in weakness.

---

* So says Mr. Carlyle, in one of the most interesting little documents in connection with the life of Watts ever published, the little pamphlet to which we have already referred.

CHAPTER XV.

Death and Burial.

HE died in 1748, at the age of seventy-four, in ripe
years, and hoary with the honours of holiness. We
are dependent upon his friend and biographer, Dr. Gibbons,
for almost all that we know of his last days and hours, but
it is very pleasant to find that the author of "The World
to Come" himself went down to the grave with all the
calmness and confidence which the words he has uttered
have so often imparted to others in the outlook towards
the better country. He says, "It is a glory to the Gospel
when we can lie down with courage in hope of its promised
blessings; dying with faith and fortitude is a noble conclusion of a life of zeal and service." "Death in the course
of nature," he says, "as well as by the hands of violence,
hath always something awful and formidable in it; flesh
and blood shrink and tremble at the appearance of a dissolution; but death is the last enemy of all the saints, and
when a Christian meets it with sacred courage he gives
that honour to the Captain of his salvation which the
saints in glory can never give, and which we can never
repeat; it is an honour to our common faith when it over-
comes the terrors of death, and raises the Christian to a

song of triumph in the view of the last enemy; it is a new
crown put upon the head of our Redeemer, and a living
cordial put into the hands of mourning friends in our dying
hour when we can take leave of them with holy fortitude,
rejoicing in the salvation of Christ."

Such were his words; such honour have not all the
saints; some who have looked forward through life with
triumph to that hour have fainted when it came, and some
who feared it most have felt it least: peculiar tempera-
ments and special forms of pain and disease sometimes
make death dreadful; and an old writer says, " We are not
glad to feel the snake, even when we know its sting is
drawn." Thomas Walsh, one of the holiest and most eminent of the early Methodists, was very angry against John
Fletcher, the seraphic vicar of Madeley, because he heard
him say that some comparatively weak believers might
die most cheerfully, and that some strong ones, for the
further purification of their faith, or for inscrutable reasons,
might have severe conflicts. " Be it done unto you according to your faith," said Walsh, " and be it done unto me
according to mine." But when the hour came to Walsh it
was clouded, and those eyes which had " looked out of the
windows were darkened;" only at the last moment he ex-
claimed, " He is come! He is come! My beloved is mine,
and I am His for ever!" And so he passed. But Fletcher
died in a rapture. " I know thy soul," said his wife, " but
if Jesus is very present with thee, lift up thy right hand."
Immediately it was raised. " If the prospects of glory
sweetly open before thee, repeat the sign." The hand was
raised a second time, and so his soul breathed itself away.
Faith survives the presence of sensible comforts. An aged
believer in Southampton, on her death-bed, complained of
the absence of sensible comforts to her pastor, the Rev. W.

Kingsbury, but so strong was her faith that she said, "It is against the whole scope of Divine revelation that my soul should be lost." Old Thomas Fuller; having surveyed the various modes of death, arrived at the short, decisive conclusion, "None please me." "But away," he adds, "with these thoughts; the mark must not choose what arrow shall be shot against it." The happiness of a clear, calm departure was given to Watts, his closing days were serene and happy; with all the imaginative glow of his mind, he had naturally a calm character. He had well grounded his convictions; he had long lived like a sunbeam amidst sunbeams in the light. Dr. Gibbons, speaking from his own knowledge, says, "Although his weakness was very great, he knew no decay of intelligence, and was the subject of no wild fancies." His biographer adds, "He saw his approaching dissolution with a mind perfectly calm and composed, without the least alarm or dismay, and I never could discover, though I was frequently with him, the least shadow of a doubt as to his future everlasting happiness, or anything that looked like an unwillingness to die; how I have known him recite with self-application those words in Hebrews, 'Ye have need of patience, that, after ye have done the will of God, ye may receive the promise;' and how often have I heard him, upon leaving the family after supper and withdrawing to rest, declare with the sweetest composure, that if his Master was to say to him that he had no more work for him to do, he should be glad to be dismissed that night. And I once heard him say, with a kind of impatience, perhaps such as might in some degree trespass upon that submission we ought always to pay to the Divine will, 'I wonder why the great God should continue me in life, when I am incapable of performing Him any further service?'"

The death-beds of great and eminent men are often hung round with curious fables and inventions; one is mentioned even to our own day, although Dr. Gibbons denies the whole story in the very first edition of his biography. Somebody conveyed it to Mr. Toplady, who says, "That little more than half-an-hour before Dr. Watts expired he was visited by his dear friend, Mr. Whitefield; he, asking him how he found himself, the dying doctor answered, 'Here am I, one of Christ's waiting servants.' Soon after a medicine was brought in, and Mr. Whitefield assisted in raising him upon the bed that he might with more convenience take the draught; on the doctor's apologizing for the trouble he gave Mr. Whitefield, the latter replied, with his usual amiable politeness, 'Surely, my dear brother, I am not too good to wait upon a waiting servant of Christ!' Soon after, Mr. Whitefield took his leave, and often regretted since that he had not prolonged his visit, which he would certainly have done could he have foreseen that his friend was but within a half-an-hour's distance from the kingdom of glory." There is not a word of truth in the whole story; Dr. Gibbons says it is entirely fictitious. "Mr. Whitefield never visited the doctor in his last illness or confinement, nor had any conversation or interview with him for some months before his decease. It were to be wished that greater care was practised by the writers of other persons' lives, that illusions might not take place and obtain the regards of truth, and lay historians who come after them under the unpleasing necessity of dissolving their figments, and thereby, in consequence, evincing to the world how little credit is due to these relations."

His dying sayings are recorded, and they were all of them of a quiet and peaceful nature. Dr. Jennings, who preached his funeral sermon, and saw him on his death-bed, mentions, that while for two or three years previous to his death his active and more sprightly powers of nature had failed, his trust in God, through Jesus the Mediator, remained unshaken to the last. To Lady Abney he said : " I bless God I can lie down with comfort at night, not being solicitous whether I awake in this world or another." And again he said : " I should be glad to read more, yet not in order to be confirmed more in the truth of the Christian religion, or in the truth of its promises, for I believe them enough to venture into eternity on them." When he was almost worn out and broken down by his infirmities he said, in conversation with a friend, that he remembered an aged minister used to say, that the most learned and knowing Christians, when they come to die, have only the same plain promises of the Gospel for their support as the common and the unlearned. " And so," said he, " I find it ; they are the plain promises of the Gospel that are my support, and I bless God they are plain promises, which do not require much labour or pains to understand them, for I can do nothing now but look into my Bible for some promise to support me, and live upon that." Dr. Gibbons naturally regrets that he did not commit to writing the words of his dying friend ; it is wonderful that he did not ; but Watts had an amanuensis who had been with him upwards of twenty years, and who, as Gibbons says, was " in a manner ever with him ; " to him and to Miss Abney, or, as she is generally called, Mistress Elizabeth Abney, the eldest daughter and successor to the Abney property, we are principally indebted for the record of his dying words. When he found his spirit tending to impatience, he would check himself, saying : " The business of a Christian is to bear the will of God as well as do it. If I were in health I could only be doing that, and that I may do now; the best thing in obedience is a regard to the will of God, and the way to that is to get our inclinations and aversions as much modified as we can." Some of his expressions were such as the following: " I would be waiting to see what God will do with me; it is good to say as Mr. Baxter, what, when, and where God pleases. If God should raise me up again I may finish some more of my papers, or God can make use of me to save a soul, and that will be worth living for. If God has no more service for me to do, through grace I am ready; it is a great mercy to me that I have no manner of fear or dread of death. I could if God please lay my head back and die without terror this afternoon or night; my chief supports are from my view of eternal things, and the interest I have in them. I trust all my sins are pardoned through the blood of Christ; I have no fear of dying; it would be my greatest comfort to lie down and sleep, and wake no more." Dr. Gibbons a short time before his death came into his room, and finding him alone sat down for conversation with him; he said not a word of what he had been or done in life, but his soul seemed swallowed up with gratitude and joy for the redemption of sinners by Jesus Christ. His visitor thought he realized the description of the apostle, " Whom having not seen ye love; in whom, though now ye see Him not, yet believing ye rejoice with joy unspeakable and full of glory."

So he continued to the close, rising into no ecstasies, nor sinking into any great depressions, in the full possession of his understanding, free from pain of body, comfortable in spirit. This was during the autumn of 1748. It was during the month of November that he was confined to his room, never to leave it any more. For three weeks he

continued in the state just described, tenderly attended
for the most part by Lady Abney or Mr. Parker.   The following extracts are from Mr. Parker's letters to the brother
of Dr. Watts, residing at Southampton, the first dated
November 24th, 1748 : " I wrote to you by the last post
that we apprehended my master very near his end, and
that we thought it not possible he should be alive when
the letter reached your hands ; and it will no doubt greatly
surprise you to hear that he still lives.   We ourselves are
amazed at it.   He passed through the last night in the main
quiet and easy, but for five hours would receive nothing
within his lips.   I was down in his chamber early in the
morning, and found him quite sensible.   I begged he would
be pleased to take a little liquid to moisten his mouth, and
he received at my hand three teaspoonsful, and has done
the like several times this day.   Upon inquiry he told me
he lay easy, and his mind was peaceful and serene.   I said
to him this morning that he had taught us how to live, and
was now teaching us how to die by his patience and composure, for he has been remarkably in this frame for several
days past.   He replied, ' Yes.'   I told him I hoped he ex-
perienced the comfort of these words, ' I will never leave
thee, nor forsake thee.'   He answered, ' I do.'   The ease
of body and calmness of mind which he enjoys is a great
mercy to him, and to us.   His sick chamber has nothing
terrifying in it.   He is an upright man, and I doubt not
that his end will be peace.   We are ready to use the
words of Job, and say, ' We shall seek him in the morning,
but he shall not be.'   But God only knows by whose
power he is upheld in life, and for wise purposes, no doubt.
He told me he liked that I should be with him.   All other
business is put off, and I am in the house night and day.
I would administer all the relief that is in my power.   He

is worthy of all that can be done for him. I am your very faithful and truly afflicted servant."

On the next day, November 25th, in the afternoon, aged seventy-four years, four months, and eight days, the gentle spirit of the Doctor passed away, and Mr. Parker wrote again to the same person : "At length the fatal news is come. The spirit of the good man, my dear master, took its flight from the body to worlds unseen and joys unknown yesterday in the afternoon, without a struggle or a groan. My Lady Abney and Mrs. Abney are supported as well as we can reasonably expect. It is a house of mourning and tears, for I have told you before now that we all attended upon him and served him from a principle of love and esteem. May God forgive us all, that we have improved no more by him, while we enjoyed him!" "May I be excused," says his biographer, "if I take the liberty of adding that I saw the corpse of this excellent man in his coffin, and observed nothing more than death in its aspect. The countenance appeared quite placid, like a person fallen into a gentle sleep, or such as the spirit might be supposed to leave behind it upon its willing departure to the celestial happiness. How justly might I have said at the moment I beheld his dead earth, as he does in an epitaph upon a pious young man, who was removed from our world after a lingering and painful illness :

> "So sleep the saints, and cease to groan,
>   When sin and death have done their worst :
> Christ has a glory like His own
>   Which waits to clothe their waking dust!"

And this was the manner in which "this silver cord was loosed, and this golden bowl broken."

They buried him, of course, in Bunhill Fields ; thither already had been borne the bodies of many of those who

had been his fellow-students, and his most familiar friends ;
and thither were to follow him at last many of those
friends who were for a few brief years to survive him.   It
was the *Campo Santo* of Nonconformity, the spot consecrated by the memories of the martyrs and confessors of
civil and religious liberty, and their tombs then were fresh.
Their graves and their memories were green and verdant.
Amidst the wilderness of indiscriminate tombs it is now
scarcely possible to decipher localities, dust has mingled
with dust, yet it would be scarcely possible to visit anywhere a spot where almost every mound recalled venerable
remains or in the course of years became haunted by such
tender and animating memories.   Bunhill Fields does not
possess the attractive and splendid tombs of *Père la Chaise*
or Munich, of Greenwood or Kensall Green, but it may be
with perfect certainty affirmed that none of these places
possess such a congregation of sainted sleepers, and such
consecrated dust.

The history of this pensive enclosure goes back to the
reign of Henry III.   It had been from a period even
anterior to this set apart as the exercising and training
ground for the archers and train-bands of the City ; indeed
it is probable, whether he knew it or not, that this is the
very spot to which Lord Lytton refers in some of the
earlier scenes of the " Last of the Barons," the archery-
ground of Finsbury ; a romantic and lovely spot, a very
easy walk from the quaint gabled houses of the old City
four hundred years since.   It was a spot surrounded by
gardens and orchards in the Manor of Finsbury or *Fens-*
bury, and on the borders of that extensive suburban tract,
the Moor Fields ; but when the Great Plague decimated
London, the Corporation set apart this field as a burial-
place for the poor.   It was a gentle acclivity, a rising spot

of ground, which affection had called the *Bon*hill, at a
time when the language of the country was very largely
held in possession by Norman influences and French
terms, as in innumerable instances mingled with Saxon.
Thus:

> In death divided from their dearest kin,
> This was a field to bury strangers in;
> Fragments from families untimely reft,
> Like spoils in flight, or limbs in battle left,
> Lay there* ———

The subsequent history of the place justifies another
characterization from the same poet:

> For they were there to this Siberia sent,
> Doomed in the grave itself to banishment.

As a humble cemetery for the purposes we have mentioned, it had been enclosed at the charge of the Corporation, but for this purpose it was not long needed; and
when the ravages of persecution succeeded to those of
disease, one Tyndall purchased it, principally for the interment of Dissenters, and it became known as Tyndall's
Burying Ground. The first interment in this second
epoch of its funereal history dates from the first distinctly
legible stone in the year 1668. Twenty years after this,
it received the beloved and revered remains of John
Bunyan; in the interim, many of those who had been
among the foremost religious actors, preachers, and writers
of the time came hither—Thomas Goodwin, Thomas
Manton, Joseph Caryl, Theophilus Gale, John Owen,
William Jenkyn, Henry Jessey, William Kiffin, Hanserd
Knollys, and many others. In this spot almost every
order of religious outlawed opinion finds some representa-

---

* Montgomery on the Cholera Mount of Sheffield.

tive : here reposes the active body of Daniel Defoe, and in
Bunhill Fields, but in a spot set apart to those of his
opinion, rests the founder of the Society of Friends, George
Fox ; and here that revered and holy woman, from whose
household in the Rectory of Epworth went forth the inspiration, as from her own life went forth the lives of the
prophet and poet of Methodism, Mrs. Susannah Wesley ;
here rest two well-beloved sweet singers, whose names are
found in all our hymn-books, Joseph Swain and Joseph
Hart. As the years passed along every one brought some
additional revenue to the wealth of the spot. Hither
came Dr. Gibbons, Watts' biographer, and, by-and-by,
John Gill, the author of the huge commentary, if wild in
fancy, still learned in all Rabbinical and Hebrew lore,
and John Macgowan, the author of the " Dialogues of
Devils ; " here rests Dr. Williams, the founder of the well-
known library, and donor of the scholarships connected
with it, and by this name we are reminded of the great
Arians who sleep very quietly here. Here lie Theophilus
Lindsay, Abraham Rees, Richard Price, Nathaniel Lardner,
and Thomas Belsham, all men of huge scholarship, whatever our estimate of their doctrines ; here lies, of another
order, the learned John Eames, the friend and fellow-
student of Dr. Watts, the friend and correspondent of Sir
Isaac Newton, and of whom Watts said that he was the most
learned man he ever knew ; Thomas Bradbury, Watts'
abusive and disingenuous traducer and adversary, found
the quiet he never permitted himself to find when living,
either in tranquil or troublesome times ; and hither, within
the memory of those living, came Matthew Wilks, quaint
and witty old preacher of the London Tabernacles, and his
fiery-hearted and earnest co-pastor, John Hyatt, and James
Upton, John Rippon, and the beloved and beautiful

Alexander Waugh and George Burder. The names we have mentioned are great, but a very small instalment from the list of those famous in holiness and scholarship and sanctified genius, to whom Bunhill Fields was the Machpelah of their lives. Indeed, until the opening of the Abney Park Cemetery, a place which derived its name and interest from its association with, and memories of, Dr. Watts, Bunhill Fields was the receptacle of every Nonconformist notability in the neighbourhood of London. It was as natural that those who had attained an eminence in its confession should receive sepulture there, as that the great statesman or poet should repose within the hallowed naves of Westminster. The significance of the spot, and the fact that it received amongst its other treasures all that was mortal of the subject of this memoir, seem to justify this lengthy loitering amongst its tombs.

Watts, by his will, directed that his remains should find their last resting-home in this place, amongst the fathers and brethren, many of whom he had so well known ; he also desired that it should be conducted as quietly as possible, but wished that his body should be attended to the grave by two Independent, two Presbyterian, and two Baptist ministers ; but an immense concourse of persons gathered, as was to be expected. Dr. Chandler gave the address at the grave, and Dr. David Jennings preached to his people the funeral sermon. Returning from the funeral, Dr. Benjamin Grosvenor was met by a friend, who said, "Well, Doctor, you have seen the end of Dr. Watts, and must soon follow him ; what think you of death ? " " Think of it !" replied he, " why, when death comes I shall smile on him if God smile on me." Other funeral sermons were preached, and they are in our possession, especially one by Dr. John Milner, of which Doddridge thought very highly,

and in whose house Oliver Goldsmith, a poor, simple young
man, his mind and heart full of worlds of shrewdness and
tenderness, for a long time lived as an usher.   To prevent
any laboured and too flattering an epitaph, which in those
days, indeed, there was plenty of cause to dread, from the
hands of partial friends, who certainly had none of the
graces of concision, Watts wrote his own modest memorial, and it was placed over his grave.   It reads as follows :

" Isaac Watts, D.D., pastor of a church of Christ in
London, successor to the Rev. Mr. Joseph Caryl, Dr. John
Owen, Mr. David Clarkson, and Dr. Isaac Chauncey, after
fifty years of feeble labours in the Gospel, interrupted by
four years of tiresome sickness, was at last dismissed to his
rest—
In uno Jesu omnia.

2 Cor. v. 8 : ' Absent from the body, and present with the
Lord.'   Col. iii. 4 : ' When Christ, who is my life, shall
appear, then shall I also appear with Him in glory.' "

" This monument, on which the above modest inscription
is placed, by order of the deceased, was erected, as a small
testimony of regard to his memory, by Sir John Hartopp,
Bart., and Dame Mary Abney."

But, shortly after his death, a monument was erected to
his memory in Westminster Abbey.   Another monument
erected in his chapel met with a singular fate : some years
since the chapel was pulled down, and all its properties
sold off.   John Astley Marsden, Esq., of Liscard Castle, in
Cheshire, passing through one of the London streets, saw
a marble tablet inscribed with the name of Dr. Watts ;
inquiring about its meaning, he found it was the very
tablet which had been set up behind his pulpit ; he purchased it as an interesting relic of a man for whom he had

a great reverence, he took it home to his residence in Cheshire, and upon his own ground he reared a church at his own expense, and there placed the old cast-aside monument, handing the church over in trust to the Congregational body. The inscription is that humble memorial which Watts himself had prepared, and to which we have referred. In addition, however, to these, a monument has been raised to his memory in Abney Park Cemetery, a cemetery which has succeeded to the reputation of Bunhill Fields as the resting-place of metropolitan Nonconformists, and is spread out upon the grounds where stood the house and park, the history of which, and its relation to the memory of Watts, we have given in an earlier part of this volume.

In 1861, principally through the active exertions of Mr. William Lankester, a monument was erected to his memory in his native town of Southampton. The statue, about eight feet high, which is three feet larger than life, is of white marble, and stands upon a pedestal of polished grey Aberdeen granite ; and the site selected has received since then the designation "Watts' Park." The movement for the erection of the monument received the co-operation of Churchmen as well as Nonconformists, and the president of the committee was Dr. Wigram, the Bishop of Rochester. The statue was uncovered by the Earl of Shaftesbury, July 17th, 1861, and the day was kept with great festivity in the town ;* it took the shape of a great local celebration in honour of a man who had conferred

---

* "Memorials, Historical, Descriptive, Poetical and Pictorial, Commemorative of the Inauguration of the Statue to Dr. Isaac Watts, in the Western Park, Southampton, by the Earl of Shaftesbury, July 17th, 1861." See also "The Proceedings connected with the Inauguration of the Memorial Statue to Dr. Isaac Watts, at Southampton, July 17th, 1861."

honour on the town by his life and writings. It is not
uninteresting to think of the change of public sentiment
since the day when the infant Isaac, in the arms of his
mother, was held up to the eyes of his father in the gaol
of the very town where, to the honoured memory of that
infant, there was offered up so large an ovation of respect,
in which not only the Mayor and Corporation, but
members, ministers, and prelates of that very Church
which had persecuted the father for his opinions, united.
It is a testimony to the change which has passed over
ecclesiastical opinion since that day.

Thus, some portion of the prophecy of Dr. Jennings in
his funeral sermon, from the text, "He being dead yet
speaketh," was fulfilled. "If I am not greatly deceived,
the same thing will be said of him in far distant ages that
is said of Abel in our text ; while he is now celebrating
the honours of God and of the Lamb in the new songs of
heaven, how many thousands of pious worshippers are this
day lifting up their hearts to God in the sacred songs that
he taught them upon earth ! Though his voice is not any
longer heard by us, yet his words, like those of the day and
night, are gone out to the end of the world. America and
Europe still hear him speak, and it is highly probable they
may continue to do so till Europe and America shall be
no more."

CHAPTER XVI.

Summary and Estimate of Prose Writings.

IN attempting any estimate of the prose writings of
Watts we give the first place to his educational works.
And without descending to adulation it may be fairly
questioned whether any one individual in English literature
has effected so much and such various work for the cause
of education as Isaac Watts. As we have seen, he gave a
system of logic to the universities, a very simple system,
but it broke up the old trammels and chains of mere verbal
logic, and taught students to look after, and how to look at
things. Johnson says: " Of his philosophical pieces his
' Logic' has been received into the universities, and therefore
wants no private recommendation. If he owes part of it to
Le Clerc, it must be considered that no man who undertakes merely to methodize or illustrate a system pretends
to be its author. Few books," continues Johnson, " have
been perused by me with greater pleasure than his ' Improvement of the Mind,' of which the radical principles may
indeed be found in Locke's ' Conduct of the Understanding,'
but they are so expanded and magnified by Watts as to
confer upon him the merit of a work in the highest degree
useful and pleasing. Whoever has the care of instructing
others may be charged with deficiency in his duty if this

book is not recommended." And in another paragraph of his memoir Johnson says: " For children he condescended to lay aside the scholar, the philosopher, and the wit, to write little poems of devotion and systems of instruction adapted to their wants and capacities from the dawn of reason through its gradations of advance in the morning of life. Every man acquainted with the common principles of human action will look with veneration on the writer who is at one time combating Locke, and in another making a catechism for children in their fourth year ; a voluntary descent from the dignity of science is perhaps the hardest lesson that humility can teach."

There is, indeed, scarcely a department of knowledge, however simple, to which he did not descend ; there is scarcely a region of thought, however subtle, through which he did not familiarly move. We have a volume on the " Art of Reading, Writing, and Pronouncing English," this is for the very youngest students ; and for the same age we have his First and Second Catechisms, and his " Divine and Moral Songs ; " we have his work on " Astronomy, Geography, and the Use of the Globes," and the " Compendium of the Assembly's Catechism, with Proofs," and his most charming and rememberable " Catechism of Scripture History," a large and yet most compendious volume : and thus we reach the period of life when he prepares the mind for its graver studies and more serious exploits.

The " Logic " is easy and delightful reading, and yet sets in order, disciplines, marshals, and reviews mental materials so admirably that it may be read with great profit as well as pleasure. When Lord Barrington told Watts that he had a purpose to read it through once every year, he said no extravagant thing. It brings the mind back to its simplicity ; it is not, and does not profess to be, a science of mind or analysis of method, or the laws of thought, but it is a treatise on logic, understanding by that term not so much the pushing inquiry into unexplored domains and fields, as the. setting forth the grammar of thought, the principles of numeration, by which a knowledge of the contents of the mind may be obtained, which is surely the true idea of logic. The affluence of illustrations and references is very great, these occur easily and rapidly, they are gathered up as a reaper gathers up a sheaf. In its method it reminds us somewhat of Bacon's "Novum Organum," for in every chapter, and every discrimination, illustration, and distinction, occur instances unfolding the intention of the author, and we venture to think that no logic has appeared since so well calculated to make a clear and honest mind. The characteristics of the "Logic" of Watts are very admirably summed up by Tissot, of Dijon, in his preface to a translation published in Paris, 1848: " Il y a aussi plus de méthode et de clarté peut-être dans la logique de Watts que dans celle d'Arnaud. Le bon sens Anglais, le sens des affaires, celui de la vie pratique, s'y révèle à un très haut degré, tandis que le sens spéculatif d'un théologien passablement scolastique encore est plus sensible dans *l'Art de Penser*. Dr. Watts a su être complet; sans être excessif, il a touché très convenablement tout ce qui devait l'être, et s'est toujours arrêté au point précis où plus de profondeur nuit à la clarté."*

As the " Logic" is a methodical and orderly arrangement

* " There is also perhaps more method and clearness in the logic of Watts than in that of Arnauld. The good English sense—the business faculty—that of practical life, repeats itself here in the highest degree ; whilst the speculative mind of a tolerably scholarly théologian is yet more full in *the art of thinking*. Now Watts is complete without being extravagant ; he has touched very adequately all that is necessary, and he always stops at the very precise point where depth might have injured transparency."

of those principles which give conduct to the understanding, as we have called it a grammar rather than an etymology of the laws of thought, a setting forth of their necessary conditions of thinking, rather than an inquiry into their first principles, so his "Improvement of the Mind" is an advance in the education of the character. The "Logic" is a code of principles, the "Improvement of the Mind" the illustration of those principles in their practice and action. No book can be better fitted to strengthen and direct the mind in the first years of mind-life. Is it ever read now? Is there an edition of it in circulation now? Are there many youths who would have patience to read it now? And yet no work has taken its place. It also, like the "Logic," is fertile in illustrations of all that the author desires to convey; every means by which the mind can be enlarged or strengthened is dwelt upon; here there seems to be no unnecessary diffuseness, but a compact presentation. The style is apothegmatical, and rather colloquial than rhetorical, and it leaves upon the mind of the reader the impression of a large world of wealth in the mind of the author of which its pages are the mere fragments and indications. There is a wisdom which rules men's lives and acts in their minds unconsciously, and ages and times vary in the method pursued for the attainment of knowledge. Perhaps, in the times in which we live the method is very much out of sight, and men become wise in spite of themselves, the faculties of character are sharpened and made intense by friction. It may also be said that character is not so much the result of certain rules laid down for practice, as the inevitable pressure of certain conditions from which it cannot well escape; life educates men more than books, and the sharp collision of society and its rough usages more than rules derived from writers. All this is true; but still some men continue to preach, and others continue to hear, it is to be supposed under the impression that the preaching and the hearing are not altogether in vain; and it is a very desirable thing frequently to draw out into the light certain principles, to give to minds, so to speak, a pictorial resemblance of the idea.

It is so in the "Improvement of the Mind," the very subjects are suggestive: general rules to obtain knowledge, —the five methods of improvement compared—rules relating to observation—books and reading—judgment of books—living instruction by teachers—learning a language —of knowing the sense of writers and speakers—conversation—of disputes in general—the Socratical way of disputation—forensic disputes—academic or scholastic disputes—study or meditation—of fixing the attention— of enlarging the capacity of the mind—of improving the memory—of determining questions—of inquiring into causes and effects—of the sciences and their use. Then follows the second part, which was posthumous; hitherto the mind has been supposed to be attaining, now it is itself communicating, and here are discussions on methods of teaching and reading lectures—of an instructive style—of convincing of truth or delivering from error—of the use and abuse of authority—of managing the prejudices of men—of instruction by preaching—of writing books for the public, etc. etc. And beneath all these subjects is spread out a mass of wise and useful observations, the result, the reader thinks, of a life of earnest and careful study. A wise and candid judgment pervades every page. A confidence in the writer as in one who is not writing merely, but who is giving to the reader a portion of himself, grows in the mind. Watts was himself an exceedingly careful student. We have seen how his practice was to condense or to amplify the volumes or the pages he him-self read. He recommended this plan to be followed with the nobler pieces of composition, and such as it seemed desirable to make the heirlooms of the mind.

We have now lying before us the "Ecclesiastics" of John Wilkins, the Bishop of Chester. The volume bears every internal evidence of being the property of Dr. Watts: it is interleaved, and in addition to the varied and singular learning of the book itself, in the handwriting of the Doctor there is a perfect storehouse of references, exhibiting the amazing world of knowledge over which his mind travelled; and not merely references, but frequently some condensed expression of sentiment and opinion. We ought to refer to this very valuable little manuscript volume again. It often seems surprising that volumes such as these have fallen into such neglect; but they only share the fate of multitudes of others in various departments equally worthy. The number of those who gaze upon the true regalia of literature is very small; our times delight in startling contrasts, antitheses and paradoxes, and illustra-tions frequently rather remarkable for their brilliancy than for their solid and abiding persuasiveness. The literature of every time has its vices and its virtues; writers even exercising a far stronger fascination and spell over their day than Watts are very seldom referred to now, they are names and little more. They are like extinct creations of other times, a kind of dodo, a being very near to our own day, but yet only known by a specimen preserved in a museum. Thus probably the two works to which we have referred will have few more readers. Yet safer and wiser charts for travelling the seas of knowledge were never pre-pared, and while they breathe a fine mental independence, a freshness wafted from undiscovered realms, they are

eminently free from all that rashness and audacity of speculation which some have chosen to regard as a pursuit of
knowledge, or as adding to the spoils of the understanding.
He kept his students within the bounds of the knowable
and provable, and if he trampled upon the ridiculous logic
which had for years held the mind of Europe in chains, by
the fetters of words which had no kind of sense either in
the heavens or the earth, and resolutely determining that
words could only be valuable when they were the real
signs of things, and things of which something could be
known ; on the other hand, he gave no encouragement to
licentiousness of thought, which is as dangerous to the
well-being of the intelligence as the servility of opinion. So
that, on the whole, whatever advances and attainments we
have made since, we may believe that for the discipline
and tutelage of the young, a better finger-post could scarcely
be set up upon the highways of knowledge than Watts'
"Logic ;" a better and more living guide a young man can
scarcely have through the cities of instruction than his
" Improvement of the Mind."

Among the pieces of our author which are least known
are the essays variously published under the title of " Re-
liquiæ Juveniles ; Miscellaneous Thoughts in Prose and
Verse, on Natural, Moral, and Divine Subjects, written
chiefly in younger years." These were published in 1734,
and dedicated to the Countess of Hertford. A similar
volume is the " Remnants of Time Employed in Prose and
Verse ; or, Short Essays and Composures on Various Subjects." All of these are very pleasing essays, in which the
writer gives a more than ordinary rein to his fancy : the
pieces are in prose and verse, and they display a considerable amount of humour ; the subjects are very various,
and display the purely literary excursions of the author's

mind. The reader will be so far interested as to enjoy some few selections. To dwell at length upon the characteristics of the essays, or to indulge in any lengthy citation, would be like writing a dissertation upon Johnson's "Rambler," or Addison's "Spectator;" indeed, there is very much of the Christian Rambler and the Christian Spectator in these papers: brief essays on manners, on certain vices or defects of character, conveyed after the usage of the time beneath names sheltered under a Greek or Latin etymology; sometimes a graceful meditation upon a text of Scripture, and sometimes a poem. We have ourselves found these essays always fresh and interesting, possessing much of the spirit and vivacity and philosophical meditativeness of Cowley, with a perpetual suffusion of Christian sentiment and doctrine, and the whole exhibiting the vigilance of the author's eye, and the active usefulness of his mind.

THE SKELETON.

"Young Tramarinus was just returned from his travels abroad, when he invited his uncle to his lodgings on a Saturday noon. His uncle was a substantial trader in the City, a man of sincere goodness, and of no contemptible understanding; Crato was his name. The nephew first entertained him with learned talk of his travels. The conversation happening to fall upon anatomy, and speaking of the hand, he mentioned the carpus and the metacarpus, the joining of the bones by many hard names, and the periosteum which covered them, together with other Greek words, which Crato had never heard of. Then he showed him a few curiosities he had collected; but

anatomy being the subject of their chief discourse, he
dwelt much upon the skeletons of a hare and a partridge.
'Observe, sir,' said he, 'how firm the joints! how nicely
the parts are fitted to each other! how proper this limb for
flight, and that for running; and how wonderful the whole
composition!' Crato took due notice of the most considerable parts of those animals, and observed the chief
remarks his nephew made; but being detained there two
hours without a dinner, assuming a pleasant air, he said,
'I wish these rarities had flesh upon them, for I begin to
be hungry, nephew, and you entertain me with nothing
but bones.' Then he carried home his nephew to dinner
with him, and dismissed the jest.

"The next morning his kinsman Tramarinus desired him
to hear a sermon at such a church, 'For I am informed,'
said he, 'the preacher will be my old schoolmaster.' It
was Agrotes, a country minister, who was to fulfil the service of the day; an honest, a pious, and a useful man, who
fed his own people weekly with Divine food, composed his
sermons with a mixture of the instructive and the pathetic,
and delivered them with no improper elocution. Where
any difficulty appeared in the text or the subject, he
usually explained it in a very natural and easy manner,
to the understanding of all his parishioners. He para-
phrased on the most affecting parts largely, that he might
strike the conscience of every hearer, and had been the
happy means of the salvation of many; but he thought
thus with himself, 'When I preach at London I have
hearers of a wiser rank, I must feed them with learning
and substantial sense, and must have my discourse set
thick with distinct sentences and new matter.' He contrived, therefore, to abridge his composures, and to throw
four of his country sermons together to make up one for

the City, and yet he could not forbear to add a little Greek
in the beginning.   He told the auditors how the text was
to be explained ; he set forth the analysis of the words in
order, showed the *hoti* and the *dioti*—that is, that it was
so, and why it was so—with much learned criticism—all
of which he wisely left out in the country ; then he pronounced the doctrine distinctly, and filled up the rest of
the hour with the mere rehearsal of the general and special
heads ; but he omitted all the amplification which made
his performances in the country so clear and so intelligible,
so warm and affecting.   In short, it was the mere joints
and carcase of a long composure, and contained above
forty branches in it.   The hearers had no time to consider
or reflect on the good things which were spoken, or apply
them to their own consciences ; the preacher hurried their
attention so fast onward to new matters that they could
make no use of anything he said while he spoke it, nor
had they a moment for reflection, in order to fix it in their
memories and improve by it at home.

"The   young gentleman was somewhat out of countenance when the sermon was done, for he missed all that
life and spirit, that pathetic amplification, which impressed
his conscience when he was but a school-boy.   However,
he put the best face upon it, and began to commend the
performance.   'Was it not,' said he, 'sir, a substantial
discourse ?   How well connected all the reasons !   How
strong all the inferences, and what a variety and number
of them !'   'It is true,' said the uncle, 'but yet methinks
I want food here, and I find nothing but bones again.   I
could not have thought, nephew, you would have treated
me two days together just alike ; yesterday at home, and
to-day at church, the first course was Greek, and all the
rest mere skeleton.'"

GOD IN VEGETATION.

" Let us first consider this as it relates to the vegetable part of the creation. What a profusion of beauty and fragrancy, of shapes and colours, of smells and tastes, is scattered among the herbs and flowers of the ground, among the shrubs, the trees, and the fruits of the field ! Colouring in its original glory and perfection triumphs here ; red, yellow, green, blue, purple, with vastly more diversities than the rainbow ever knew, or the prism can represent, are distributed among the flowers and the blossoms. And what variety of tastes, both original and compounded, of sweet, bitter, sharp, with a thousand nameless flavours, are found among the herbs of the garden ! What an amazing difference of shapes and sizes appears among the trees of the field and forest in their branches and their leaves ! and what a luxurious and elegant distinction in their several fruits ! How very numerous are their distinct properties in their uses in human life ! And yet these two common elements, earth and water, are the only materials out of which they are all composed, from the beginning to the end of nature and time. Let the gardener dress for himself one field of fresh earth, and make it as uniform as he can ; then let him plant therein all the varieties of the vegetable world, in their roots or in their seeds, as he shall think most proper ; yet out of this common earth, under the droppings of common water from heaven, every one of these plants shall be nourished, and grow up in their proper forms ; all the infinity, diversity of shapes and sizes, colours, tastes, and smells, which constitute and adorn the vegetable world, would the climate permit, might be produced out of the same clods. What rich and surprising

wisdom appears in that Almighty Operator, who out of the
same matter shall perfume the bosom of the rose, and give
the garlic its offensive and nauseous powers; who from the
same spot of ground shall raise the liquorice and the worm-
wood, and dress the cheek of the tulip in all its glowing
beauties! What a surprise, to see the same field furnish
the pomegranate and the orange tree, with their juicy fruit,
and the stacks of corn with their dry and husky grains;
to observe the oak raised from a little acorn into its stately
growth and solid timber; and that pillars for the support of
future temples and palaces should spring out of the same
bed of earth that sent up the vine with such soft and
feeble limbs as are unable to support themselves! What
a natural kind of prodigy it is, that chilling and burning
vegetables should arise out of the same spot; that the fever
and frenzy should start up from the same bed where the
palsy and the lethargy lie dormant in their seeds! Is it
not exceeding strange that healthful and poisonous juices
should rise up, in their proper plants, out of the same common glebe, and that life and death should grow and thrive
within an inch of each other? What wondrous and inimitable skill must be attributed to that Supreme Power, that
First Cause, who can so infinitely diversify effects, where
the servile second cause is so uniform and always the same!
It is not for me in this place to enter into a long detail of
philosophy, and show how the minute fibres and tubes of
the different seeds and roots of vegetables take hold of,
attract, and receive the little particles of earth and water
proper for their own growth; how they form them at first
into their own shapes, sending them up aspiring above
ground by degrees, and mould them so as frame the stalks,
the branches, the leaves, and the buds of every flower, herb,
and tree. But I presume the world is too weary of sub-

stantial forms, and plastic powers, and names without ideas, to be persuaded that these mere creatures of fancy should ever be the operators in this wondrous work. It is much more honourable to attribute all to the design and long forethought of God the Creator, who formed the first vegetables in such a manner, and appointed their little parts to ferment under the warm sunbeams, according to such established laws of motion as to mould the atoms of earth and water which were near them in their own figure, to make them grow up into trunk and branches, which every night should harden into firmness and stability; and, again, to mould new atoms of the same element into leaves and bloom, fruit and seed, which last, being dropped into the earth, should produce new plants of the same likeness to the end of the world."

FOOD.

" If the food of which one single animal partakes be never so various and different, yet the same laws of motion which God has ordained in the animal world, convert them all to the same purposes of nourishment for that creature. Behold the little bee gathering its honey from a thousand flowers, and laying up the precious store for its winter food. Mark how the crow preys upon a carcase, anon it crops a cherry from the tree; and both are changed into the flesh and feathers of a crow. Observe the kine in the meadows feeding on a hundred varieties of herbs and flowers, yet all the different parts of their bodies are nourished thereby in a proper manner : every flower in the field is made use of to increase the flesh of the heifer, and to make beef for men ; and out of all these varieties there is a noble milky juice flowing to the udder, which provides nourishment for

young children.   So near akin is man, the lord of the creation, in respect of his body, to the brutes that are his slaves,
that the very same food will compose the flesh of both of
them, and make them grow up to their appointed stature.
This is evident beyond doubt in daily and everlasting
experiments.   The same bread-corn which we eat at our
tables will give rich support to sparrows and pigeons, to
the turkey and the duck, and all the fowls of the yard :
the mouse steals it and feeds on it in its dark retirement ;
while the hog in the sty, and the horse in the manger,
would be glad to partake.   When the poor cottager has
nursed up a couple of geese, the fox seizes one of them for
the support of her cubs, and perhaps the table of the land-
lord is furnished with the other to regale his friends.   Nor
is it an uncommon thing to see the favourite lap-dog fed
out of the same bowl of milk which is prepared for the
heir of a wealthy family, but which nature had originally
designed to nourish a calf.   The same milky material will
make calves, lap-dogs, and human bodies."

CHRIST AS A SUN.

" I cannot deny myself, in this place, the pleasure of pub-
lishing to the world a very beautiful resemblance, the first
hints and notices whereof I received formerly in conversation from my reverend and worthy friend Mr. Robert
Bragge, whereby the person of Christ as God-man in His
exalted state may be happily represented.   The sun in the
heavens is the most glorious of all visible beings : his
sovereign influence has a most astonishing extent through
all the planetary globes, and bestows light and heat upon
all of them.   It is the sun that gives life and motion to all

the infinite varieties of the animal world in the earth, air,
and water. It draws out the vegetable juices from the
earth, and covers the surface of it with trees, herbs, and
flowers. It is the sun that gives beauty and colour to all
the millions of bodies round the globe; by its pervading
power perhaps it forms minerals and metals under the
earth. Its happy effects are innumerable; they reach
certainly to everything that has life and motion, or that
gives life, support, or pleasure to mankind. Now suppose
God should create a most illustrious spirit, and unite it to
the body of the sun, as a human soul is united to a human
body : suppose this spirit had a perceptive power capacious
enough to become conscious of every sunbeam, and all the
influences and effects of this vast shining globe, both in its
light, heat, and motion, even to the remotest region; and
suppose at the same time it was able, by an act of its will,
to send out or withhold every sunbeam as it pleased, and
thereby to give light and darkness, life and death, in a
sovereign manner, to all the animal inhabitants of this our
earth, or even of all the planetary worlds. Such may be
the 'glorified human soul of our blessed Redeemer united
to His glorified body;' and perhaps His knowledge and
His power may be as extensive as this similitude represents, especially when we consider this soul and body as
personally united to the Divine nature, and as one with
God. Now this noble thought may be supported by such
considerations as these. As our souls are conscious of the
light, shape, motions, etc., of such distant bodies as the
planet Saturn or the fixed stars, because our eyes receive
rays from thence ; so may not a human soul united to a
body as easily be supposed to have a consciousness of anything, wheresoever it can send out rays or emit either fluids
or atoms from its own body ? May not the sun, for instance,

if a soul were united to it, become thereby so glorious a complex being, as to send out every ray with knowledge, and have a consciousness of everything wheresoever it sends its direct or reflected rays ?   And may not the human soul of our Lord Jesus Christ have a consciousness of everything wheresoever it can send direct or reflected rays from His own shining and glorified body ?   To add yet to the wonder, we may suppose that these rays may be subtle as magnetic beams, which penetrate brass and stone as easily as light doth glass ; and at the same time they may be as swift as light, which reaches the most amazing distance of several millions of miles in a minute.   By this means, since the light of the sun pervades all secret chambers in our hemisphere at once, and fills all places with direct and reflected beams, if consciousness belonged to all those beams, what a sort of omniscient being would the sun be ! I mean omniscient in its own sphere.   And why may not the human soul and body of our glorified Saviour be thus furnished with such an amazing extent of knowledge and power, and yet not be truly infinite ?   Let us dwell a little longer upon these delightful contemplations.   If a soul had but a full knowledge and command of all the atoms of one solid foot of matter, which according to modern philosophy is infinitely divisible, what strange and astonishing influences would it have over this world of ours ?   What confusions might it raise in distant nations, sending pestilential streams into a thousand bodies, and destroying armies at once ?   And it might scatter benign or healing and vital influences to as large a circumference.   If our blessed Lord, in the days of His humiliation, could send virtue out of Him to heal a poor diseased woman, who touched the hem of His garment with a finger, who knows what healing atoms, or what killing influences, He may send from His dwelling in glory to the remotest distances of our world, to execute His Father's counsels of judgment or mercy ? It is not impossible, so far as I can judge, that the soul of Christ in its glorified state may have as much command over our heavens and our earth, and all things contained in them, as our souls in the present state have over our own limbs and muscles to move them at pleasure. Let us remember that it is now found out, and agreed in the new philosophy of Sir Isaac Newton, that the distances are prodigious to which the powerful influence of the sun reaches in the centre of our planetary system. It is the sun who holds and restrains all the planets in their several orbits, and keeps in those vast bodies of Jupiter and Saturn in their constant revolutions—one at the distance of 424 millions, and the other at the distance of 777 millions of miles— besides all the other influences it has upon everything that may live and grow in those planetary worlds. It is the sun who reduces the long wanderings of the comets back again near to himself from distances more immensely great than those of Saturn and Jupiter. And why may not the human nature of our Lord Jesus Christ, both in soul and body, have a dominion given Him by the Father larger than the sun in the firmament ? Why may not the Son of God be endued with an immediate consciousness and agency to a far greater distance ? Thus if we conceive of the human soul of Christ, either in the amazing extent of its own native powers or in the additional acquirements of a glorified state, we see reason to believe that its capacities are far above our old usual conceptions, and may be raised and exalted to a degree of knowledge, power, and glory suitable and equal to His operations and offices, so far as they are attributed to His human nature in the word of God."

APPARENT FOLLY REAL WISDOM.

" This very man, this Gelotes, a few days ago, was carried by his neighbour Typiger, to see a gentleman of his acquaintance ; they found him standing at the window of his chamber, moving and turning round a glass prism, near a round hole which he had made in the window-shutter, and casting all the colours of the rainbow upon the wall of the room.   They were unwilling to disturb him, though he amused himself at this rate for half an hour together, merely to please and entertain his eyesight, as Gelotes imagined, with the brightness and the strength of the reds and the blues, the greens and the purples, in many shifting forms of situation, while several little implements lay about him, of white paper and shreds of coloured silk, pieces of tin with holes in them, spectacles and burning-glasses.   When the gentleman at last spied his company, he came down and entertained them agreeably enough upon other subjects, and dismissed them.   At another time, Gelotes beheld the same gentleman blowing up large bubbles with a tobacco-pipe out of a bowl of water well impregnated with soap, which is a common diversion of boys.   As the bubbles rose, he marked the little changeable colours on the surface of them with great attention, till they broke and vanished into air and water.   He seemed to be very grave and solemn in this sort of recreation, and now and then smiled to see the little appearances and disappearances of colours, as the bubbles grew thinner towards the top, while the watery particles of it ran down along the side to the bottom, and the surface grew too thin and feeble to include the air, then it burst to pieces and was lost.   ' Well,' says Gelotes to his friend, ' I did not think you would have carried me into the acquaintance of a madman ; surely he can never be right in his senses who wastes his hours in such fooleries as these. Whatsoever good opinion I had conceived of a gentleman of your intimacy, I am amazed now that you should keep up any degree of acquaintance with him, when his reason is gone and he is become a mere child. What are all these little scenes of sport and amusement, but proofs of the absence of his understanding ? Poor gentleman! I pity him in his unhappy circumstances; but I hope he has friends to take care of him under this degree of distraction.' Typiger was not a little pleased to see that his project, with regard to his neighbour Gelotes, had succeeded so well; and when he had suffered him to run on at this rate for some minutes, he interrupted him with a surprising word : ' This very gentleman,' says he, ' is the great Sir Isaac Newton, the first of philosophers, the glory of Great Britain, and renowned among the nations. You have beheld him now making these experiments over again by which he first found out the nature of light and colours, and penetrated deeper into the mysteries of them than all mankind ever knew before him. This is the man, and these his contrivances, upon which you so freely cast your contempt, and pronounce him distracted. You know not the depth of his designs, and therefore you censured them all as fooleries, whereas the learned world has esteemed them the utmost reach of human sagacity.'

" Gelotes was all confusion and silence ; whereupon Typiger proceeded thus : ' Go now and ridicule the lawgiver of Israel, and the ceremonies of the Jewish Church, which Moses taught them ; go, repeat your folly and your slanders, and laugh at these Divine ceremonies, merely because you know not the meaning of them, go, and affront the God of Israel, and reproach Him for sending

Moses to teach such forms of worship to the Jews.   There is not the least of them but was appointed by the Greatest of Beings, and has some special design and purpose in the eye of Divine Wisdom.   Many of them were explained by the Apostle Paul, in his letter to the Hebrews, as types and emblems of the glories and blessings of the New Testament ; and the rest of them, whose reason has not been discovered to us, remain, perhaps, to be made known at the conversion of the Jews, when Divine light shall be spread over all the ancient dispensations, and a brighter glory diffused over all the rites and forms of religion which God ever instituted among the race of Adam.' "

A PLEA FOR CHRISTIANIZING HORACE.

" It is a piece of ancient and sacred history which Moses informs us of, that when the tribes of Israel departed from the land of Egypt, they borrowed of their neighbours gold and jewels by the appointment of God, for the decoration of their sacrifices and solemn worship when they should arrive at the appointed place in the wilderness.   God Himself taught His people how the richest of metals which had ever been abused to the worship of idols might be purified by the fire, and being melted up into a new form, might be consecrated to the service of the living God, and add to the magnificence and grandeur of His tabernacle and temple.   Such are some of the poetical writings of the ancient heathens ; they have a great deal of native beauty and lustre in them, and through some happy turn given them by the pen of a Christian poet may be transformed into Divine meditations, and may assist the devout and pious soul in several parts of the Christian life and worship.   Amongst all the rest of the

Pagan writers, I know none so fit for this service as the odes of Horace, as vile a sinner as he was. Their manner of composure comes nearer the spirit and force of the Psalms of David than any other; and as we take the devotions of the Jewish king, and bring them into our Christian churches, by changing the scene and the chronology, and superadding some of the glories of the Gospel so may the representation of some of the heathen virtues, by a little more labour, be changed into Christian graces, or, at least, into the image of them, so far as human power can reach. One day, musing on this subject, I made an experiment on the two last stanzas of Ode xxix, Book iii.

> ' Non est meum, si mugiat Africis
> Malus procellis, ad miseras preces
> Decurrere, et votis pacisci,
> Ne Cypriæ Syriæque merces
>
> Addant avaro divitias mari ;
> Dum me, biremis præsidio scaphæ,
> Nudum per Ægeos tumultus
> Aura ferat, geminusque Pollux.'

THE BRITISH FISHERMAN.

> Let Spain's proud traders, when the mast
> Bends groaning to the stormy blast,
> Run to their beads with wretched plaints,
> And vow and bargain with their saints,
> Lest Turkish silks or Tyrian wares
>   Sink in the drowning ship,
> Or the rich dust Peru prepares,
> Defraud their long projecting cares,
> And add new treasures to the greedy deep.
>
> My little skiff that skims the shores,
> With half a sail and two short oars,
> Provides me food in gentler waves ;
> But if they gape in watery graves
> I trust the Eternal Power, whose hand
>   Has swelled the storm on high,
> To waft my boat and me to land,
> Or give some angel swift command
> To bear the drowning sailor to the sky."

A work like this would be incomplete if it did not attempt some general estimate, however feeble, of our author's works, which are, however, so various that it is difficult to bring their relation to their author's mind beneath one classification. The remark Dr. Jennings made in his funeral sermon is simply just, when he says he " questions whether any author before Dr. Watts ever appeared with a reputation on such a variety of subjects as he has, both as a prose writer and a poet. However," he adds, "this I may venture to say, there is no man now living of whose works so many have been diffused at home and abroad, which are in such constant use, and translated into such a variety of languages, many of which I doubt not will remain more durable monuments of his great talents than any representation I can make of them, though it were to be graven on pillars of brass. Thus did he shine as an ingenious man and a scholar."

This circumstance of *the variety of his writings* constitutes them an element of his character : he was more various than intense, acute rather than profound. There are some of his works upon which we need not permit ourselves to be detained, they illustrate his readiness in turning to every kind of labour which seemed to give the promise of usefulness, for usefulness was evidently in everything the object he set before himself. Regarded by the immense apparatus now at hand for every kind of mental exercise Watts' labours do some of them seem needless ; but regarded from his own age, it appears as if he created, originated, and gave effect to almost every department of religious or improving knowledge. If the reader looks round the literary horizon of that day, he will learn rightly to estimate the benefits conferred by this writer ; and these works, the smallest, the most inferior of his mental exercises, were not one of them a mere compilation, they were all the emanations of that perpetually active mind, which, whether the body were well or ill, must be employed for some useful object and end. None of his books were made out of other books, excepting, indeed, so far as almost every volume must imply the knowledge of a subject and the mind of an author; and at the same time it must be said that some of his books for the young have been dropped but not surpassed; they might still furnish the best hints and the best arrangements for obtaining and imparting knowledge.

Being a literary man, Watts falls beneath a class of observations which are not either necessary or applicable in forming an estimate of almost any of his brethren, such as Howe, or Jacomb, or Bradbury, or, indeed, any of the writers of his order or day. The *wisdom* of his mind was remarkable; it was " a city, built four square." In this useful purpose, which he ever kept before him, whatever charges may be preferred against him on the score of the indulgence of fancy (and many of his writings reveal how capable he was of such excursions), he kept his mind singularly free from the literary vanities of his times, and his times as singularly illustrate at once the vanity and the glory of literature. If anybody would know what vanities there were, let him take down the volumes of the Athenian Oracle,* and he will find few other volumes which will

* " The Athenian Oracle, being an entire collection of all the valuable Questions and Answers in the old Athenian Mercurys, intermixed with many cases in Divinity, History, Philosophy, Mathematics, Love, and Poetry, and never before Published," etc. 4 vols. Printed for Andrew Bell, at the Cross Keys.

" Athenian Sport; or, Two Thousand Paradoxes Merrily Argued, by a Member of the Athenian Society."

" Memoirs for the Ingenious; containing several Curious Observations in Philosophy, Mathematics, Physic, Philology, and other Arts and give so lively an impression of the literary folly of those times. Old Samuel Wesley, John Wesley's father, did not disdain to contribute largely to those pages; they are affluent in absurdities, while they have a show of learned ignorance. Select a few; most of the essays are in the way of question and answer. "Balaam being a Moabite, how could he understand the ass speaking to him in Hebrew? How came the two disciples to know Moses and Elias on the mount? I am resolved to go round the earth on foot; I desire to know whether my head or my feet will travel the most, and how much the one more than the other? Whether or no there is a vacuum? Whether it is more proper to say the soul contains the body, or the body the soul? Whether the quadrature of the circle be possible? Pray, why does *a n d* not spell *t u m? t h e, m e d?* etc. etc. Whether Adam was a giant? How a silkworm lives when it has left off eating and is enclosed in its web? Whether it is prudent to live in a room haunted by spirits? Whether, since mermen and mermaids have more of the human shape than other fishes, they may be thought to have more reason? Where extinguished fire goes to? Where was the land of Nod? How is it the spaniel knows its master's horse? Whether a finite creature is capable of enduring infinite loss?" etc. etc.

These volumes, perhaps, constitute the most amazing collection of nonsense in our own or any other language; nor are they without a certain value as illustrating, not only the time, then in possession of men, but the ridiculous way in which they used it. Of course there are questions, and many of them, of a more grave and serious character, but for the most part they are the very soap-bubbles of the

Sciences, in Miscellaneous Letters." Printed for H. Rhodes, and for J. Harris, at the Arrow, in the Poultry.

most foppish and foolish imaginations, the most undisci-
plined and frequently prurient and indecent fancies.   The
indulgence in these was quite a phase of the intellectual
life of the time.   A singular chapter in the curiosities
of literature and science a reader may find in such volumes
as the " Philosophical Conferences of France ;" * and the
vanities of theology were quite equal to the vanities of
literature, as may be seen in the innumerable productions
of the time.

   With a mind so disposed to imaginative excursions,
it is quite worthy of notice that Watts preserved a
wise balance of all his powers and faculties ; he lived
on the confines of the age of the wildest mysticism our
literature has known.   From some words in his works
he appears to have been well acquainted with the writings
of Henry More, and also to have entertained for them that
reverence and respect which assuredly many of them command ; but from their singular and erratic fancies he kept
himself quite free.   Very strange are the matters with
which we find these old men entertained themselves,
affirming " that God of Himself is a dale of darkness,
were it not for the light of the Son ;" " that the star-
powers are Nature, and the star-circle the mother of all
things, from which all is, subsists, and moves ;" " that the
waters of the world are mad, which makes them rave and
run up and down, so as they do in the channels of the
earth ;" " that they, at last, shall be calcined into crystal ;"
" that the pure blood in man answers to the element of
fire in the great world, his heart to the earth, his mouth to

   * " Another Collection of Philosophical Conferences of the French
Virtuosi, upon Questions of all sorts for the Improving of Natural Knowledge, made in the Assembly of the Beaux Esprit of Paris, by the most
ingenious persons of that nation, rendered into English." Sold at the
George, in Fleet Street, and the Mitre, Middle Temple, 1665.

the Arctic pole; and "—but we will not finish this sublime
stretch of metaphysical imagination—"that there be two
kinds of fires, the one a cold fire and the other hot, and
that death is a cold fire;" "that everything has sense,
imagination, and a fiducial knowledge of God in it—
metals, meteors, and plants not excepted." Also the like
pleasant excursions of fancy are found in "Paracelsus," as
"that the stars are, as it were, the phials, or cucurbits, in
which meteorical sal, sulphur, and mercury are contained,
and that the winds are made out of these by the ethereal
vulcans, are blown forth out of these emunctories, as when
a man blows or breathes out of his mouth;" "that the stars
are, as it were, the pots in which the archeus, or heavenly
vulcan, prepares pluvious matter, which, exhaled from
thence, first appears in the form of clouds, and after con-
denses to rain;" "that hail and snow are the fruits of the
stars, proceeding from them as flowers and blossoms from
trees;" "that the lightning and thunder are, as it were,
the deciduous fruits of the ethereal stars;" "that the stars
eat and are nourished," etc. etc.

All this, and a good deal more to the like purpose. Since
the beginning of the world, men have asked of themselves
and others strange questions, like those Southey discovered
in Luys de Escobar: "When God made dresses for Adam
and Eve, how did He get the skins of which those dresses
were made, seeing that beasts were not yet killed?" "Perhaps," says the respondent, "He made skins on purpose."
"Why are there three persons in the Trinity rather than
four or five?" "St. Cosmas and St. Damian cut off a black
man's leg and fastened it on a white man; which will have
the leg at the resurrection?" "How did Adam learn
Hebrew?" Queer curiosities these, all of which will remind the reader of the madness of Elinora Melorina, a

lady of Mantua, who, being fully persuaded she was married to a king, would kneel down and talk with him, as
if he had then been present with his retinue.   Nay, if she
by any chance found a piece of glass upon a dunghill, or if
she came upon a piece of oyster-shell or tin, or any such
thing that would glisten in the sunshine, she would say it
was a jewel sent from her lord and husband, and upon this
account she would fill her cabinet full of this kind of rubbish.   The cabinets of the mystics, amidst some worthier
matter, are full of the kind of rubbish we have quoted
above, which, when instanced as solutions of things psychi-
cal or physical, seem to be as satisfactory as the old story of
the foolish person who, riding an ass to the pond to drink
by the light of the moon, and some clouds intervening, and
hiding the moon while the ass was drinking, arrived at the
grave conclusion that the ass had swallowed up the moon,
and took it clean out of being.   When such grave problems
and questions are the result of so much of fasting and
devotion, they only remind us of the question preferred
by a monk on one occasion to a higher Church dignitary :
" How many keys did Christ give to Peter ? " which brought
the satisfactory reply, that " he ought to prepare himself
by a course of physic for such grave, sweet, and savoury
questions ! "   Illustrative as they are of the literary vanities
and follies of the time, follies to which even scholarly
clergymen and eminent writers lent themselves, and as
illustrating also not only the freedom of Watts from such
epidemical foolishness, but the work he did in calling the
mind to healthful methods of thought, the writer trusts
their quotation here may be forgiven.

He appears to have preserved his mind in great stillness.
It is the quiet and still mind which is wise and prudent ;
and, like Henry More, to whom we have referred. his life

would repeat what that great man was wont to say, " In the more peaceful spirit, when it is also a quick and perceptive one, will always reside those faculties which are to the soul vision and power. In the deep and calm mind alone, in a temper clear and serene, such as is purged from the dregs, and devoid of the more disorderly tumults of the body, doth true wisdom or genuine philosophy, as in its own proper tower, securely reside." Hence the first great attribute of Watts' mind is *clearness*.

He ever kept before him a purpose of *usefulness*, alike in teaching men what to think about, and how to think about it ; indeed, it is simply true, as Gibbons has remarked, that *perspicuity* was eminently a feature of his intellect ; and it must be admitted that upon whatever he speaks or writes, he is always clearly to be understood—as we have seen, it was by no means a great virtue of his age, or of his contemporaries ; and if he discoursed upon the more lofty and difficult subjects of thought or philosophy, they seem to acquire clearness in their passage through his mind. He did not crowd words upon each other, and images of every order were used by him, not to add to the splendour of a paragraph, or to set off a division, but for the purpose of reflecting light on the reader's mind. He has dwelt himself upon the prime importance of perspicuity. In his " Improvement of the Mind," he says : " He that would gain a happy talent for the instruction of others must know how to disentangle and divide his thoughts, if too many are ready to crowd into one paragraph ; and let him rather speak three sentences distinctly and clearly, which the hearer receives at once with his ears and his soul, than crowd all the thoughts into one sentence, which the hearer has forgotten before he can understand it." It is a prime virtue in Watts' style that it is clear ; it ought to be a chief virtue in every writer. In him it illustrated the character of his mind. He seemed even to be impatient of the dark and obscure, and he never would permit himself to repose near the absolutely incomprehensible without attempting in some way to understand it ; so, also, as he attempts to express his mind upon any subject, his sentences instantly appear to be the very windows of the intellect. And this accounts for that other noticeable characteristic of his style —*its perfect ease.* There was smoothness and grace, the entire absence of the turgid and the bombastic; his sentences flowed along in happy harmony. Very frequently such a style conveys the impression that a man has nothing to say, when, perhaps, it is by immense labour, and by the study of the finest writers, and by conversation, that he has attained to that grace and natural ease of manner in which all who listen or who read are instantly able to apprehend the meaning. Thus he himself translates his favourite Horace :

> Smooth be your style, and plain and natural,
> To strike the sins of Wapping or Whitehall;
> While others think this easy to attain,
> Let them but try, and with their utmost pain,
> They'll sweat and strive to imitate in vain.

Another attribute, to which Gibbons alludes, in Watts' style is his *dignity,* especially in the use of his metaphors and in the restraint he puts upon himself in his most ardent and animated passages. A wise use of the passions is a marked characteristic of his writings, as he says, " Did the Great God ever appoint statues for His ambassadors to invite sinners to His mercy ; words of grace written upon brass or marble would do the work almost as well; where the preachers are stone no wonder if the hearers are motionless." And in a fine passage in which he reprobates the philosophy of the Earl of Shaftesbury, under the name of Rhapsodus, who affirms that neither the fear of future punishment, nor the hope of future reward, can possibly be called good affections, Watts exclaims :

" Go, dress up all the virtues of human nature in all the beauties of your oratory, and declaim aloud on the praise of social virtue and the amiable qualities of goodness, till your hearts or lungs ache, among the looser herds of mankind, and you will ever find, as your *heathen fathers* have done before you, that the wild appetites and passions of men are too violent to be restrained by such mild and silken language. You may as well build up a fence of straw and feathers to resist a cannon-ball, or try to quench a flaming granado with a shell of fair water, as hope to succeed in these attempts. But an eternal heaven and an eternal hell carry a Divine force and power with them. This doctrine, from the mouth of Christian preachers, has begun the reformation of multitudes. This Gospel has recovered thousands among the nations from iniquity and death. They have been awakened by these awful scenes to begin religion, and afterwards their virtue has improved itself into superior and more refined principles and habits by Divine grace, and risen to high and eminent degrees, though not to consummate state. The blessed God knows human nature better than *Rhapsodus* doth, and has throughout His Word appointed a more proper and more effectual method of address to it by the passions of hope and fear, by punishments and rewards."

His *ideas* are large and ample ; thoughts thronged through his pages. Admirable as his prose is, he writes still like a poet, and he speaks of the value of poetry as not a mere amusement or the embroidery of the mind, he says how it " brightens the fancy with a thousand beautiful images,

how it enriches the soul with great and sublime sentiments
and refined ideas, and fills the memory with a noble variety
of language, it teaches the art of describing well, of
painting everything to the life, and presenting the pleasing
and frightful scenes of nature and providence, vice and
virtue, in their proper charms and horrors ; it assists the
art of persuasion, leads to a pathetic mode of speech and
writing, and adds life and beauty to conversation."

And hence his style is so *attractive ;* it has often been
an enjoyment to us to turn over the pages of his prose
writings. What a variety of topics is presented to us in his
interesting inquiry " Concerning Space," and how interesting his treatment makes the discussion, however abstract
the topic. It is the same with his philosophic essays on
" Innate Ideas," and on the " Nature of Substance," and in
that on the " Strength and Weakness of Human Reason."
His sermons, we have before said, have not the pomp
and glow of Jeremy Taylor, but they resemble, and certainly do not fall inferior to, those of John Donne, in a
quiet metaphysical subtlety and a happy use of images
supplied by fancy ; but let us select a few :

THE SOUL AND GOD.

" My soul is touched with such a Divine influence that it
cannot rest, while God withdraws, *as the needle trembles,
and hunts after the living loadstone."*

A SENSITIVE HEART.

" Nothing could displease Phronissa (so this good mother
is called) more than to hear a jest thrown upon natural
infirmities. She thought there was something sacred in
misery, and it was not to be touched with a rude hand."

IMPULSIVE CHRISTIANS.

" Such Christians as these (such who are weak and too much under the influence of their passions) live very much by sudden fits and starts of devotion, without that uniform and steady spring of faith and holiness which would render their religion more even and uniform, more honourable to God and more comfortable to themselves.   They are always high on the wing, or else lying moveless on the ground. They are ever in the heights or in the depths, travelling on the bright mountains with the songs of heaven on their lips, or groaning and labouring through the dark valleys, and never walking onward as on an even plain towards heaven."

THE FULFILMENT OF DIVINE PREDICTIONS.

" How easy it will be for our blessed Lord to make a full accomplishment of all His predictions concerning His kingdom ; salvation shall spread through all the tribes and ranks of mankind, as the lightning from heaven in a few moments would communicate a living flame through ten thousand lamps or torches placed in a proper situation and neighbourhood."

He had an eminent *power in description ;* the following meditation is a rich illustration of this.   The whole meditation is far too long to quote—his descriptions of the awakening life of leaves, and birds, and insects—but he closes :

THE FIRST OF MAY.

" 'Tis a sublime and constant triumph over all the intellectual powers of man, which the great God maintains every moment in these inimitable works of nature, in these impenetrable recesses and all mysteries of Divine art ; and the month of May is the most shining season of this triumph. The flags and banners of Almighty wisdom are now displayed round half the globe, and the other half waits the return of the sun to spread the same triumph over the southern world. The very sun in the firmament is God's prime minister in this wondrous world of beings, and he works with sovereign vigour on the surface of the earth, and spreads his influence deep under the clods to the very root and fibre, moulding them in their proper forms by Divine direction. There is not a plant, nor a leaf, nor one little branching thread above or beneath the ground, which escapes the eye or influence of this benefi- cent star. An illustrious emblem of the omnipresence and universal activity of the Creator."

The following strikes us as very pleasing:

ON DISTANT THUNDER.

" When we hear the thunder rumbling in some distant quarter of the heavens, we sit calm and serene amidst our business or diversions; we feel no terrors about us, and apprehend no danger. When we see the slender streaks of lightning play afar off in the horizon of an evening sky, we look on and amuse ourselves as with an agreeable spectacle, without the least fear or concern. But lo! the dark cloud rises by degrees; it grows black as night, and big with tempests; it spreads as it rises to the mid-heaven, and now hangs directly over us; the flashes of lightning grow broad and strong, and, like sheets of ruddy fire, they blaze terribly all round the hemisphere. We bar the doors and windows, and every avenue of light, but we bar them all in vain. The flames break in at every cranny, and threaten swift destruction; the thunder follows, bursting from the cloud with sudden and tremendous crashes; the voice of the Lord is redoubled with violence, and overwhelms us with terror; it rattles over our heads as though the whole house was broken down at once with a stroke from heaven, and was tumbling on us amain to bury us in the ruins. Happy the man whose hope in his God composes all his passions amid these storms of nature, and renders his whole deportment peaceful and serene amidst the frights and hurries of weak spirits and unfortified minds."

Many pages might be filled with such passages in which the compactness of the proverb, or the pleasantry of the fancy, or the richness of the description, is remarkable. It comes out of such characteristics as we have noticed, that he reformed the preaching of his day, especially as to the structure of sermons; it was the age of, what he calls very felicitously, "branching sermons;" and even John Howe, as both Robert Hall and Henry Rogers* have remarked, " far outwent many of his most extravagant contemporaries in minute and frivolous subdivision; we have sometimes heads arranged rank and file, half a score deep." Henry Rogers continues, " If any would wish to see the full extent to which Howe carried this fault, they may look into the ' scheme' (a very accurate one), which his publishers prefixed to the first edition of the ' Delighting in God,' and by the time the student has thoroughly digested and mastered that, he will find little difficulty I apprehend in any of the first books of Euclid." It was the characteristic of nearly all the great Puritan preachers before Watts. He speaks of some who would draw out a long rank of particulars in the same sermon under one general, and run up the number to eighteenthly! or seven and twentiethly! until they cut all

* Rogers' "Life of Howe," p. 476.

their sense into shreds, so that everything they say of anything is a new particular; and he says, he has sat under this preaching until he has thought of Ezekiel's vision in the valley full of bones, " behold they were very many and very dry." He adds, " A single rose bush, or a dwarf pear, with all their leaves, flowers, and fruit about them, have more beauty and spirit in themselves, and yield more food and pleasure to mankind, than the innumerable branches, boughs, and twigs of a long hedge of thorns." In the same manner he satirizes another kind of preaching, in which there are no breaks and pauses. " Is there no medium," he says, " between a sermon made up of sixty dry particulars, and a long loose declamation without any distinction of the parts of it? Must a preacher divide his works by the breaks of a minute watch, or let it run on incessantly like the flowing stream of sand in the hour-glass ? " And thus he inquires, " Can a long purling sound awaken a sleepy conscience ? Can you make the arrow wound where it will not stick ? Where all the discourse vanishes from the remembrance, can you imagine the soul to be profited or enriched ? When you brush over the closed eyelid with a feather, did you ever find it give light to the blind ? have any of your soft harangues, your continued threads of silken eloquence, ever raised the dead ?" Very happily he says, " Preachers talk reason and religion to their auditories in vain, if they do not make the argument so short as to come within their grasps, and give a frequent rest to their thoughts; they must break the Bread of Life into pieces to feed children with it, and part their discourse into distinct propositions, to give the ignorant a plain scheme of any one doctrine, and enable them to comprehend or retain it. The auditors of the first kind of preacher have some confusion in their knowledge, the hearers of the last have scarce any knowledge at all."

The reader will not fail to notice, in this nervous passage, the happy imagery by which the writer gives point to his ideas.

But that which we have said hitherto refers rather to the style, the vehicular frame-work in which Watts set forth his thoughts; it is more important to enter into the mind and spirit of the man; and, first, no attribute seems more remarkable than the seraphic *reverence* of his nature. It is not easy to mention a writer who more distinctly realises to the mind one of those six-winged seraphs Isaiah saw, who with twain covered his face, with twain his feet, and with twain stood ready to fly; Watts appeared ready for any flight; but reverence, an awful sense of the mysterious and inscrutable, governed every movement of his soul. The Unitarians have, with singular audacity, sought to drag him through the Serbonian bog of creedless Christianity.* It is a fine remark, quoted by Southey, that " such doubts as troubled him he subdued, not in a martial posture, but upon his knees." It is very certain that he had a large speculative disposition; he approached very near to the veil which hides from man the incommunicable light; there is not a line in his writings which displays a tendency towards Arianism. Towards the doctrine of Socinianism he does not condescend to give a single glance. His complaint was, and we apprehend it to be a more common one than even those who are troubled with it are aware, not that he could not believe all that is revealed, but that

---

* The matter, we suppose, is long since set at rest; it may be very distinctly set at rest by a study of Watts' works, discussing the great question of the Trinity. " Watts not a Socinian," by the Rev. S. Palmer, puts the matter in a popular and concise form; but when his monument was erected in Southampton, a lecture was delivered and published on " His Life, Character, and Religious Opinions," by the Rev. Edmund Kell, M.A., F.S.A., the late Unitarian minister of Southampton, in which the old exploded dishonest statements were all reiterated.

revelation had not conferred more light upon the subjects of even incomprehensible knowledge. But his prayer, his " solemn address to the great and ever-blessed God, upon what he had written concerning the great and ever-blessed Trinity," is certainly an extraordinary, a passionate and most humble utterance of an ardently devout mind. It is too lengthy for entire quotation, but some of the closing paragraphs will convey the spirit of the entire piece, and the whole may be read, if read in the spirit in which it was written, with profit to every one : " Blessed and faithful God, hast Thou not promised that ' the meek Thou wilt guide in judgment, the meek Thou wilt teach Thy way ?' Hast Thou not taught us by Isaiah, Thy prophet, that Thou wilt ' bring the blind by a way they know not, and wilt lead them in paths which they have not known ? ' Hast Thou not informed us by the prophet Hosea, that ' if we follow on to know the Lord, then we shall know Him ?' Hath not Thy Son, our Saviour, assured us, that our Heavenly Father will give His Holy Spirit to them that ask Him ? And is He not appointed ' to guide us into all truth?' Have I not sought the gracious guidance of thy Good Spirit continually ? Am I not truly sensible of my own darkness and weakness, my dangerous prejudices on every side, and my utter insufficiency for my own conduct ? Wilt Thou leave such a poor creature bewildered among a thousand perplexities, which are raised by the various opinions and contrivances of men, to explain Thy Divine Truth ? Help me, Heavenly Father, for I am quite tired and weary of these human explainings, so various and uncertain. When wilt Thou explain it to me Thyself, O my God, by the secret and certain dictates of Thy Spirit, according to the intimation of Thy Word ? Nor let any pride of reason, nor any affectation of novelty, nor any

criminal bias whatever, turn my heart aside from hearken-
ing to these Divine dictates of Thy Word and Thy Spirit.
Suffer not any of my native corruptions, nor the vanity of
my imagination, to cast a mist over my eyes while I am
searching after the knowledge of Thy mind and will, for
my eternal salvation.

"I entreat, O most merciful Father, that Thou wilt not
suffer the remnant of my short life to be wasted in such
endless wanderings in quest of Thee and Thy Son Jesus, as a
great part of my past days have been; but let my sincere
endeavours to know Thee, in all the ways whereby Thou
hast discovered Thyself in Thy Word, be crowned with
such success that my soul, being established in every
needful truth by Thy Holy Spirit, I may spend my remaining life according to the rules of Thy Gospel, and may, with
all the holy and happy creation, ascribe glory and honour,
wisdom and power, to Thee who sittest upon the throne,
and to the Lamb for ever and ever."

We have stated the matter fairly as in relation to Watts'
entireness of faith, but justice has not been done to Watts
in relation to that dilemma and agitation of public opinion
and sentiment which forced him into controversy. It was
not that he himself doubted, neither was it that he for
himself approached the confines of a discussion of which
it might be said—

> Dark with excessive light its skirts appear.

Arianism was vexing the church in general in England
in that age.* Many of the churches, especially those to
which Watts stood related, indicated a close proclivity to
Arian sentiment. The peculiar spirit of the times had

---

* This is illustrated and manifest by the writings of Waterland,
which are almost contemporary with the discussions of Watts.

created this degeneracy of sentiment; there was little of
what we are now accustomed to denominate practical
Christianity—the activities created by Methodism were
quite unknown. All over the country were Nonconformist
churches (nooks of retreat), where some learned, scholarly,
and philosophical minister was at the head of a class of
thoughtful minds. Numbers of them seemed to have
little to do but to think; the heart did not minister much
to the head in many instances. The Unitarianism of our
day was unknown. It thus represented very much the
high Arian sentiment of reverence to Christ without the
acknowledgment of His Godhead. The hymns of Watts
abound in expressions of praise to Christ and to the
Holy Spirit. He was called upon to vindicate that which
he himself had done; he was called upon to defend that
whole scheme of doctrine which accepted the Three Persons
in the Divine Godhead. Perhaps the defect in all such
efforts is, that the very attempt to embody some doctrines
within the forms of the understanding naturally and
essentially depraves them. If we say, as we often do, a
God understood is no God at all—and this remark applies
to mere natural religion—the same holds true of those
higher doctrines of revelation which are the adumbrations
of " the light which no man hath seen or can see." There are
doctrines in Theology, even as there are doctrines in Science,
the demonstration of which is rather negative than positive. Chemists tell us of an element essential to our life—
we breathe it every moment; it contributes to the balance of
all the powers of the atmosphere; it tames the subtle,
fiery-tempered oxygen, the wild and vehement hydrogen;
it represses, allays, and composes, but itself has no colour,
no odour; it has no active properties, no chemical affections; it is one of the greatest mysteries in nature. It

is invisible, and yet it proclaims its presence ; the chemist cannot touch it, but he is sure of its existence.   It may well fill our minds with awe that we are ever in the presence of such an agent, that before it the lamp of science is darkened, like a man with a dim light in a room in which he sees phantoms he cannot touch, and hears voices the causes of which he cannot detect, and as he holds up his lamp he is aware of a presence that disturbs him, that will not enter into his knowledge, and for which he cannot account.   Only he knows that it is.   Such is nitrogen.   It is thus we apprehend the doctrine of the Trinity.

All efforts must fail to apprehend the doctrines involved in the idea of the Trinity, which insist upon either the idea of personality or numeration, as they are understood by us.   Watts, with the Bible in his hand, stood on the defensive against the aggressions of Arianism, and having attempted to unfold the Christian doctrine of the Trinity, he published his further dissertation, " The Arian Invited to the Orthodox Faith ; a plain and easy method to lead such as deny the Proper Deity of Christ into the belief of that Article."   Those who charge Arianism upon Watts can only do so, because throughout the argument he has conducted it in a strain of eminent courtesy and charity.   He approached the matter in no spirit of disputation, but with a cordial desire to promote, if possible, healing and unity ; nor do we think that there are any indications, in the course of any of his discussions, that his own mind or faith was unhinged ; but the discussions around him compelled him to direct his attention to questions certainly not uncongenial to his speculative and analytic order of mind. Probably the reader feels that there is a sufficient correspondence between the sense of our own spiritual wants and the revelation given to us in the Divine Word to make us feel that the Trinity of Persons in the Godhead is a necessity of our moral nature, and that it is a doctrine, as we have already intimated, best held, as most satisfactory to the mind and conscience, when held *im*plicitly rather than *ex*plicitly.

The claim which the Unitarians put forth to find in Watts one of themselves is not less than audacious and dishonest. It is, however, founded—very ridiculously, we venture to think—upon some expressions reported after his death, which implied that he would have been willing, had he been able, to have altered some expressions in his hymns. Truly it is amazing that the author could survive the publication of his first volume forty years, and not alter many barbarisms of metre and expression. It may, perhaps, be partly accounted for from the fact that the copyright of the hymns had passed at once from his hands. We can very well believe there were certain expressions in his hymns he would have been not indisposed to alter, without touching at all upon matters of doctrine. It will be time enough for Unitarians to claim Watts when they are able to set aside his last published words, and to reconcile them with that faith which they call theirs, or to account, upon such principles as they would make him hold, for the sentiments which fell from his lips when dying.

But as a study of Watts' mind, these pieces of his are like all that emanated from his pen, characterized by exceeding reverence for the subject he attempted to elucidate, and by charity, respect, and courtesy towards his opponents. Johnson says : " I am only enough acquainted with his theological works to admire his meekness of opposition, and his mildness of censure. It was not only in his books, but in his mind, that orthodoxy was united with charity." Some will, perhaps, almost think that this width of charity in Watts degenerated into a vice; we hope this book has made it evident that he both had strong convictions and knew how to act upon them steadily. But his heart was very inclusive in its love. It was not merely that he lived within the shadows of persecution, and belonged to an order whose opinions were only tolerated; he represented the mildest type of Nonconformity. Perhaps we shall surprise some readers not very well acquainted with his writings, by informing them that one of the latest efforts of his mind and pen was upon the inquiry, "Whether an Establishment is altogether an Impossibility." This was in his Essay, published in the year 1739, on "Civil Power in Things Sacred." It is a singular scheme, and the question is discussed with great moderation and candour ; but it is rather a plea for a system of national education than the establishment of a national religion. He inquires, indeed, whether there might not be established a religion consistent with the just liberties of mankind, and practicable with every form of civil government. He thinks that officers should be appointed by the State to explain and enforce the great duties and sanctions of morality, and that the citizens should be compelled to receive such lessons as are unquestionably at the foundation of a national well-being, the welfare, strength, and support of the State, and that such teachers, as public benefactors, should be sustained at the charge of the State.

Watts' philosophical works exhibit him in the same light as his theological. They are marked by a vivid disposition to analysis and speculation, and by that elevated reverence of thought which appertains to all his writings. Instance his "Inquiry Concerning Space ; whether it be

Something or Nothing, God or a Creature." Most minds are quite unequal to such discussions, and many regard them as unwise, irreverent, and dangerous. They are a kind of intellectual Matterhorn which certain daring spirits assault from age to age—the origin of evil, liberty, and necessity—the nature of substance, and time, and space. It would surely be a dangerous and a doubtful doctrine to teach that such questions are only the territories or hunting-grounds of the bold masters of sceptical negations. It does not derogate from the greatness of Isaac Watts to admit that he was neither a Joseph Butler, a William de Leibnitz, nor a Jonathan Edwards ; but in his mind such studies became means of usefulness. He fashioned Alpenstocks for climbers among those higher mountain ranges, through which he had himself travelled. In such studies a reverent mind may at once enlarge the understanding while learning the limitation of its powers. A wise guide will here, too, guard against the dangerous *crevasse,* while he hath himself

> The secret learned
> To mix his blood with sunshine, and to take
> The wind into his pulses.*

Johnson quotes a passage from Mr. Dyer, charging Watts with confounding the idea of space with empty space, and that he did not consider that though space might be without matter, yet matter, being extended, could not be without space. But in reply to this, it may be remarked that this is the whole question, and extended matter falls rather beneath the denomination of substance. It appears certainly the case that Watts, in his discussion, deals with infinite space, or say, certainly, indefinite space—that is, extension abstracted from phenomena. Such space Sir Isaac Newton

* J. R. Lowell.

reverently regarded as the sensorium of God. Newton was so essentially reverent even in thought that it was not possible for him to indulge an idea which was capable of depraving religious conceptions; but all minds, even religious minds, have not been equally reverent. Hence some have gone on to regard space as the immensity of God, as a property of God. But it would follow from this that as space is extended, so God, too, must be extended; and whatever tends to conform God with nature, or to place Him in contact with it, in any other way than as in relation to His wisdom and His will, is essentially unscriptural, and it is a dangerous proclivity below which yawn the fearful gulfs of Pantheism and Atheism. In these discussions our writer anticipated many of those shadows which in the course of a few years were to project themselves over the whole domain of philosophy and theology; and, indeed, only a few years before, in the great work of Spinosa, ominous indications had been given; and the second part of the "Living Temple" of John Howe bore immediately upon the coming questions. Watts' essay penetrates into the stronghold of Pantheism. Newton and Pascal, both looking up into the infinite spaces, felt their nature called on to reply to the questions suggested. The silence terrified Pascal; Newton's calmer nature gathered up even infinite space into the great idea, that it was but a mode, or attribute, of God. Some such doctrines govern the Essays of Watts: Space, he argues, cannot be God; we cannot indeed conceive that infinite space ever began to be, we have an idea of it as eternal and unchangeable; according to Watts it seems to contain what existence it has in the very idea, nature, or essence of it, which is one attribute of God, and whereby we prove His existence. It appears to be a necessary being and has a sort of self-existence, for we cannot tell how to conceive it not to be. It seems to be an impassible, indivisible, immutable essence, and therefore according to the ghastly pantheistic philosophy it is argued that space is God. This idea Watts concisely set aside, because it involves the absurdity of making the blessed God a Being of infinite length, breadth, and depth, and ascribing to Him parts of this nature measurable by inches, yards, and miles. Perhaps this is not so clear to all readers as it was to the writer himself; but the close seems more satisfactory when he says, "Strongest arguments seem to evince this, that it must be God, or it must be nothing." Watts, then, was an Idealist, and the remark of Johnson arises from a misapprehension of the drift of the essay. He argues that space is only the shadow cast by substance —we are sure that shadow or darkness is a mere nothing, and space is nothing but the absence of body, as shade is the absence of light, and both are explicable without supposing either to be real beings : it is therefore merely an abstract idea, or, as we should say, a "thought-form;" it will follow from this that such an idea of space dissolves one of the charming illusions of Pantheism, and that there rises from the midst of this universe of unidentical being the personality of man.

Some critics have entertained a grim joke at the expense of Watts, that having annihilated space, he proceeded in the next place to annihilate substance, anticipating at once Berkeley and Hume. Let it then be remembered that he engaged in none of these excursions in a vain or Pyrrhonistic spirit : his essays were written not to unhinge, but to rest and settle and give repose to the mind ; indeed he says, "There are mysteries wherein we bewilder and lose ourselves by attempting to make something out of nothing;" substance is one of these. He goes for some distance on the way with Locke, especially in refuting the idea that substance is something real in nature; with Locke he argues that " all the ideas we have of particular, distinct sort of substances, are nothing but several combinations of simple ideas co-existent in such, the cause of their union, which makes the whole subsist of itself." Only then comes in the important question, "what is it that supports the accidents and qualities of being?" At this point Watts parts company with Locke. His ideas of substance seem to be antago-nistic to Locke, and dangerously sustaining Spinosa, who taught, as our readers know, that the whole universe, God and this world, may be the same individual substance— " How can I be sure that God and the material world have not one common substance?" But, very singularly, Watts himself in tracing the mistakes upon this matter to their origin, seems to fall into the very error he seeks to ex-plode, the idea of a real, invisible abstract or concrete, seems to stand behind all things; he says, the mistakes which men make arise from the occult quality in the termination of names, *ity* in solidity, *sion* in extension, which imply a quality without including the substance; as white*ness*, without including the substance or the thing that is white; the word white is concrete, and denotes the thing or substance together with the quality, and he says, " We ought to remember that *things* are made by God, or Nature, *words* are made by man, and sometimes applied in a way not exactly agreeable to what things and ideas require." The object of Watts in his discussion of the idea of substance, was the same as that in his discussion in the idea of space, to disarm Spinozism of its gross and crude ideas of God. But we do not feel that the same success closes the discussion. Perhaps it will be sufficient to admit at once that space and substance are both modes of Divine operation. Push the inquiry to any extent, and the most absolute Spinozist is compelled to halt in some such conclusion. That God is extended, that He is a mere infinite extension, is an absurdity; but it seems that no injustice is done to the most reverent and infinite thought of God by regarding Him as the essential *sub-stans*, the substance as of all souls, so of all being.

That about the philosophic essays which interests us is their freshness, and the clear, easily lucid, and charmingly illustrated style in which the doctrines are conveyed. They assuredly are a very happy commentary upon Locke, from whom he often separates, as in the essay on "Innate Ideas;" he agrees with Locke in the main, and then proceeds to discourse upon many simple ideas which are innate in some sense. His essay to prove that the "Soul never Sleeps," and "On the Place and Motion of Spirits, and the Power of a Spirit to move Matter," are interesting ; that on the "Departing and Separate Soul" is a sublime piece of writing, and on the "Resurrection of the same Body," and on the "Production and Nourishment of Plants and Animals." Few persons now, it may be supposed, even know of the existence of these essays ; they seem to us pieces of truly delightful reading, most instructive, suggestive, and entertaining, singularly free from hard and unpleasant lines of dogmatism, full of delightful and suggestive pictures ; take the following :

SUNBEAMS AND STARBEAMS.

" What a surprising work of God is vision, that notwith-standing all these infinite meetings and crossings of star-

beams and sunbeams night and day, through all our solar
world, there should be such a regular conveyance of light
to every eye as to discern each star so distinctly by night,
as well as all other objects on earth by day! And this
difficulty and wonder will be greatly increased by con-
sidering the innumerable double, triple, and tenfold reflections and refractions of sunbeams, or daylight, near our
earth, and among the various bodies on the surface of it.
Let ten thousand men stand round a large elevated
amphitheatre; in the middle of it, on a black plain,
let ten thousand white round plates be placed, of two
inches diameter, and at two inches distance; every eye
must receive many rays of light reflected from every
plate, in order to perceive its shape and colour; now, if
there were but one ray of light came from each plate,
here would be ten thousand rays falling on every single
eye, which would make twenty thousand times ten
thousand, that is, two hundred millions of rays crossing
each other in direct lines in order to make every plate
visible to every man. But if we suppose that each plate
reflected one hundred rays, which is no unreasonable
supposition, this would rise to twenty thousand millions.
What an amazing thing is the distinct vision of the shape
and colour of each plate by every eye, notwithstanding
these confused crossings and rays! What an astonishing
composition is the eye in all the coats and all the humours
of it, to convey those ten thousand white images, or those
millions of rays so distinct to the retina, and to impress
and paint them all there! And what further amazement
attends us if we follow the image on the retina, conveying
itself by the optic nerves into the common sensory without confusion? Can a rational being survey this scene
and say there is no God? Can a mind think on this

stupendous bodily organ, the eye, and not adore the Wisdom that contrived it ?"

And the following is not only most interesting, but anticipates, with much strength, a line of argument important to the sceptical philosophy of our own day. The German Buchner binds up his atheistic philosophy between the two covers of Force and Matter; and many in our own country follow in the same train of singularly forgetful thought: forgetful because force and matter are really not sufficient to constitute a universe; the regulative and directive power which controls force and manipulates matter to its will is assuredly as essential a factor as either force or matter.* Thus Dr. Watts argues in his remarks:

THE DIRECTION OF MOTION A PROOF OF DEITY.

"Yet, after all, I know it may be replied again, that gravitation is a power which is not limited in its agency by any conceivable distances whatsoever; and therefore, when these starbeams are run out never so far into the infinite void by the force of their emission from the star, yet their gravitation towards the star, or some of the planetary worlds, which sometimes, perhaps, may be nearer to it, has perpetual influence to retard their motion by degrees, even as the motion of a comet is retarded by its gravitation towards the sun, though it flies to such a prodigious distance from the sun, and in time it is stopped and drawn back again and made to return towards its centre. And just so, may we suppose, all the sunbeams and starbeams that ever were emitted, even to the borders

---

* This matter has been well argued against the Atheistic view, in a very interesting little pamphlet, "Croll on the Conservation of Force."

of the creation, to have been restrained by degrees by this principle of gravitation till, moving slower and slower, at last they are stopped in their progress and made to return toward their own or some other planetary system. And if so, then there is a perpetual return of the beams of light towards some or other of their bright originals, an ever-lasting circulation of these lucid atoms, which will hinder this eternal dilation of the bounds of the universe, and at the same time will equally prevent the wasting of the substance of the lucid bodies, the sun or stars. Well, but if this power of restraining and reducing the flight of star-beams be ascribed to this principle of gravitation, let us inquire what is this gravitation, which prevents the universe from such a perpetual waste of light? It cannot be supposed to be any real property or natural power inhering in matter or body, which exerts its influence at so prodigious a distance. I think, therefore, it is generally agreed, and with great reason, that it is properly the influence of a Divine power upon every atom of matter which, in a most exact proportion to its bulk and distance, causes it to gravitate towards all other material beings, and which makes all the bulky beings in the universe, viz., the sun, planets, and stars, attract the bodies that are near them towards themselves. Now this law of nature being settled at first by God the Creator, and being constantly maintained in the course of His providence, it is esteemed as an effect of nature, and has a property of matter, though in truth it is owing to the almighty and all-pervading power of God exerting its incessant dominion and influence through the whole material creation, producing an infinite variety of changes which we observe among bodies, con-fining the universe to its appointed limits, restraining the swift motion of the beams of light, and preserving this vast system of beings from waste and ruin, from desolation and darkness. If there be a world, there is a God ; if there be a sun and stars, every ray points to their Creator ; not a beam of light from all the lucid globes, but acknowledges its mission from the wisdom and will of God, and feels the restraint of His laws, that it may not be an eternal wanderer. But I call my thoughts to retire from these extravagant rovings beyond the limits of creation. What do these amusements teach us but the inconceivable grandeur, extent, and magnificence of the works and the power of God, the astonishing contrivances of His wisdom, and the poverty, the weakness, and narrowness of our own understandings, all which are lessons well becoming a creature ?"

In the same manner, also, he replies to the modern doctrine of *traducianism* in his remarks on

CREATION OR CONSERVATION.

"It has been a very famous question in the schools, whether conservation be a continual creation, *i.e.*, whether that action, whereby God preserves all creatures in their several ranks and orders of being, is not one continued act of His creating power or influence, as it were, giving being to them every moment ? Whether creatures, being formed out of nothing, would relapse again into their first estate of nonentity if they were not, as it were, perpetually reproduced by a creating act of God ? Now there is one plain and easy argument whereby, perhaps, this controversy may be determined, and it may be proposed in this manner. In whatsoever moment God creates a substance, He must create with it all the properties, modes, and accidents which belong to it in that moment ; for in the very moment of creation the creature is all passive, and cannot give itself those modes. Now if God every moment create wicked men and devils, and cause them to exist such as they are, by a continued act of creation, must He not, at the same time, create or give being to all their sinful thoughts and inclinations, and even their most criminal and abominable actions ? Must He not create devils, together with the rage and pride, the malice, envy, and blasphemy of their thoughts ? Must He not create sinful men in the very acts of lying, perjury, stealing, and adultery, rapine, cruelty, and murder ? Must He not form one man with malice in his heart ? Another with a false oath on the tongue ? A third with a sword in his hand, plunging it into his neighbour's bosom ? Would not these formidable consequences follow from the supposition of God's conserving providence being a continual act of creation ? But surely these ideas seem to be shocking absurdities, whereas, if conservation be really a continued creation, the modes must be created together with their substances every moment, since it is not possible that creatures, who every moment are supposed to be nothing but the immediate products of the Divine will, should be capable in every one of those very moments in which they are produced or created to form their own modes in simultaneous co-existence with their subjects. I own there are difficulties on the other side of the question ; but the fear of making God the author of sin has bent my opinion this way. We must always inviolably maintain it for the honour of the blessed God, that all spirits, as they come out of His hand, are created pure and innocent ; every sinful act proceeds from themselves, by an abuse of their own freedom of will, or by a voluntary compliance with the corrupt appetites and inclinations of flesh and blood. We must find some better way, therefore, to explain God's providential conservation of things than by representing it as an act of proper and continual creation, lest we impute all the iniquities of all men and devils, in all ages, to the pure and holy God, who is blessed for evermore."

There are two other pieces well worth a study—his remarks on Mr. Locke's "Essay on the Human Understanding," and a "Brief Scheme of Ontology." The essay on ontology, like that on logic, is a most interesting hand-book and guide to thought. Watts thought so clearly that it often seems as if he were only putting things neatly. Sometimes, as in his "Philosophic Essays," and in his pieces on the Trinity, he is eminently translucent ; you see that there is light behind. This is the impression conveyed by his dissertation on "Space," "Substance," and "Concerning Spirits, their Place and Motion ;" but in his Ontology and Logic he is transparent, the objects are brought distinctly into view. When he presents before you his greater thoughts his style is indeed clear, but you feel that it is as when "morning is spread upon the mountains" before sunrise, or as when evening lingers in the soft and rosy light after sunset, there is something somewhere behind, some orb of light which spreads out all that roseate glow ; in his Ontology and Logic he is concise and dis-tinct, as we have said ; you may almost call him a neat writer. He has a wonderful power of accumulating par-ticulars, a singular felicity in discriminating ideas. This gives to him a very nice sense of words, as he says, "We must search the sense of words. It is for want of this that men quarrel in the dark, and that there are so many con-tentions in the several sciences, and especially in divinity." His power of discrimination is so nice that it often becomes as amusing as it is instructive ; regarded thus, his Logic

is a most interesting book, we suppose quite the most
delightful to read of any treatise on logic in our language.
Of this amusing cumulative power let the reader take the
following :

NAMES AND NAMING THINGS.

" Do not suppose that the natures or essences of things
always differ from one another as much as their names
do. There are various purposes in human life for which
we put very different names on the same thing, or on
things whose natures are near akin ; and thereby often-
times, by making a new nominal species, we are ready to
deceive ourselves with the idea of another real species of
beings, and those whose understandings are led away by
the mere sound of words fancy the nature of those things
to be very different whose names are so, and judge of them
accordingly. I may borrow a remarkable instance for my
purpose out of every garden which contains a variety of
plants in it. Most of all plants agree in this, that they
have a root, a stalk, leaves, buds, blossoms, and seeds : but
the gardener ranges them under very different names, as
though they were really different kinds of beings, merely
because of the different use and service to which they are
applied by men, as for instance those plants whose roots
are eaten shall appropriate the name of roots to themselves, such as carrots, turnips, radishes, etc. If the leaves
are of chief use to us then we call them herbs, as sage,
mint, thyme ; if the leaves are eaten raw they are termed
salad, as lettuce, purslane ; if boiled they become pot-
herbs, as spinage, coleworts ; and some of those same
plants which are pot-herbs in one family are salads in
another. If the buds are made our food they are called

heads or tops; so cabbage heads, heads of asparagus, and artichokes. If the blossom be of most importance we call it a flower, such as daisies, tulips, and carnations, which are the mere blossoms of those plants. If the husks or seeds are eaten they are called the fruits of the ground, as peas, beans, strawberries, etc. If any part of the plant be of known or common use to us in medicine we call it a physical herb, as cardamus, scurvy-grass; but if we count no part useful we call it a weed, and throw it out of the garden; and yet perhaps our next neighbour knows some valuable property and use of it, he plants it in his garden and gives it a title of an herb or a flower. You see here how small is the real distinction of these several plants considered in their general nature as the lesser vegetables, yet what very different ideas we vulgarly form concerning them, and make different species of them, chiefly because of the different names given to them."

Exactly the same characteristics meet us in his Ontology, but here there is yet more of this kind of amusement; its pages are crowded with illustrations. It was perhaps in the nature of the subject that he scarcely mentions a particular for which he does not furnish one or twenty illustrative examples : take his curious discrimination of causes into the deficient, the permissive, and the conditional :

CLASSIFICATION OF CAUSES.

" *A deficient* cause is when the effect owes its existence in a great measure to the absence of something which would have prevented it, so that this may be reckoned a negative rather than a positive cause : the negligence of a gardener, or the want of rain, are the deficient causes of

the withering of plants; and the carelessness of the pilot,
or the sinking of the tide, is the cause of a ship's splitting
on a rock; the forgetfulness of a message is the cause of
a quarrel among friends, or of the punishment of servants; the not bringing a reprieve in time is the cause of
a criminal's being executed; and the want of education is
the cause why many a child runs headlong into vice and
mischief; the blindness of a man, or the darkness of the
night, are the causes of stumbling; a leak in a boat is a
deficient cause why the water runs in and the boat sinks;
and a hole in a vessel is called a deficient cause why the
liquor runs out and is lost. Man is the deficient cause of
all his sins of omission, and many of these carry great
guilt in them.

"*A permissive cause* is that which actually removes
impediments, and thus it lets the proper causes operate.
Now this sort of cause is either natural or moral. A
natural permissive cause removes natural impediments
or obstructions, and this may be called a deobstruent
cause. So opening the window shutters is the cause of
the light entering the room; cleaning the ear may be the
cause of a man's hearing music who was deaf before;
breaking down a dam is the cause of the overflowing of
water and drowning a town; letting loose a rope is the
cause of a ship's running adrift; leaving off a garment is
the cause of a cold and a cough; and cutting the bridle of
the tongue may be the cause of speech to the dumb.

"*Note.*—The cause which removes natural impediments
may be a proper efficient cause with regard to that removal, yet it is not properly efficient, but merely permissive with regard to the consequences of that removal.

"*A moral permissive cause* removes moral impediments,
or takes away prohibitions, and gives leave to act: so a

master is a permissive cause of his scholars going to play ;
a general is the same cause of his soldiers plundering a
city ; and a repeal of a law against foreign silks is the
permissive cause why they are worn.

" *Query.*—Was not God's permission of Satan to afflict
Job rather natural than moral, since his mischievous
actions did not become lawful thereby, and since it is now
become his nature to do mischief where he has no natural
restraint ?

" *A condition* has been usually caused *causa sine quâ
non,* or a cause without which the effect is not produced.
It is generally applied to something which is requisite in
order to the effect, though it hath not a proper actual
influence in producing that effect. Daylight is a condition
of ploughing, sowing, and reaping ; darkness is a condition
of our seeing stars and glowworms ; clearness of the
stream is the condition of our spying sand and pebbles
at the bottom of it ; being well dressed with a head uncovered is a condition of a man's coming into the presence
of a king ; and paying a peppercorn yearly is the condition of enjoying an estate. How far the perfect idea of
the word condition, in the civil law, may differ from this
representation is not my present work to determine.

" *Note.*—These three last causes may possibly be all
ranked under the general name of conditions, but I think
it more proper to distinguish them into their different
kinds of causality."

We perhaps repeat ourselves in these last remarks, for
all is an illustration of that perspicuity which we mentioned as Watts' first characteristic ; but in him perspicuity
was not the attribute of a small mind, or a limited range
of vision ; perspicuous speech is the natural instrument of
perspicuous thought : how can that man express himself

clearly who does not see clearly? Hence dark language must be the companion of dark vision; but the perspicuity of a child amongst its playthings, in its playground or its garden is one thing, and the perspicuity of the pilot of a vessel, or a gifted astronomer, is quite another. However wide or vast the subjects upon which Watts wrote, it seemed he had cleared thought in his own mind, by the clearness with which speech served him in making the things in his own mind the property of others; and upon whatsoever he wrote there was always the same suffusing light of the devoutness of the spiritual mind. Here is no flippancy; here are no impertinent epigrams, no hard words even for opponents; we have to search a long way through his works before we find an expression of severity, we will not say of contempt—perhaps there are such—but we are sure they will only be used of those who, by some abandonment of sentiment, had separated themselves from the common feeling of mankind. Yet there was considerable nervousness in his speech, he was a great preacher, he commanded attention; judging from the testimony of Johnson, he must have been, to cultivated minds, one of the most distinguished preachers of his day: his enunciation was clear, forcible, and distinct, and what was wanting to an imposing presence was made up from the earnestness of the manner, the calm luminousness, elevation, and we would even say, the sustained but subdued vehemence of his diction. His sermon on the " Reformation of Manners," to which Southey has referred, not in his life of Watts but in one of the volumes of his " Common-place Book," as " an extraordinary piece," is an illustration of this. It was preached at the time when we were in conflict with Louis XIV. He gives the following side-glance to the wars in Flanders, and on the borders of the Rhine, and he refers to the import-

ance, not only of fighting the enemy abroad, but resisting
vice at home.   He exclaims, in a remarkable passage :

"But was there ever any war without danger, or victory
without courage ?   Besides, the perils you run here are
almost infinitely less than those which attend the wars of
nations, where the cause is not half so Divine.   The fields
of battle in Flanders, and almost all over Europe, have
drunk up the blood of millions, and have furnished graves
for large armies ; but it can hardly be said that *you* have
hitherto 'resisted unto blood striving against sin.'   In a
war of more than twelve years' continuance (*i.e.*, against
vice at home) there has but one man fallen.   The
providence of God has put helmets of salvation upon
your heads.   Some of you can relate wonders of deliver-
ance to safety when you have been beset by numbers,
and their rage has kindled into resolutions of revenge ;
the Lord has taken away their courage in a moment,
the 'men of might have not found their hands;' thus
He has caused 'the wrath of man to praise Him, and
the remainder of wrath He hath restrained.' *   Read over
this psalm, and with Divine valour pursue the fight.   But
if your life should be lost in such a cause as this, it will be
esteemed martyrdom in the sight of God, and shall be thus
written down in the book of the wars of the Lord. Believe
me, these red lines will look well in the records of heaven,
when the judgment shall be set, and the books opened in
the face of men and angels."

Watts in the pulpit ought to furnish the subject for a
distinct chapter—it must fall into this feeble attempt to
realize the man's mind in his works.   His sermons were
evidently carefully prepared and admirably arranged ; it
was not possible for him to speak without thought, but he

* Psalm lxxvi. 5, 10.

used very few notes in the pulpit, preparing carefully so
that the mind and memory were fully charged, giving to
such a mind as his freedom, instantaneous propriety, and
fulness of expression; many men who exhibit fulness of
wisdom, both in thought and language, in the study, find
all fail them when they come to speak in public.   On
every hand we hear that this was not the case with Watts,
and that his deliverances in public corresponded to his
great powers in the study; and his sermons are of that
nature that they assure us if the delivery corresponded to
the strength of the matter and the felicity and harmony of
the composition, they must have been very impressive.   As
some of the great sermons of Jeremy Taylor appear to have
been prepared to preach when he was in exile at the Golden
Grove in Wales, in the drawing-room of Lord Vaughan, so
some of Watts' sermons were prepared for delivery at the
evening worship at Theobalds ; one of the noblest of these
is a commanding piece on the Scale of Blessedness, or
Blessed Saints, Blessed Saviour, Blessed Trinity.   In this
subduing sermon occurs one of the passages which excited
the wrath of Thomas Bradbury, and to which we have
referred.   Here it is; the note is evidently intended to
justify himself from his coarse assailant, although he does
not say so.

A SCALE OF BLESSEDNESS.

"Can we ever imagine that Moses the meek, the friend
of God, who was, as it were, His confidant on earth, His
faithful prophet to institute a new religion, and establish a
new Church in the world, who, for God's sake, endured
forty years of banishment, and had forty years' fatigue in
a wilderness; who saw God on earth face to face,
and the shine was left upon his countenance: can we

suppose that this man has taken his seat no nearer
to God in Paradise than Samson and Jephthah, those
rash champions, those rude and bloody ministers of
Providence ?*   Or can we think that St. Paul, the greatest
of the apostles, 'who laboured more than they all,' and
'was in sufferings' more abundant than the rest ; who
spent a long life in daily services and deaths for the sake of
Christ, is not fitted for, and advanced to a rank of blessedness superior to that of the crucified thief, who became a
Christian but a few moments at the end of a life of im-
piety and plunder ?   Can I persuade myself that a holy
man, who has known much of God in this world, and
spent his age on earth in contemplation of the Divine ex-
cellences, who has acquired a great degree of nearness to
God in devotion, and has served Him, and suffered for
Him, even to old age and martyrdom, with a sprightly and
faithful zeal : can I believe that this man, who has been
trained up all his life to converse with God, and is fitted
to receive Divine communications above his fellows, shall
dwell no nearer to God hereafter, and share no larger a
degree of blessedness, than the little babe who has just
entered into this world to die out of it, and who is saved,
so far as we know, merely by spreading the veil of the
covenant grace, drawn over it by the hand of the parent's
faith ?   Can it be that the Great Judge who 'cometh and
His reward is with Him, to render to every one according

* " These expressions may be sufficiently justified if we consider Jephthah's rash vow of sacrifice, which fell upon his only child ; and Samson's rude or unbecoming conduct in his amours with the Philistine
woman at Timnath, the harlot at Gaza, and his Delilah at Sorek; his
bloody quarrels and his manner of life.   The learned and pious Dr.
Owen, as I have been often informed by his intimate friend, Sir John
Hartopp, called him a rude believer.   He might have strong faith of
miracles, but a small share of that faith which purifies the heart.".

to his works,' will make no distinction between Moses and Samson, between the apostle and the thief, between the aged martyr and the infant, in the world to come ? And yet, after all, it may be matter of inquiry, whether the meanest saint among the sons of Adam has not some sort of privilege above any rank of angels by being of a kindred nature to our Emmanuel, to Jesus the Son of God."

And the following is a fine passage on the Trinity, which may be read with pleasure, although some years after he says that "it is a warmer effort of the imagination than riper years would indulge. What distinctions there may be in this one Spirit I know not ; I am *fully established in the belief of the Deity of the Blessed Three,* though I know not the manner of the explication."

THE TRINITY.

" The Father is so intimately near the Son and Spirit, that no finite or created natures or unions can give a just resemblance of it. We talk of the union of the sun and his beams, of a tree and its branches ; but these are but poor images and faint shadows of this mystery, though they are some of the best that I know. The union of the soul and the body is, in my esteem, still farther from the point, because their natures are so widely different. In vain we search through all the creation to find a complete similitude of the Creator.

" And in vain may we run through all parts and powers of nature and art, to seek a full resemblance of the mutual propensity and love of the Blessed Three towards each other. Mathematicians, indeed, talk of the perpetual tendencies and infinite approximations of two or more lines on the same surface, which yet never can entirely concur in one line : and if we should say that the Three Persons of the Trinity, by mutual indwelling and love, approach each other infinitely in one Divine nature, and yet lose not their distinct personality, it would be but an obscure account of this sublime mystery. But this we are sure of, that for three Divine Persons to be so inconceivably near one another in the original and eternal spring of love, goodness, and pleasure, must produce infinite delight. In order to illustrate the happiness of the Sacred Three, may we not suppose something of society necessary to the per-fection of happiness in all intellectual nature ? To know and be known, to love and to be beloved, are, perhaps, such essential ingredients of complete felicity that it cannot subsist without them. And it may be doubted whether such mutual knowledge and love, as seems requisite for this end, can be found in a nature absolutely simple in all respects. May we not then suppose that some distinctions in the Divine Being are of eternal necessity, in order to complete the blessedness of Godhead ? Such a distinction as may admit, as a great man expresses it, of delicious society. 'We, for our parts, cannot but hereby have in our minds a more gustful idea of a blessed state, than we can conceive in mere eternal solitude.'

" And if this be true, then the three differences, which we call personal distinctions, in the nature of God, are as absolutely necessary as His blessedness, as His being, or any of His perfections. And then we may return to the words of my text, and boldly infer, that if the man is blessed who is chosen by the free and sovereign grace of God, and caused to approach, or draw near Him, what immense and unknown blessedness belongs to each Divine Person, to all the Sacred Three, who are by nature and unchangeable necessity so near, so united, so much one, that the least moment's separation seems to be infinitely impossible, and, then we may venture to say, it is not to be conceived : and the blessedness is conceivable by none but God !

" This is a nobler union and a more intense pleasure than *the Man* Jesus Christ knows or feels, or can conceive, for He is a creature. These are glories too Divine and dazzling for the weak eye of our understanding, too bright for the eye of angels, those morning stars ; and they, and we, must fall down together, alike overwhelmed with them, and alike confounded. These are flights that tire souls of the strongest wing, and finite minds faint in the infinite pursuit ; these are depths where our tallest thoughts sink and drown ; we are lost in this ocean of being and blessedness that has no limit on either side, no surface, no bottom, no shore. The nearness of the Divine Persons to each other, and the unspeakable relish of their unbounded pleasures, are too vast ideas for our bounded minds to entertain. It is one infinite transport that runs through the Father, Son, and Spirit, without beginning, and without end, with boundless variety, yet ever perfect and ever present without change, and without degree ; and all this because they are so near to one another, and so much one with God.

"But when we have fatigued our spirits and put them to the utmost stretch, we must lie down and rest, and confess the great incomprehensible. How far this sublime transport of joy is varied in each subsistence ; how far their mutual knowledge of each other's properties, or their mutual delight in each other's love, is distinct in each Person, is a secret too high for the present determination of our language and our thoughts : it commands our judgment in silence, and our whole souls into wonder and adoration."

He frequently indulged in a warmth of expression; he did not disdain ornament, although all was held in a wise check, and indeed with a severe rein, and his sermons were not less practical than beautiful. They abound in such passages as the following, in which he so sweetly and mildly expostulates with

CENSORIOUS CHRISTIANS.

" Be not too severe in your censures, you who have been kept from temptation, but pity others who are fallen, and mourn over their fall. Do not think or say the worst things you can of those who have been taken in the snare of Satan, and been betrayed into some grosser iniquities. When you see them grieved and ashamed of their own follies, and bowed down under much heaviness, take occasion then to speak a softening and a healing word. Speak for them kindly, and speak to them tenderly. ' Have compassion of them, lest they be swallowed up of over much sorrow.' And remember, too, O censorious Christian, that thou art also in the body. It is rich grace that has kept thee hitherto, and the same God, who for wise ends has suffered thy brother to fall, may punish thy severity and reproachful language by withholding His grace from thee in the next hour of temptation, and then thy own fall and guilt shall upbraid thee with inward and bitter reflections, for thy sharp censures of thy weak and tempted brother. This life is the only time wherein we can pity the infirmities of our brethren, and bear their burdens. This law of Christ must be fulfilled in this world, for there is no room for it in the next : ' Wherefore bear ye one another's burdens, and so

fulfil ye the law of Christ.' This world is the only place
where different opinions and doctrines are found amongst
the saints; disagreeing forms of devotion, and sects, and
parties, have no place on high: none of these things can
interrupt the worship or the peace of heaven. See to it
then, that you practise this grace of charity here, and love
thy brother, and receive him into thy heart in holy fellowship, though he may be weak in faith, and though he may
observe days and times, and may feed upon herbs, and
indulge some superstitious follies while thou art strong in
faith, and well acquainted with the liberty of the Gospel.
Let not little things provoke you to divide communions on
earth: but by this sort of charity, and a Catholic spirit,
honour the Saviour and His Church here in this world; for
since there are no parties, nor sects, nor contrary sentiments among the Church in heaven, this Christian virtue
can never find any room for exercise there. This kind of
charity ends with death."

But such delineations as these might be pursued to a
great length, and we have scarcely dwelt at all upon that
aspect of his public teaching which the last quotation
instantly suggests, its eminent practical character; his discourses on "Christian Morality," his beautiful discourse
on "Humility," for which he received the hearty thanks
of the Bishop of London; his "Caveat against Infidelity,"
his "Guide to Prayer;" summarily, it may be said, he
touched everything with an exquisite delicacy of conscience,
and with the elevation of a saint. His mind cannot be
summed in one attribute, neither his piety, nor his genius
can be said to find an adequate illustration in one work;
he was one of a race of men of whom, indeed, the history
of the literature of those times furnishes many illustrations,
whose learning and labours were alike vast; they must

have caught the earliest daybeam, and trimmed the lamp far beyond the hours of midnight, pursuing their industrious toil, devouring libraries. Their works formed a library; they had not the necessities of our times to call them away, nor was it the age of magazines and reviews, and the lighter shallops of literature. The age immediately preceding that of Watts, and his own age, present to us the forms of many men, who in some sheltered nook passed a life unprofitable—ought we to say inglorious?—satisfied with the spoils of learning, they lived a life of barrenness; they sought wisdom for her own sake, neither for the use it enabled them to confer on others, or the fame it conferred on themselves; or, if they published, it was not so much from the benevolent idea of the transfusion of knowledge, but really from their interest only in their own idea. These were the men and those the times which may be best described in the words of Milton:

> Whose lamp at midnight hour
> Is seen in some high lonely tower,
> Where he may oft outwatch the Bear
> With thrice great Hermes, or unsphere
> The spirit of Plato, to unfold
> What worlds or what vast regions hold
> The immortal mind that hath forsook
> Her mansion in this fleshly nook.

But to this order of mind Watts added that which altogether changed it; he possessed in an eminent degree the love of books and thought, lofty imaginations, and excursions through the far-off continents of knowledge; but he added to the volitions of genius, and the accumulations of the scholar, the doing " all for the glory of God;" few lives so useful and even so obvious seem to have been so sanctified from every human passion and selfish isolation; and hence with powers which might have found their gratifi-

cation had he chosen to move like some remote and
solitary planet in an unilluminating orb, he preferred
rather to be a satellite, shedding a useful lustre on his
serene way, and in the language of a well-known writer,
"singing while he shone." The amiable critic to whom we
have already referred says that the whole lesson of Watts'
life might be condensed into the apostolic injunction,
"Study to be quiet and mind your own business;" and the
estimate is greatly true. He was a firm Nonconformist,
but he was no agitator; he lived and wrought laboriously
in his vocation, and that vocation was to bring about "the
union of mental culture and vital piety." As he did not
write pamphlets to expose the evils of the hierarchy, or
the defects of his own ecclesiastical system, so neither
did he attempt to rebuke in print such assailants as
Bradbury. He was the first in England who set the
Gospel to music; and many who knew not the meaning of
the words yet found their hearts melted by the melody of
genius. There is a saintly dignity and peaceful purity
about his life which it is not invidious to say gives to him,
even in writers of his own order, a high pre-eminence.
He seems to have been one whom "the peace of God
which passeth all understanding" kept. And surely he
has won a place in the universal Church—no Church
repudiates him; his eulogy has been pronounced, and his
life recorded, by Samuel Johnson, and Robert Southey,
and Josiah Conder. If his hymns crowd the "Congregational Hymn Book," they are to be found in the "Hymns
Ancient and Modern;" and, as we have seen, his monument adorns not only the "conventicle" but the cathedral.

Ages differ, and men differ with their age. This is the
place neither to compare nor to contrast; but in an
eminent sense Watts appears to have fulfilled himself.

He drank deep from every kind of learning : we have seen
that he wrote upon every kind of subject ; and although it
is the fashion now to pass him by, and even to underrate
many of those pieces in prose and verse which were long
held as the most cherished heirlooms of the Church, we
shall have to search long and far to discover a more ample
and consecrated intelligence, a more conscientious and
laborious worker, than the mild, the modest, yet majestic
hermit, philosopher, and sweet singer of Theobalds and
Stoke Newington.

MONUMENT OF DR. WATTS IN WESTMINSTER ABBEY.

TABLE OF COINCIDENTS.

Mention has been made in p. 14 of a curious Autobiographical Table prepared by Dr. Watts of the chief incidents in his life, together with contemporaneous events of public interest. We give a fac-simile of the first page, and the contents of the remainder.

Coincidents

Memorable Affairs in my Life —

I was Born.	July. 17. 1674.
Began to Learn Latin of my father —	1678
Co Latin School to be Instructed in Writing —	1680
Was Proportion of Latin School	1683
Began to Learn Greek	1683 or before
Had & Small Pox —	1683
Learnt — French —	1684, 1685 ?
Learnt Hebrew —	1687, 8

1683: My father persecuted & imprisoned for Nonconformity 6 months, after that forced to leave his family & live privately in London for 2 years

1683 ½ : R: Ch: 2: Dyd. & K: Ja: 2: pool

1688: Nov: 5: Prince of Orange landed in Engl

Fell under Considerable Convictions of Sin ⎱ — 1688

& was taught to trust in Christ I hope, — 1689

Had a great & dangerous sickness 1689

Left ye grammar school & came to Londō to Mr Rowe, to study Philos. ⎱ — 1690.

Paid a 6 weeks visit to Southā ⎱ 1692

1692: Sept: 8: at noon an Earthquake felt England & in other nations —

COINCIDENTS.

1693 : July 13 : Grandmo. Watts dyed

1697. Jun. 11: Grandfa. Tanton dyed
      12   Cousin Isaac Watts dyed
1697 Peace at Reswic concluded

1698 Cousin John Chapmā of Portsm dyed
$\frac{}{9}$

1699 Feb: Mr Wⁿ Adams dyed
$\overline{1700}$

MEMORANDA.

I was admitted to Mr. T. Rows Church.	Dec. 1693
I went into yᵉ Country	June. 1694
Dwelt at my father's house 2 years & ¼.	
Came to Sʳ John Hartopp's to be a Tutor to his Son at Newington	Oct: 15. 1696
Began to preach, after I had pursued University Studys above 8 years.	July.17.1698.
Went to Southampton and preached there severall times in a visit to my friends.	Augᵗ. 1698.
Preacht as Dr. Chanceys Assistant in yᵉ Church at Mark Lane, & a little after that my fever and weakness began.	Feb. 1698/9
Paid another Visit to Southampton of 5 weeks.	July 1699

CONCIDENTS.	MEMORANDA.	
	Another.	June 1700
	Went to y^e Bath by y^e advice of Physicians.	June. 9. 1701.
1700. March 30. Grandmo. Tanton [died.] May 22. Mr John Pook Nov^r: 11: Mr Tho. Gunston	From y^e Bath to Southampton Thence to Tunbridge. returned to Newington & to preaching at Mark Lane. So y^t I was detained from Study & preaching $5 \frac{\circ}{}$ m by my Weakness. Except one very short discourse at Southto. in extreme necessity. Dr. Chancy having left his people, Aprill 1701. & I being returned to preach among 'em, they Call'd me to y^e Pastorall office.	July. 1701 Sept 3 1701. $\left.\begin{array}{c}\text{Nov. 3:}\\ \text{Nov: 1701}\end{array}\right\}$
	Accepted it & was ordained	Jan. 15. 1701 $\overline{2}$ March 8 ——— March 18. 1701 $\overline{2}$
1702 March 8th, Morning: King W^m dyed	Visited my friends at Southampton Seiz'd wth violent Jaundice & Cholic 3 weeks after my return to London & had a very slow recovery—8 or 9 weeks Illness $\left.\begin{array}{c}\text{}\end{array}\right\}$ This year (viz) 1702 by Slow degrees removd from Newington to Mr Tho: Hollis's in the Minories.	July. 1702. from $Sept^r$ 8 or thereabout to Novr 27 or 8 1702
Mrs. Owen Dr Owen's Widow dyed Jan^r. 18: 170 $\frac{3}{4}$	June—Mr Sam^{ll} Price was chosen by y^e Church to assist me in preaching Augt I went to Tunbridge and stayd there 7 weeks with scarce any benefitt, for the waters thro some defect of my stomach did not digest well. Dec^r: after having intermitted in a great measure a method of study and pursuit of Learning, 4 years, by reasō of my great indispositions of body and weakness of head (excep^t w: was of absolute necessity for my Constant preaching) & being not satisfyd to live so any longer, after due consideratiō &	1703
1703 Novr 26 Friday night and Saturday morning, the Great and Dreadfull Storm		

COINCIDENTS.

Augt. 31. 1704 Bro: Richard marryd

Br. Joseph Brandley my first servt went away Decr 1704 : & Edwd. Hitchin came

Augt 1705 Mr Tho: Rowe my Tutor dyed

Mr Benoni Rowe my intimate friend dyed Apll 1706

Bro: Thomas marry'd, May 9th: 1706

Union of E & Scot: May 1st 1707

This year yr French prophetts made a great noise in our nation, and drew in Mr Lacy, Sir R. Bulckley &c. 200 or more had yr agitations, 40 had yr inspiration—Prov'd a delusion of Satan at Birminghā Feb 3 or 4th 1707 $\frac{}{8}$

Sister Sarah marryed. Feb: 1707 $\frac{}{8}$

Pretender's invasion disappointed. March: 1708

May 25 1708 The Prophetts disappointed by Mr Eams not rising frō the Dead

Terrible long snowy winter 1708 $\frac{}{9}$

Bro R: came to settle in Londō: Oct 7 1709

Mar: 1 1709 $\frac{}{10}$ yr Mob rose & pulled down yr pews and gallerys of 6 meeting houses (viz) Mr Burgess, Mr Bradbury, Mr Earle, Mr Wright, Mr Hamilton, & Mr Chr: Taylor but were dispersed by yr Guards under Capt: Horsey at 1 or 2 in yr morning.

Mr Arthur Shallot senr dyed : 4th Feb 1710 $\frac{}{11}$ and Mr Tho: Hunt merchant & his wife dyed about yr same time.

Mrs Ann Pickford dyed Apll. 7th 1711.

My Lady Hartopp dyed Novr: 9th: & Mrs Gould, Novr 15th 1711.

MEMORANDA.

prayer, I took a boy to read to me & write for me, whereby my studies are much assisted. Decr 1703

Visited my friends at Southto. May. 1704

Remov'd our Meeting place to pinners hall and began expositions of Scripture. June 1704

Visited Southton July 1705

Published my Poems Decr 1705

Went to Southton May. 18th 1706 returned agn wth but small recruit of health. July 5th

went to Tunbridge Augt 8th. Returned much stronger Augt 30.

Publisht essay against Uncharitableness Apll 1707.

Went to Southton July, returned July Went to Tunbridg: Augt: returned Sepr 3d

All this Year my health has been encouraging

Publisht my Hymns & Spll Songs July 1707

Overturned in a coach without hurt. Oct. 5. 1707

Preached a reformation Sermō: Oct. 6. 1707, and printed it

Went to Southton—and afterward to Tunbr: Augt 1708

Removed our Meeting place to Bury Street Sepr 29 : 1708.

Printed 2d Edition of Hymns & 2d ed: of Poems: Apll & May 1709.

Went to Southton: June : Tunbridg, Augt 1709

Edwd Hitchen my Servt went away Decr: 31.

I bought a horse for my health Apll. 1710

I rode down to Southton, & back agn June & according to yr accott. I kept I rode above 800 mile frō Apll 13th to Sepr 28th

I removed from Mr. Hollis's & went to live wth Mr Bowes att Dec. 30th & John Merchant my Servt. came to me

Went to Southton June, returned July

Went to Tunbridge Augt: returned 7 Sepr being under a disorder of my stomach, and freqt pains of yr head. Found some relief at Tunbr: waters.

INDEX.